How do our ideas about Shakespeare inform our understanding of the limits of performance? This stimulating and original book asks how both text and performance are construed as vessels of authority. In Shakespeare studies the notion of the text as a fixed site of authority and intention has long been controversial; nonetheless, the author finds that our understanding of Shakespearean performance – in the work of actors and directors, as well as of performance scholars – retains a surprising sense of the possibility of being "faithful" to Shakespearean texts, and so to "Shakespeare."

Worthen considers three activities where the relationship between dramatic texts and stage performances has been negotiated: directing, acting, and scholarship. An opening theoretical chapter uses contemporary editorial theory to pose the problem of authority in performance. Worthen then examines how some prominent theatre directors articulate their role as *régisseur* under the sign of Shakespeare. Next he looks at how actors read Shakespeare's plays, and how their training provides a strategy for investing that reading with "Shakespearean" authority. In the final chapter he inspects performance-oriented criticism of Shakespeare since the 1960s. In each case, Worthen considers how fidelity to the "author" stabilizes and limits the potential work of performance.

This undogmatic and exploratory book represents an important theoretical advance in the performance criticism of Shakespeare. Contributing to the scholarly study of acting and directing, *Shakespeare and the authority of performance* makes a critical intervention in the wider discourse of performance studies.

SHAKESPEARE AND THE AUTHORITY OF PERFORMANCE

SHAKESPEARE AND THE AUTHORITY OF PERFORMANCE

W. B. WORTHEN

University of California at Davis

CAMBRIDGE
UNIVERSITY PRESS

PUBLISHED BY THE PRESS SYNDICATE OF THE UNIVERSITY OF CAMBRIDGE
The Pitt Building, Trumpington Street, Cambridge CB2 IRP, United Kingdom

CAMBRIDGE UNIVERSITY PRESS
The Edinburgh Building, Cambridge CB2 2RU, United Kingdom
40 West 20th Street, New York, NY 10011–4211, USA
10 Stamford Road, Oakleigh, Melbourne 3166, Australia

First published 1997

Typeset in 11/12.5pt Baskerville

A catalogue record for this book is available from the British Library

Library of Congress cataloguing in publication data
Worthen, William B., 1955–
Shakespeare and the authority of performance / W. B. Worthen.
p.   cm.
Includes bibliographical references and index.
ISBN 0 521 55134 X (hardback). – ISBN 0 521 55899 9 (paperback)
1. Shakespeare, William, 1564–1616 – Dramatic production.
2. Shakespeare, William, 1564–1616 – Criticism, Textual.
3. Theatre – Production and direction.
4. Acting.
I. Title.
PR3091.w67 1997
792.9'5 – dc21   97-45571   CIP

ISBN 0 521 55134 X   hardback
ISBN 0 521 55899 9   paperback

Transferred to digital printing 2002

Contents

Acknowledgments

This book has been written in various places, through a number of vicissitudes, and it's a pleasure to be able to thank some of the people whose friendship helped sustain it. I'm happy to thank several colleagues – especially James Bulman, Anthony Dawson, Barbara Hodgdon, Richard Paul Knowles, Cary Mazer, and Carol Rutter – who participated in seminars of the Shakespeare Association of America in which some of this work was first presented. Their encouragement and skepticism on those occasions and elsewhere have been invaluable to me. I have also had the good fortune to discuss some of this material with the Performance Analysis working group of the International Federation for Theatre Research, and with audiences at New York University and at the University of California at Davis. I am particularly grateful to Pirkko Koski and my colleagues in the institute on national theatre and theatre historiography at the University of Helsinki for entertaining some of these ideas on Shakespeare and performance. My thanks to James Bulman and Edward Pechter for sending advance copies of their two recent anthologies of Shakespeare criticism, and to Shannon Steen and Amy Wegener for graciously providing copies of work in progress so that I might engage it here. During much of the writing, I had the benefit of the daily stimulation of students in the Interdisciplinary Ph.D. in Theatre and Drama program at Northwestern University. The Northwestern University School of Speech and the College of Arts and Sciences generously supported a leave of absence under unusual circumstances that enabled me to complete this work.

My thanks, finally, to Sarah Stanton of Cambridge University Press, not only for her patience, but for her probing, occasionally alarming, questions about the direction of the book. To Sharon Achinstein, Una Chaudhuri, Jules Law, James Loehlin, Peggy Phelan, Janelle Reinelt, Sandra Richards, Freddie Rokem, Jo Anne Shea, Shannon Steen, Mary Trotter, Wendy Wall, and Frank Whigham, my thanks for good reading, conversation, and criticism; you know how much farther my debts to each of you extend.

Evanston and Berkeley, 1997

Several parts of this book were published in rather different form as articles. Portions of chapter 1 appeared as "Disciplines of the Text/Sites of Performance," *The Drama Review – The Journal of Performance Studies* 39:1 (Spring 1995): 13–28; portions of chapter 2 appeared as "Invisible Bullets, Violet Beards: Reading Actors Reading," *Textual and Theatrical Shakespeare: Questions of Evidence*, ed. Edward Pechter (Iowa City: University of Iowa Press, 1996): 210–29, and as "Staging 'Shakespeare': Acting, Authority, and the Rhetoric of Performance," *Shakespeare, Theory, and Performance*, ed. James Bulman (London: Routledge, 1996): 12–28. Part of the argument of chapter 4 was first explored in "Deeper Meanings and Theatrical Technique: The Rhetoric of Performance Criticism," *Shakespeare Quarterly* 40 (1989): 441–55, and in reviews of Harry Berger, Jr., *Imaginary Audition: Shakespeare on Page and Stage, Shakespeare Quarterly* 42 (1991): 96–99, and Susan Bennett, *Performing Nostalgia: Shifting Shakespeare and the Contemporary Past, Theatre Journal* 48 (1996): 391–92. I am grateful to the publishers for allowing me to use this material here.

CHAPTER I

Authority and performance

What is in fact curious about all these gestures, these angu-
lar and abruptly abandoned attitudes, these syncopated
modulations formed at the back of the throat, these musical
phrases that break off short, these flights of elytra, these
rustlings of branches, these sounds of hollow drums, these
robot squeakings, these dances of animated manikins, is
this: that through the labyrinth of their gestures, attitudes,
and sudden cries, through the gyrations and turns which
leave no portion of the stage space unutilized, the sense of a
new physical language, based upon signs and no longer
upon words, is liberated. These actors, with their geometric
robes seem to be animated hieroglyphs.

Antonin Artaud, "On the Balinese Theater" (54)

Observing the Balinese dancers, Antonin Artaud evokes the challenge of intercultural reading. On the one hand, what impresses
Artaud is the immediacy of the performers, the sense that their
performance is not an act of re-presentation, but instead a kind
of "pure theater, where everything, conception and realization
alike, has value, has existence only in proportion to its degree of
objectification *on the stage*" (53). At the same time, though, Artaud
also sees their performance hollowing out the dancers, objectify-
ing them; they become "animated manikins" making "robot
squeakings," and undergo a thorough and "systematic deperson-
alization" (58). Although their gestures "make useless any translation into logical discursive language" (54), Artaud's account of the
dancers nonetheless attempts such a translation: their movements
demonstrate the value "of a certain number of perfectly learned
and above all masterfully applied conventions," they have the
"evocative power of a system," a system that verges, surprisingly

I

enough, on "mathematics" (55). Artaud, the theorist of "no more masterpieces," working to evacuate the logos-like authority of scripted texts, nonetheless *reads* the Balinese dancers' bodies and their performance as a *text*.[1]

Artaud's reading is arresting for other reasons, too, not least for its imperial dimension; we might suspect that the Balinese bodies become texts so readily because, for Artaud, the Balinese are already just things. I open with Artaud's wild ethnology as a way to tease out some contemporary assumptions about the relationship between texts and stage performances. The relationship between texts, textuality, and performance is deeply inflected by notions of authority – not so much professional authority, but the stabilizing, hegemonic functioning of the Author in modern cultural production. Here, I want to explore some of the ways in which notions of authority are inscribed in discussions of performance, often at just those moments when the apparent insurgency of performance seems most urgently opposed to that Trojan horse of the absent author, the text. How does the Author, whose texts are consumed, transgressed, rewritten by performance, figure in the ways we account for the work of the stage?

This is a book about theatrical performance at the end of the twentieth century. More precisely, it is about how a well-defined and established collection of voices – scholars and journalists, actors and directors – talk about a certain kind of performance: the staging of Shakespearean drama. To be sure, this is an artificial narrowing of the field of performance, sidestepping not only the global variety of nontheatrical performance, but also the range of stage performances that have nothing to do with the representation of dramatic texts, let alone the canonical plays of Shakespeare. Yet, in the West, ideas of performance – both in popular parlance and in more formal academic discourse – are troped by the institutions and practices of Western stage traditions: by a sense of the asymmetry between "acting" and behavior, by a characteristically permeable boundary between mimesis and semiosis, by the slippage between reading plays and staging them. Precisely because "Shakespeare" stands at the center of two articulate and contentious traditions – of reading and the criticism of texts; of performance and the staging of scripts – Shakespearean theatre affords a powerful way to bring questions of authority and performance into view.

In this book, I listen to how a variety of institutionalized voices – university professors and newspaper critics, actors and directors with the Royal Shakespeare Company, the Royal National Theatre, the Stratford Shakespeare Festival, and similarly visible platforms – talk about the role of "Shakespeare" in the work of performance. Describing performance, performers, scholars, critics, teachers, and directors invoke surprisingly literary valuations of a stable text, and an intending author. The sense that performance transmits Shakespearean authority remains very much in play, most strongly perhaps when the ostensibly free and disruptive activity of the stage is at hand. For despite the "death of the author" (Barthes), or the author's functional absorption into the systems of cultural and ideological production (Foucault), "Shakespeare" – sometimes coded as the "text," its "genre," or the "theatre" itself – remains an apparently indispensable category for preparing, interpreting, and evaluating theatrical performance, at least as much for practitioners as for scholars and critics.

Harry Berger, Jr. remarks that recourse to the author, in accounts of performance as well as in readings of texts, enacts a "principle of closure, of semiotic inhibition, employed in the conflict of interpretations to privilege certain readings and control 'unruly meanings'" ("Bodies and Texts" 153). While the theatre is often described as licentious, promiscuous, innovative, imaginative, or merely haphazard in its representation of texts, to think of performance as conveying authorized meanings of any kind, especially meanings authenticated in and by the text, is, finally, to tame the unruly ways of the stage. In *Shakespeare and the authority of performance*, I consider how both scholars and performers take the stage to be authorized in this way, as a place for authentically Shakespearean meanings. I ask how authority arises in stage Shakespeare, how the interface between page and stage is imagined at three moments in the cultural production of theatrical Shakespeare: in the role of the modern director, in the training and practice of actors, and in the interpretive practice of performance scholarship. How do directors, actors, and scholars represent the authority of Shakespeare in the action of performance?

And, more important, what are the consequences for an understanding of performance – and drama – of seeing the theatre as a
kind of paper stage, its work and the audience's response already
scripted by the hand of "Shakespeare"? At the end of this chapter,
I will have more to say about listening to directors, actors, and
scholars, and will chart the specific contours of the argument to
follow. First, though, I want to raise some more basic questions
about the page, the stage, and the acting of authority.

Stage versus page, literature versus theatre, text versus performance: these simple dichotomies have less to do with an intrinsic
opposition between writing and enactment than with habitual
ways of describing dramatic performance, of understanding the
relationship between the meanings that arise from reading or
criticism and the shapes of meaning in the theatre. Not surprisingly, both "literary" and "performative" accounts share an
essentializing rhetoric that appears to ground the relationship
between text and performance. In a schematic sense, a literary
perspective takes the authority of a performance to be a function
of how fully the stage expresses meanings, gestures, and themes
located ineffably in the written work, the source of the performance and the measure of its success. Though performance may
discover nuance and meaning not immediately available through
reading or criticism, these meanings are nonetheless seen as
latent potentialities of the words on the page. From the performative perspective, stage production is, in a sense, the final cause
for the writing of plays, which are fully realized only in the circumstances for which they were originally intended: theatrical performance. Stanley Wells nicely epitomizes this position in his General
Introduction to the Oxford *William Shakespeare: The Complete Works*,
remarking that "it is in performance that the plays lived and had
their being. Performance is the end to which they were created"
(xxxviii).[2] Much as the text-centered view universalizes reading or
interpretive practice (the meanings of the play are *in* the text,
regardless of the ways readers have been conditioned to read it),
so the performance-oriented view universalizes notions of stage
performance (the meanings of the play emerge *on* the stage, regardless of how performers and audiences have been conditioned to

produce and see them). In the literary view, performance has an accidental, merely "ministerial" dependence on qualities essential to the text; in the performative view, the text has a heuristic, merely "ministerial" value in helping to reframe the work's animating design, a stage performance.[3]

I have phrased this dichotomy crudely, in part to suggest how notions of authority – a seminal intention, an instigating structure of meaning – trace thinking about dramatic performance, even when "performance" as a critical conception has become widely disseminated in performance art, literary theory, and theatre and performance studies.[4] Although literary critics are sometimes dismissive of what they take to be the vagaries of the theatre relative to the intrinsic meanings of the text, theatre practitioners and performance scholars sometimes indulge in a related romance, opposing "performance" (transgressive, multiform, revisionary) to the (dominant, repressive, conventional, and canonical) domain of the "text" and its minions, scholars and critics of literature. Think of actors, for example, dismissing some baroque interpretation of *Hamlet* or *Trifles* or *Waiting for Godot* as unactable, unassimilable to the discourse of contemporary stage production, and so illegitimate to the realities of drama-in-practice. Or of theatre reviewers dismissing a "conceptual" production as merely trendy, somehow not faithful to the intentions of Shakespeare and/or his play. Or of stage directors talking about letting the stage release the intentions of the author. Or of the more theatrically oriented stage directions of the Oxford *Shakespeare* as opposed to the editorial procedures of earlier editions. Or of the critical and legal fireworks touched off by some productions of Samuel Beckett's plays – *Endgame* at the American Repertory Theatre, *Footfalls* at London's Royal National Theatre – when the plays' dialogue was observed, but stage directions (concerning the setting of *Endgame*, and the pattern of movement in *Footfalls*) were disregarded or revised (where does the "author's" text end and the "director's" text begin?). Or of the controversy surrounding whether Anna Deavere Smith, who uses the recorded words of her interview subjects as the text of her performance, should be considered for the Pulitzer Prize for Drama as "author" of *Twilight: Los Angeles, 1992* (she was not). The volatility of these controversies suggests that texts and performances are not really the issue, but how they are construed as vessels of authority, of canonical values, of hegemonic consensus.

The desire to ground the meaning of theatrical production by attributing it either to the authorial work or to the authorized institutions of stage practice transforms the historically and culturally labile relationship between these modes of production into an inert, apparently ontological opposition. Part of this confusion stems from three interlaced ways of thinking about a text: (1) as a canonical vehicle of authorial intention; (2) as an intertext, the field of textuality; (3) as a material object, the text in hand. In "From Work to Text," his now-classic celebration of textuality, Roland Barthes provides a convenient discrimination between the first two senses, that informs recent discussions of textuality and performance. Barthes describes an "epistemological slide" (155) in the conception of written texts, from "the traditional notion of the *work*" to the more relativized sense of the *text* (156). The *work*, that "fragment of substance, occupying a part of the space of books (in a library for example)" (156–57), is the vehicle for authorized cultural reproduction, a "signified" approached through interpretation; the work discloses a "secret, ultimate, something to be sought out" (158). The *text*, on the other hand, is the field of production rather than interpretation; its "field is that of the signifier," governed by a metonymic rather than a hermeneutic logic, best approached through "the activity of associations, continuities, carryings-over," through "*playing*" (158). As an object of authorized interpretation, the *work* is "normally the object of a consumption" (161); the *text* is not an object but a field, "that *social* space which leaves no language safe, outside, nor any subject of the enunciation in position as judge, master, analyst, confessor, decoder" (164). If the *work* is authorized, interpreted, consumed, the *text* is encountered as a field of "play, activity, production, practice" (162).

It's not surprising that Barthes's opposition between the work (authoritarian, closed, fixed, single, consumed) and the text (liberating, open, variable, traced by intertexts, performed) proves so useful to contemporary thinking about performance, in part because Barthes's sense of the text is self-consciously performative.

Barthes's text is the field of the signifier, of textuality, of play, of production, of *jouissance*, that "pleasure without separation" (164). Where interpretation is earnest, concerned with fidelity and "filiation" (160), performance is insouciant, rewriting and disseminating the work in various ways. Contemporary "studies" – literary and theatre studies as well as performance and cultural studies – have gained analytical and theoretical leverage from this textualization of performance, the sense that performed events operate discursively, and that meanings arise from the interplay of signifying formalities.[5]

Despite the widespread application of "textuality" to reading the body and performance, these two conceptions of the text (text-as-*work*, text-as-*textuality*) often become compacted in one another, and compacted with a third sense of the text, the material object in history, the printed text, the *book*. Part of the problem in the way that text and performance are conceived has to do with reductive assumptions of the formal consistency of published texts, of texts as material objects that house the work of the author. For although it is now commonplace to see performance as traced by a variety of gestural, figural, and ideological textualities, the notion that there *is* a text to produce onstage, and that this text is reproduced in some relatively direct manner ("page to stage"), is pervasive, a powerful – even dominant – way of imagining the meanings of the stage. To think of performance either as transgressing the text or as a means of reproducing the text requires a certain confidence in the identity of the text itself. Over the past twenty years, however, editorial theory has widened Barthes's interruption of the identity of works and texts, by challenging the relationship between texts as material objects and the authorial works they represent, multiplying the ways of attributing authority to the text, and the consequences of thinking of any text as an authoritative version of a literary work. Much of this discussion in English studies surrounds the production of Shakespearean dramatic texts, how editorial practice from Heminge and Condell through the "new" bibliography of W. W. Greg and Fredson Bowers evokes the materialization of authority, a strategy for producing books that claim to embody the original, or best, or closest approximation to, the author's intended

inscription, a fleshing out of the spiritualized work. But as Leah
Marcus asks,

What if, rather than flowing effortlessly and magically from
Shakespeare's mind onto the unalterable fixity of paper, the plays were
from the beginning provisional, amenable to alterations by the playwright or others, coming to exist over time in a number of versions, all
related, but none of them an original in the pristine sense promised by
Heminge and Condell? Nothing we know about conditions of production in the Renaissance playhouse allows us to hope for single authoritative versions of the plays. (*Puzzling Shakespeare* 44)

Marcus suggests that the notion of a printed text as the embodiment of an organic authorial work is foreign to the circumstances
of Renaissance publishing, and perhaps to all textual production,
in Shakespeare's era.[6]

The conditions of production in the Renaissance playhouse
militate against the final ascription of an ideal, coherent, work to
a single animating *author*, and the texts of Shakespeare's plays are
the result of dialogue and collaboration, of authorial and non-
authorial revision and of the demands of theatre practice.
Michael Bristol argues that these circumstances can be deployed
as evidence for a variety of reconceptualizations of the field of the
author, including a call for a more fully historicized application of
Foucault's critique of authorship to the specific situation of dramatic production in Shakespeare's era (see "How Good" 39–43).
Indeed, the contingencies of playwriting specific to Shakespeare's
theatre hardly exhaust the promise of editorial theory for thinking about authority and performance. Contemporary editorial
theory is concerned with the ways that authority is made manifest in texts, the ways that printed texts – and the notions of
authorship, literature, and culture they convey – enact changing
rather than fixed representations of literary works. For this
reason, I want to turn to what D. C. Greetham has called the
"antidiscipline" of textual scholarship ("Textual Forensics" 32) to
explore some further implications of the relationship between
works, texts, and books for thinking about performance. This
may seem a surprising move to those who regard textual scholarship, editing, and bibliography as the epitome of the "literary," a

gray and recondite world well removed from the energies of live performance. Even a brief encounter, though, with recent work in this area reveals that editorial theory has provoked unusually searching and meticulous reflection on the authority of various manifestations of a work of art. Textual theory considers how the reproduction of texts encodes and transmits both the literary work and a framework of valuation, an ideology of authority. Moreover, it provides more dynamic models of the relation between works, texts, and performances than the static "text versus performance" or "text to performance" paradigms that have afflicted most discussions of drama and theatre, and of Shakespearean performance in particular. Finally, editorial theory challenges the understanding of the relationship between authority and representation that informs many of the ways both scholars and performers talk about theatrical performance.

In producing a new edition of, say, a Shakespeare play, editors want to establish a consistent relationship between the edited text and the work of the author. This is considerably more difficult than it may at first appear, in large part because the work is always absent, an ideal category known only through manifestations – manuscripts, various printed forms, performances – which can be assigned various kinds and degrees of authority, and stand in various relations to any authorial act of writing.[7] G. Thomas Tanselle, for example, describes verbal works such as poems and novels as employing "an intangible medium. Any tangible representation of such a work – as in letterforms on paper – cannot be the work itself, just as choreographic notation or traditional musical scores are not works of dance or music. The media involved – language, movement, and sound – being intangible, these works can be stored only through conversion to another form, which in effect becomes a set of instructions for reconstituting the works" ("Editing" 5). For Tanselle, a set of editorial practices and commitments follow from this sense of the work, but rather than tracing those, I would like to consider more closely the moment at which the "intangible" *work* is materialized, performed so to speak, as a *text*.[8]

A sense that the text stores the dramatic work, so that it can be released – as works of dance and music are – in the theatre will be familiar to performers and to many critics of performance as well. Nonetheless, the fact that dramatic texts can be actualized as works in at least two different modes of production, as reading and as stage performance, suggests that musical scores and choreographical notation provide a somewhat misleading analogy to the relationship between dramatic texts and their stage performance. For as Tanselle implies, the "instructions" provided by these forms of storage are not sufficient in themselves to produce the work: without an understanding of the conventional workings of production, these "instructions" are illegible. We need an understanding of theatre practice to see the text of *Hamlet* as providing "instructions" that can lead to a staging – *any* staging, let alone one a particular audience might find adequate or authoritative – of the work. What kind of theatre practice can be used to "follow" *Hamlet*'s "instructions" in the most effective (authoritative) way? The habits of the late twentieth-century (British, Canadian, American) theatre? Some reconstruction or adaptation of early-modern performance practice? How can we speak of an actress in the role of Ophelia (or Lady Macbeth, or Juliet, or Cleopatra) delivering an authentically Shakespearean performance, when an actress cannot be following any conceivably authentic Shakespearean "instructions"? Two moments of ideological labor intervene between the text's "instructions" and the realized work: a conventionalized practice for using those "instructions," and the rhetorical assignment of "authority" to practices that follow the "instructions" in a particular way.

As Peter Shillingsburg argues in *Scholarly Editing in the Computer Age*, to see the work as having "no substantial existence," something "only partially represented by any one given printed or written form" (46), is to undermine a traditional sense of the stability of the work itself. A work may be expressed in a variety of texts, but the multiplication of texts complicates the unity of the work and its relation to authorial intention (think of all the different texts of *Hamlet* you may own, have taught from or studied, as well as the different quarto versions published in Shakespeare's lifetime, and the different versions of the 1623 Folio, for that matter). Although the "redundancy of its various printed and written forms gives a sense of unity which helps us to conceive of the range of forms as one work," the variance between these forms also suggests the "haziness" of the work's "outlines" (46) – this haze deepens if you also think of translations, the marked-up copy you used when you played Ophelia or Laertes in your college production, of your videotape collection of Kenneth Branagh, Mel Gibson, Derek Jacobi, Laurence Olivier, and the different scripts of *Hamlet* they follow. To consider the relationship between the immaterial work and its manifestations, Shillingsburg proposes a series of intermediate terms – *version, text, document* – which localize the action of authority in the transmission of works, and help to clarify the complex relationship between works, texts, and performances.

A "version is one specific form of the work – the one the author intended at some particular moment in time" (47). Since a version is only *intended*, it is also intangible: "A version has no substantial existence, but it is represented more or less well or completely by a single text as found in a manuscript, proof, book, or some other written form. In other words, a version is the ideal form of a work as it was intended at a single moment or period for the author" (47). The *text* might at first appear to be the moment when the intangible work becomes concrete, but Shillingsburg describes the text as a purely formal entity: the moment at which authorial "intention" is rendered in a specific form, in the case of literary works, the ordering of graphic symbols.

A text is the actual order of words and punctuation as contained in any one physical form, such as manuscript, proof, or book. A text is the product of the author's, or the author-and-others', physical activity in the attempt to store in tangible form the version the author currently intends. And yet a text (the *order* of words and punctuation) has no substantial or material existence, since it is not restricted by time and space. That is, the same text can exist simultaneously in the memory, in more than one copy or in more than one form. The text is contained and stabilized by the physical form, but is not the physical form itself. Each text represents more or less well a version of the work. A manuscript may actually contain two or even more texts: that represented by the original reading including those portions now cancelled and that represented by the final revision or that represented by intermediate readings. (49–50)

The *text* in this sense is an intermediate category. Representing an authorial version, the text is both immaterial – two editions of *Hamlet* published decades apart containing an identical order of symbols represent the same texts – and the point of a version's materialization as a *document*, "the physical material, paper and ink, bearing the configuration of signs that represent a text" (51).

Shillingsburg may seem to be multiplying categories here, but these distinctions are needed to clarify the theoretical problem of how works are transmitted, and what the various, often incompatible, texts mean relative to the performance of the work. Texts can be "accurately reproduced" or not; they "may be transmitted by an authoritative or nonauthoritative agent," and whether "a transmitting agent is authoritative or nonauthoritative will depend on the definition being used for authority" (172). The theatre might seem to be a fully nonauthoritative transmitting agent: using texts Shakespeare never fashioned (modern editions), personnel Shakespeare never knew (the director, actresses), theatres Shakespeare never imagined (modern technology, architectural and scenic conventions), and actors and audiences informed by 400 years of history, how can *any* production claim to stage an authoritative *work* of Shakespeare? Let me quickly point out that this is not to say that readers and critics have any better access to authoritative production: reading and writing about Shakespeare's texts happens under a similar congeries of conditions remote from the circumstances under which Shakespeare and company generated the texts of these plays, making any claim to come to an authentic *reading* of a Shakespearean work equally problematic (especially if what we mean by *reading* is something that approximates what Shakespeare's audiences might have been doing when they sat down to read a *play*). In what sense is a modern Shakespeare scholar, sitting in the Folger Shakespeare Library, holding a text of what is now "the First Folio" in his or her hands, engaging in an authoritative experience of the original work? In what sense is this a more authentic transmission of the work than I might engage, sitting in my office using the apparatus of a modern edition, or consulting several texts and performances on a CD-ROM? I don't mean to imply here that questions of authority are irrelevant or "undecidable." I do mean to suggest that "authority" is – or can be – part of the rhetorical contingency of transmission. It is the function of transmitting agents – some transmitting agents at least – to claim to reproduce authority: a "definition being used for authority" intervenes in most acts of transmission. We might wonder whether the theatre departs from editing at this point or exemplifies the crisis in which editors now find themselves. Is the theatre engaged in *transmitting* the work, or *producing* it?[9]

The question of how the nonmaterial – author or work – is materialized outlines the ideological problematic of modern stage performance: how the verbal text (a version of the work whose text is recorded in specific documentary form) is transformed into a nontextual event, while this event nonetheless claims to reproduce text, work, author. Is a text or a performance the vehicle of the work, or does it produce the work anew? Jerome McGann has directly addressed this question, in an influential critique of editing that revalues the relationship between work and text. McGann asks, "must we regard the channels of communication as part of the message of the texts we study? Or are the channels to be treated as purely vehicular forms whose ideal condition is to be transparent to the texts they deliver? How important for the reader of a novel or any other text, are the work's various materials, means, and modes of productions?" ("Case" 153–54). Resisting the notion that the text is transparent to the work, McGann moves the work from origin to consequence in the process of production: the work at any time consists in the multiplicity of its versions, the history of its transmission, reception, consumption. Like Shillingsburg, McGann sees the text as intangible, a specific order of symbols. Unlike Shillingsburg, McGann sees each text as restricted by time and space – "a 'text' is not a 'material thing' but a material event or set of events, a point in time (or a moment in space) where certain communicative interchanges are being practiced" (*Textual Condition* 21). Like performances, texts produce the work as an event in time, an event which has its immediate participants (say, the first readers of a given edition of Shakespeare's *Works*), but also becomes part of the ongoing negotiation of the work's changing identity in history (the implicit dialogue between the Pelican, Bevington,

Riverside, Oxford, New Cambridge, and Signet *Shakespeares* on my shelf). The work's authority is also temporal, a function of the rhetorical structure of each textual event, how the event – production and reception – generates its own version of the authoritative experience of the work.

The "text" is the literary product conceived as a purely lexical event; the "poem" is the locus of a specific process of production (or reproduction) and consumption; and the "work" comprehends the global set of all the texts and poems which have emerged in the literary production and reproduction process. (*Textual Condition* 31–32)

The work is not necessarily immanent in the material text, waiting to be actualized in a performance-as-reading (the "poem"). McGann sees the work as the entire complex of a culture's past and present encounters both with the text and the poem. As D. C. Greetham puts it, for McGann "the concrete is not only the way in which we may know the work but *is* the work itself" ("[Textual] Criticism" 10).

McGann's sense of the work is reminiscent of the condition of Shakespearean performance, where any staging necessarily produces a new work, one in dialogue both with a panoply of texts, and with all other performances, including parodies, spoofs, and allusions in popular culture, as well as stagings in the "legitimate" theatre. This sense of the text is common in the theatre as well, as Philip McGuire notes:

The playtext of a Shakespearean play is not its enduring essence abstracted from the particularities that inhere in all performances. It is a verbal (rather than mathematical) construct that describes that ensemble of possibilities. It establishes a range, a distribution of possible events during a performance, including acts of speaking, but it does not determine in minute and complete detail all of the events that happen during a specific performance. (*Speechless Dialect* 138–39)

But McGuire sees the text as enabling only new versions, not new works. McGuire's text describes – as a mathematical formula describes a circle – the limits of possible forms which the work

might take in performance, and so limits performance to reproducing a "work" which is somehow already inscribed in the text.
McGann suggests a more profound reorientation away from the
completeness of the text, and its ability to describe – and so pro-
hibit – subsequent works. Much as the work is a record of a
culture's representations, it also records a culture's contestation
of authority, the various ways in which the "author" has been
claimed and reclaimed, disowned, ignored, rejected, compromised,
fetishized, scorned, worshiped. McGann implies that rather than
seeing performance as a derivative re-versioning of the work, one
doomed to be compromised by the untenable claims of the theatre to authoritative reproduction, performance is definitive of
the process of cultural negotiation through which works have
their continued existence, their ongoing and changing life. To see
performance in this way, however, is to see the question of a production's fidelity – to "the play," to "Shakespeare" – as purely
tautological. If the stage constitutes the work, it constitutes a
sense of "authority" or "fidelity" (or, for that matter, "transgression," or "experiment") as a rhetorical effect, part of the *way*
it produces the work rather than as an innate quality being
transmitted with (or frustrating the transmission of) the work.
"Shakespeare" can speak in the theatre only in the idiom of
theatre, an idiom inscribed (or not) with its own contingent
rhetoric of authenticity. The only thing we can be sure of is that
as audiences change, as a culture and its theatres change,
Shakespeare will speak in different accents, in different forms of
visibility and embodiment that may (or may not) assert their own
(in-)authentic claims to "Shakespeare."[10]

Theorists since Aristotle have been troubled to define the
authentic medium of dramatic performance. Is a stage production the original and authentic form of the work, of which the
text is merely a record? Is it a variant version of the work, which
transmits the work by reproducing a text in a different mode of
production? Is it a separate work, which nonetheless asserts a
kind of likeness to other productions? This tension is perhaps felt
in Shillingsburg's definition of a literary work: "the message or
experience implied by authoritative versions of a literary writing.
Usually the variant forms have the same name. Sometimes there

will be disagreement over whether a variant form is in fact a variant *version* or a separate work" (*Scholarly Editing* 173). Shillingsburg's definition informs one conventional view of the relationship between stage and page: the authority of performance is lodged in the work as manifest in the text. Performance in this view is an authoritative *version* to the extent it appears to echo a particular reading or interpretation of the work, a reading which makes a claim to authenticity. However, Shillingsburg's definition also implies something like McGann's line of questioning: to what extent is a performance not a *version* of the work (let alone a *version* of the text), but a separate iteration of the work, as though each production were a new event in the work's emergence in history?

The situation of textual editing may appear to be a long way from the situation of contemporary performance, but the issues raised here – how to ground the authority of texts in a notion of the work, how the figure of the author does or does not provide an instrument for producing texts – are in many respects the issues traced by recent discussions of performance, especially the performance of plays, and especially the performance of Shakespeare's plays. Editorial theory elaborates the sense that what Barthes means by a *text* is more like what we usually mean by a *performance*: a production of a specific version of the work in which a variety of intertextual possibilities are materialized, and which produces a variety of ways of understanding the work. Editorial critics frequently invoke "performance" to characterize the relationship between works and texts, how texts appear to assume an authentic relation to works, or become the vehicles of authorized meanings. Ralph G. Williams, for example, suggests that "every enunciation or inscription, and every experience of a work is a *performance*, and is always by the nature of time and attention partial and evanescent"; much as any "edition of a work is a *tranche de texte*, the 'slice' being arbitrary with reference to the various criteria that might be privileged as basic to an edition. Similarly, our experience of a work of art, whether or not we are aware of it as necessarily a performance, is always partial and fleeting" ("I Shall Be Spoken" 51, 55). *Performance* dramatizes the complex, concrete decisions made to produce the immaterial work in a given material state (the printed text, the text on the page, the book). Performance signifies an absence, the precise fashioning of the material text's absence, at the same time that it appears to summon the work into being, to produce it as performance (remembering that reading is as much a performance, a production of the work, as a stage performance is), a performance that summons one state of the work while it obviates others.[11]

Exploring the relationship between works and texts, textual theory confronts issues of authority and its dissemination that continue to haunt discussions of performance. It implies a rethinking not only of the relationship between text and performance, but also of the ways we talk about performance, what performance does and how "authority" seems to be preserved or invoked by it. For texts – or editions of texts – claim to produce the authority of a work in different ways, in part depending on how they represent the status of work, text, and transmission. Gary Taylor describes editing as a science of "proximity," an effort "to establish a proximate text":

The question then becomes: proximate to what? Proximate to something we value. Proximate to the individualized authorial text valued by Tanselle, or to the socialized collaborative text valued by McGann; proximate to the original spelling and punctuation valued by [Fredson] Bowers, or to the modernized spelling and punctuation favored by [Stanley] Wells. This conception of proximity allows us to recognize that there is no single source of editorial legitimacy; but that does not mean that every edition is as good as every other. Editions can be judged, can be measured, by their proximity to their chosen goals; most editions are lazy, incompetent, incoherent, or derivative. Likewise, the use of editions, by critics, can be judged by the proximity of the edition's goals to the critic's. It is incoherent for any historicist critic to quote Shakespeare in *modern* spelling; it is absurd for any critic interested in theatrical values to use an edition, like the Riverside, that is systematically *anti*-theatrical. ("End of Editing" 129–30)

Taylor accounts here for the ideological work of editing, the way in which the production of a text-as-object encodes acts of interpretation that represent, reflect, reinforce, or resist the values of a given (sector of) culture. For better or worse, editions not only document a version of the work, they declare a vision of the work, erecting a kind of monument to "something we value." In this respect, editions resemble performances, in that a performance stages the work and asserts something about it, usually that this production is "proximate" to "something we value," some value lodged in a particular reading of the text, or a kind of value associated with a given author, or values held to be intrinsic to the (changing) nature of theatre. Performances are not opposed to texts, nor are they "proximate" to them: performances assert or deflect "proximity" to texts (or to "authors") as an act of legitimation, a means of claiming "something we value" – whoever the "we," whatever the "value" – in theatrical terms. The conventional term for this "proximity" in the theatre is "fidelity," and the contradictory ways in which stage productions are seen to be "faithful" to a play dramatizes the extent to which the assertion of authority is a fully rhetorical act, absorbed in the register of ideology.

Though eccentric in the history of publishing, in many ways dramatic texts are normative of the "textual condition." Shakespeare's plays may seem like a special case, but they're really not: the publication of a play is usually guaranteed to violate any sense of a stable relation between published text, organic work, and authorial intention. As Philip Gaskell has remarked in his study of Tom Stoppard's *Travesties*, contemporary plays often exist in several quite different, ambiguously authoritative printed versions: a pre-production text, a text published in conjunction with the premiere, subsequent editions published after later productions, texts incorporating revisions which may or may not have been made directly by the author, collected editions, acting editions.[12] The acting editions common in the theatre usually include much non-authorial material (property plots, for example), and trade editions always include much writing of dubious provenance. Stage directions (which often derive from the practice of the initial production, rather than having been "written" by the author) are notably suspect, though many directors (but usually not scholars) regard them as dispensable anyway. The publisher generally prescribes the overall format of the play on the page. Plays are much less conventionalized in their layout than novels, but are not usually susceptible to the kinds of idiosyncratic layout that frequently accompanies modern poetry (Ntozake Shange and Heiner Müller are two exceptions that prove this rule). A publisher's production team determines the punctuation and positioning of speech prefixes, the amount of space between speeches, the typography, location, and positioning of stage directions, and so on: to this extent, the dramatic text as the "*order* of words and punctuation" (Shillingsburg, *Scholarly Editing* 49) is heavily infiltrated by non-authorial agents. And, of course, plays now appear in a variety of electronic formats, which enable readers both to read a text and to view video performances – usually several performances using several different texts – more or less simultaneously on a computer screen. These accidentals may seem truly incidental to the integrity of the work, but they are only incidental if we regard the printed text as the poorly materialized body of the work's spirit. If, on the other hand, we are interested in how texts are produced in the world, these accidents are the record of that production: they encode the publisher's sense of the audience and purpose of the volume, as well as the means by which it will be read, be performed. To read *Endgame* in the familiar Grove Press edition, in the double-column format of a drama anthology, or on a computer screen – where, of course, the reader may be able to interact with, *change* the text while reading it – is to recognize how deeply the material form of the text affects the kinds of attention we bring to bear on it, the ways we read it, the ways we produce the work in the world.[13]

To see the book itself as a "production" complicates traditional notions of authority, since any work turns out to be not the origin of the text, but its effect, an effect of a panoply of textualizations, of performances. To engage the text textually, to think of the text as producing the work, is to attribute to the text (and to its performance as reading or as editing) the functions of performance: performance works rhetorically, to accomplish "the *appearance of substance*," the "compelling illusion" of a motivating identity which is, of course, always absent (Butler, "Performative Acts" 271). Although textual theory has tended to multiply and complicate the relationship between author, work, version, and text, discussions of stage performance have surprisingly tended to see the

transmission of authority – either authorial intention, or meanings latent in the text signified by the author, "Shakespeare" – as
a relatively straightforward process. One version of this account
involves linking the transmitting agent – theatrical performance –
to the genesis of the work itself. In this view, plays are "written
for" stage performance and so assume their authoritative form in
(only in? in any? in all? equally throughout history?) performance. The transmitting agent is authoritative in this view because
he/she/it – director or actor or "the theatre" itself – duplicates
the work's theatrical genesis. The theatre reproduces authoritative versions of the work because it produces them in a sanc-
tioned medium. To think of "the Shakespeare experience" in the
modern theatre as having its foundation in Shakespeare's sense
of the stage is to attribute to the transmitting agents (stage practice, director, actor, designers, audiences) the ability to recover
"authorial" meanings through the lens of theatre practice merely
because it is "theatre practice." The stage speaks "Shakespeare,"
despite alterations in texts, the massive development of stage
technology, the resituation of the theatre as an institution in
Western culture, changes in social organization outside the
theatre, and perhaps despite changes in the central categories
of Shakespearean representation (such as "character") – events
which should lead us to ask how, or whether, the artisans of
Shakespeare's Globe and the professionals of the Barbican are in
fact engaged in the same practice, treading the same stage.

More plausibly, we might consider the stage as producing the
work, through the application of a historically specific, ideologically
contoured instrument: theatre practice. The work that is produced
onstage in any performance of *Hamlet* is part of the history of the
work, but is also invariably a new work as well. Mapping the relationship between ideology and literature in *Criticism and Ideology*,
Terry Eagleton helpfully considers the relationship between texts
and productions in a passage worth recalling at length here:

Text and production are incommensurate because they inhabit distinct
real and theoretical spaces. Nor is the dramatic production to be conceived of as an "interpenetration" of these two spaces, textual and theatrical, or as a "realisation" or "concretisation" of the text. The relation

between text and production is not imaginable as that of an essence to an existence, soul to body: it is not simply a question of the production "bringing the text alive," revitalising and de-reifying it, releasing it from its suspended animation so that the imprisoned life it contains becomes fluid and mobile. The production is not in this sense the soul of the text's corpse; nor is the converse relation true, that the text is the informing essence of the production. The text does not contain, *in potentia*, dramatic "life": the life of the text is one of literary signifi-cations, not a typographical "ghosting" of the flesh of production. The text is not the production "in rest," nor is the production the text "in action"; the relation between them cannot be grasped as a simple binary opposition (rest/motion, soul/body, essence/existence), as though both phenomena were moments of a single reality, distinct articulations of a concealed unity. (64–65)

What intervenes between texts and performances – and here we should regard *reading* as one way of producing the text, and of *stage performance* as another – is labor. A reading of the text is not the text itself, but a new production of the work. Similarly, "theatrical instruments (staging, acting skills and so on) transform the 'raw materials' of the text into a specific product which can-not be mechanically extrapolated from an inspection of the text itself" (65). It is not the case that *no* relationship can be "extrapo-lated," only that all relationships between texts and performances are contingent, a function of the intervening practices of produc-tion, practices which transform the text into a new representation of the work. Although text and performance – reading and stage production – each construct the work, they do so in ways that may be comparable but are not directly commensurable. As "dis-tinct formations – different material modes of production, between which no homologous or 'reproductive' relationship can hold" (66), reading and performance apply a variety of histori-cally discrete, conventional, and changing practices *to* the text in their production of the work. No production speaks the text in an unmediated, or faithfully mediated, or unfaithfully mediated way. All productions betray the text, all texts betray the work.

To consider the role of authority in modern performance is not only to see how readily it has been stabilized by a simplified, even genetic, understanding of the relationship between work, text, and performance, but also to reflect on alternative ways of understanding how such authority might be imagined. Although editorial theory has troubled the clear stream of transmission (performance manifests text manifests work; good performance manifests an authentic work, bad performance doesn't), there is both theoretical and historical warrant to link these forms, to be able to frame a relationship, say, between the panoply of textual and performed *Hamlets* on our horizon. Although these *Hamlets* – say, those constructed by Robert Weimann, Charles Marowitz's collage play, and the Mel Gibson film – are indeed not readily "homologous" with one another nor with any single sense of *Hamlet*, they do register in various ways a process of negotiation with the play.[14] Developing McGann's sense of the work as "the global set of all the texts and poems which have emerged in the literary production and reproduction process" (*Textual Condition* 32), Joseph Grigely describes texts and performances as "iterations" of the work, rather than as opposing forms of its materialization. Arguing that the "work is not equivalent to the *sum* of its texts (which would create some kind of hybridized eclectic text), but instead is an ongoing – and infinite – manifestation of textual appearances *whether those texts are authorized or not*," Grigely argues that "a work of literature cannot be 'finished,' just as a building is never finished: it evolves into textual states of being, in which case even ruins are an additional text along this line of time." A work like Shakespeare's *The Tempest*, for instance,

is defined by the manifestation of texts, in which case we can say there is no "text" of *The Tempest*, but only a series of texts that comprise *The Tempest*'s polytext. *The Tempest* is a work, and a copy of the First Folio represents one text of that work. Nor is it necessary to exclude performances from this formulation. Where a series of performances is based on a specific text (what Goodman might call a score), and given

$$W \rightarrow T_1, T_2, T_3, \ldots T_N$$

then we might say that

$$T_x \rightarrow P_1, P_2, P_3, \ldots P_N$$

What is important about such formulas is that they remind us we do not normally conceive a book in terms of itself as a work, but in terms of its texts, or in any case the specific texts with which we have had encounters. ("Textual Event" 176–77)

Grigely's schema points to the difficulty of characterizing the interaction between work, text, and performance. As John Rouse remarks, although it is commonplace to speak about stage productions as productions "'of' a preexisting play text. Exactly what the word *of* means in terms of theories and practices is, however, far from clear" ("Textuality and Authority" 146). In most cases, when a Shakespeare play is produced, various published texts of the play (Shillingsburg's *documents*) are consulted, even when one document is being used as the basic script. The director and designers may consult several editions before choosing one as the basic script; this script is often cut and altered (even modern editions often need additional modernization of individual words and phrases) before being subjected to the necessarily modernizing rigors of rehearsal and performance. These changes are often (but not always) made in consultation with other editions. Once the rehearsal begins, other documents come into play: the actors are holding (and annotating) their own copies, and (like the director) may well consult other editions to help with specific line readings. Everyone involved will be aware, too, of how other stage productions have tried to resolve particular problems in the play's staging. In other words, the "text" that a performance is "based on" – in the end, the promptbook – finally might iterate a range of documentary and stage forms of the play, as well as inscribing the production's own cuts, modernizations, and inventions. A sense of the work or of the author often intervenes as a principle of "proximity" in making these decisions – how to choose between various published texts, the solution discovered by another production, the actor's hunch, and the director's instincts where an obscure line reading needs decisive clarification.[15] A script in this sense is not merely a "destabilization of text" (Coursen, *Reading Shakespeare* 46); in its instability it defines the condition of texts. Each Shakespeare performance is an independent *production* of the work, part of an emerging series of texts/performances rather than a restatement or return to a single source. Performance – like reading, like interpretation – is always a putting of the play into the shifting framework of "something we value" through the complex and changing systems of theatre practice, which have their own ways of claiming (and deflecting) proximity to the text, and proximity to Shakespeare.[16]

To regard performance not as an authorized *version* – better or worse – of the work, but as an iteration inscribed by the practice of theatre significantly alters the paradigmatic ways in which the meanings of performance have been related to those of texts: rather than reproducing the work, stage performance produces it anew. In part, performative iteration produces a new work because, as Patrice Pavis suggests, "text and performance adhere to different semiotic systems. *Mise en scène* is not the reduction or the transformation of text into performance, but rather their confrontation" (*Theatre at the Crossroads* 26). Like textuality but incommensurable with it, performance is a mode of production, not merely a mode of enunciation, and unless "the distinction between them is kept in mind, one is tempted to equate the text/performance relationship with other traditional relationships such as signifier/signified, body/soul, content/form, literary/theatrical, etc." (25). This temptation is difficult to resist, for despite the fact that the "semiotics of the dramatic text and of the performance" occupy different "methodologies and fields of study" (25), audiences, critics, and performers naturally try to understand them in tandem, to relate the experiences derived from reading to the experience of performance in some way. What Pavis points out, however, is the persistence of a certain *kind* of thinking – in formal and informal, popular and academic discourse, in the writing of performers and of scholars – about dramatic performance: the effort to see performance as a repetition of the text, so that text and performance are versions of the *same* work. Grigely's sense of the work's iteration as texts and performances articulates a powerful sense of the duplicity of this repetition, the dialectical possibility of difference ("or") given shape by the assertion of continuity and likeness ("and"). In this way, asking whether "all readings, all performances," must "fail to release the 'or' for which 'and' creates the potential," Terence Hawkes locates the work of criticism and of performance – even when claiming to repeat the authentic meanings of the text, performance "effectively creates a potential space for 'or': there is no escape from metamorphosis" (*Meaning by Shakespeare* 38). Precisely because performance is not an incarnation of the text (as vehicle of the work), but an iteration of the work, performance is necessarily traced by a gesture of difference. This gesture might be read in a variety of ways, though in the twentieth century it has often been reduced to a single shape: performance repeats the text, and so can only either subvert or recuperate its authority. To consider performance as an iteration of the work (rather than as a repetition of the text) is to consider its emergence historically, not only to ask whether texts and performances are essentially related in this way, but also whether in eras prior to the institution of "literature" the stage *could* be understood as a vehicle for the reproduction of textual, literary authority at all.

The dialectic between texts and performances that I have been working to frame here is not new, but the modern construction of it is, dependent precisely on the rise of print culture and, more critical to theatrical performance, on the institutionalization of "literature" as a rival means of producing drama, especially Shakespeare, that came to fruition in the nineteenth century. Michael Bristol has argued that the "historical success of textuality and of the powerful institutional apparatus that supports it" – both the institution of editing and the larger apparatus of canonical *literature* as an institution of cultural production – "coincides with the virtual collapse of the theater as a strong, independent center of cultural authority," to the extent that "the power of the text has been used against the theater, disabling its capacity as the site of cultural and social institution-making, and cancelling its function in the creation of an alternative agential space":

This is, I take it, the real meaning of the incessant border disputes, skirmishes, and raids carried out between advocates of performance-oriented interpretation and the practitioners of more strictly literary and textually based hermeneutic procedures. The text versus performance debate, like so many other professional disputes, is in fact a quarrel over precedence and the allocation of authority. One reason for the largely trivial character of this debate is that the question of authority is never openly addressed, nor is there any sense among advocates of the autonomy of performance where their own authority might come from. (*Shakespeare's America* 97)

Bristol's remarks here reflect more accurately on the production of Shakespeare in England and North America, perhaps, than they do on other kinds of theatrical production, but his point is well taken. In a variety of ways, the success of a dramatic performance is imagined, described, calibrated through reference to the text of the play, to a sense of the play's literary identity, an identity that lies outside and beyond performance. The argument that the theatre is a *more* authoritative vehicle for the production of Shakespeare merely replicates a desire to locate the authority of its production of the work somewhere else, in "Shakespeare," a ground that has already been ceded to "literature." To ask where the authority of performance might come from, then, is not to look for some essential relationship between the stage and "Shakespeare," but instead to recognize the specific interpretive contingency of theatre characteristic of the past 150 years or so. The fact that performance should be held to criteria of *literary* authenticity at all, that theatre should be taken to (re)produce meanings located in the text or in "Shakespeare," is a measure of the theatre's changing historical relation to literature, a relationship specifically characteristic of Anglo-North American Shakespeare production, and specifically characteristic of the modern era.

In his influential essay "The Authentic Shakespeare," Stephen Orgel asks, "what does a play represent?" He concludes that each of the five performances he considers "makes claims to authenticity but means something quite different by the concept. Each also includes an embedded attitude toward the text that conditions, and ultimately determines, the terms of its realization." But that embedded attitude is only apparently to the "text"; it is to "an authentic Shakespeare" standing behind the text, determining how the text is seen, and the terms of its authentic reproduction (13, 24). Authenticity in performance is a function of the rhetoric of performance, the way in which a performance claims "authority" by asserting "proximity" to "something we value." In the case of modern Shakespeare performance, this "something" is, for example, what we – the producers, performers, audiences, and scholars of a given staging – now take the play to mean in other encounters with it (as readers or critics), or, more generally, what we take "Shakespeare" – as an individual writer, as a mystified "author," as the cultural sign of a historically changing frame of value – to be about. The rough-and-ready hermeneutic, the sense that stage performance *can* enact the text (and so enact "Shakespeare"), which performers and scholars alike use to describe performance, tropes performance as a belated, merely interpretive mode of production. How can theories of textuality reframe the relationship between text and performance? A critique of the function of authority in Shakespearean performance must strike a different relationship between the forms of Shakespearean cultural production, texts and performances. For performance has no intrinsic relation to texts. The fact that in the twentieth century performance has been seen to succeed when it recaptures or restates the authority of the text is a distinctive, modern way of situating text and performance, literature and theatre, one that represents a characteristically modern anxiety about the cultural status of drama – and the dramatic "author" – in the theatre.

The text versus performance paradigm, and the theoretical concern for authority it traces, may have arisen in the "mingle-mangle conditions of authorization" typical of Shakespeare's theatre (Weimann, "Bifold" 406), but today it is inflected by the rise of literature as a competing mode for the production of dramatic texts finally accomplished sometime during the nineteenth century. In earlier periods of the English theatre, as in more fully conventional theatres like the Noh, the technologies of stage production had an immanent rather than a hermeneutic relation to "the play": the theatre staged "the play" in the terms appropriate to the stage. While plays could be played in various ways, for better or worse, they were not generally seen to "interpret" the play in the modern sense. When Hamlet directs the players to "Suit the action to the word, the word to the action," he is less concerned that they interpret the text faithfully than that they rightly consider "the purpose of playing": to put the words of the play into theatrical discourse in ways that are effectively *theatrical,*

that use the means of theatre to "hold as 'twere the mirror up to
nature" (*Hamlet* 3.2.17–22). Indeed, he has little compunction
against asking them to "study a speech of some dozen lines, or
sixteen lines, which I would set down and insert" in *The Murder of
Gonzago* (2.2.541–42). As Orgel remarks, in Shakespeare's era, the
"dependency" of performance "on the text was often in doubt"
("Authentic" 7); actors – who, after all, owned the play – were
"literally as well as metaphorically" free to "appropriate the text
of the play to their own needs" (Weimann, "Performance-Game"
69).[17] Performance had an independent tradition, and much
Shakespearean performance in the later seventeenth and
eighteenth centuries claimed to stage "Shakespeare" precisely by
violating the text, rewriting and augmenting it in ways that – like
editing in the same period – staged a Shakespeare purged of the
accidents of time, publishing practices, and taste. Although the
theatre was increasingly preoccupied with Shakespeare, it did not
express this interest in terms of a performance's fidelity to literature, to the text. As a theatrical commodity, Shakespearean
authority could speak in theatrical terms, often with only indirect
reference to the mediating specificity of an authoritative text, or
to values arising from the study of plays as literature. Garrick
could succeed or fail in the role of King Lear, but his *King Lear*
could be neither a "faithful" nor a "revisionist" production of the
text: it was a *theatrical* production of the play, in Nahum Tate's
sturdy revision for the stage. Since performance was not seen to
be sustained by its text, nor by a uniform relation to its author,
the question of authenticity – if relevant at all – had to do with
how the stage articulated its Shakespeare with the theatrical
tastes of its audience. Miranda's sister, the disappearance of
Rosencrantz and Guildenstern, the popularity of Cibber's *Richard
III*, the longevity of Tate's *King Lear* all testify to the condition of a
theatre not rivaled by the institutions of literary authority: the
stage was an independent site for the production of the work, not
strictly bound to an "interpretive" role.[18]
   The possibility that a performance's authenticity could be
judged through reference to the text or, more precisely, through
reference to literary values thought to lie in the text develops
with the evolving status of literature as a recognized and distinct

mode of production, and of the author as its normative agent.
Shakespeare's mutation into – an oxymoron – a dramatic poet is
a critical part of this narrative. The evolving relationship between
plays, literature, and stage production could be traced through
events like the extraordinary publication of Ben Jonson's *Works*
in 1616 and of the Shakespeare Folio in 1623, the series of
Shakespeare editions (and the accompanying controversies) of the
eighteenth century, the effects of theatrical monopoly and the
Stage Licensing Act, Garrick's Shakespeare Jubilee of 1769,
Charles Lamb's impatience with *King Lear* in the theatre, the novel-
ization of Shakespeare's characters (in Helen Faucit [Martin]'s
On Some of Shakespeare's Female Characters, for example), to the
modern intersection between publishing and theatre characteristic not only of Ibsen's careful scheduling of his published plays for
the Christmas book trade or Shaw's novelistic stage directions,
but of more recent controversies like those surrounding Samuel
Beckett and Anna Deavere Smith. Though accomplished gradu-
ally, the transformation of Shakespeare's (and drama's) status is
particularly visible in the changing patterns of dramatic publishing that took place in the late nineteenth century. By the last
decade of the century, the theatrical "acting editions," replete
with technical stage directions, odd abbreviations, and theatrical
jargon were increasingly replaced by texts designed for an emerging market: readers. As John Russell Stephens remarks, on "the
assumption that the older form inhibited public demand, the new
reading editions were an attempt to educate a novel-buying public into the purchase of plays" (*Profession of the Playwright* 132).
Ibsen's and especially Shaw's plays, while providing lucid practical direction for theatre production, were clearly printed with a
reading audience in mind. Their status as "books" going into
stage production was emphasized, much like the increasing, even
novelistic coherence attributed to Shakespeare's plays.

The burgeoning publication of plays manufactured in forms
accessible to a reading public is one sign of a wholesale change in
the relationship between dramatic texts and stage performance.
Although the history of Shakespearean editing tends to concentrate
on scholarly publishing, Laurie E. Osborne has argued that the
"performance editions" of Shakespeare common in the eighteenth

and nineteenth centuries not only "link text to performance," but "simultaneously reveal the ambiguity of that linkage" ("Rethinking" 171). Intended for a reading and a play-producing audience these editions advertise the play's proximity to the theatre, incorporating not only cuts, adaptations, emendations, and additions to the text made in a given production, but usually extensive stage directions and cast lists as well. These editions are part of a tradition established both by the quartos published in Shakespeare's lifetime and by the Folio, in which published plays were not seen to offer a purified, "literary" text to rival the theatrical versions, but versions that specifically "haue had their triall alreadie, and stood out all Appeales; and do now come forth quitted rather by a Decree of Court, then any purchas'd letters of commendation" – the decree of stage performance ("To the great Variety of Readers," *Riverside Shakespeare* 63).[19] In *Bell's Shakespeare* (1774) and *Select British Theatre* (1815), the versions of Shakespeare that appeared in various series throughout the nineteenth century (including editions published by actors like John Philip Kemble and Henry Irving), editors sought to convey, as the introduction to Bell's *Select British Theatre* puts it, the plays "as they are acted," so that "the Work may form a rational companion to the Theatre" (quoted in Osborne, "Rethinking" 178). While these editions were purchased by general readers, they also provided the working scripts for most stage productions of the plays, driving a further wedge between Shakespeare's theatrical and literary texts. Yet as Osborne argues, while these editions "assure their purchasers that they are buying a copy of the play as performed *now*" (173), they came increasingly to mirror the "involved annotations and materials which appeared in successive scholarly editions, culminating in the variorums" (176), precisely marking an anxiety about the ability of this form of publication to produce a legitimate Shakespeare.

Indeed, the waning of the "performance edition" – they have not disappeared, of course – was offset by the expansion of editions that, in expunging the trials of the stage, claimed to produce a more fully literary author.[20] Gary Taylor notes the series of inexpensive multi-volume editions of Shakespeare produced on both sides of the Atlantic in the 1830s and 1840s, the rise of

Shakespearean specialists in conjunction with the Cambridge edition (1863–66) and the spin-off Globe edition, and correlates the reading public of these editions with the inauguration of Shakespeare instruction – and of English literature as a subject – at major universities, and the appearance of English language and literature as a subject for civil service examinations in Britain (*Reinventing Shakespeare* 182–96). And as Hugh Grady has shown, the rise of "English literature" as a discipline and Shakespeare's place in it were characteristic of the "modernizing" tendency of professions in the nineteenth century, a tendency that required the formation of specifically "literary" techniques of analysis, forms of study, and standards of evaluation, in order to legitimate literary scholarship as a profession (see *Modernist Shakespeare* chs. 1 and 4).

But while Taylor sees these developments as part of a "professorial appropriation of Shakespeare" (187), it is also part of a changing understanding of drama and its staging. For it wasn't only Shakespeare and self-promoters like Shaw who were making their way into books, into literature. As Stephens convincingly demonstrates, only in the nineteenth century does the profession of playwright – of the playwright making his or her living as a writer of plays rather than as an actor/investor (Shakespeare), as a court poet (Jonson), or as a theatrical manager (Sheridan) – come into being in the modern sense. The professionalization of playwriting implies a transformation in the legal and cultural status of plays as property. Although playwrights had traditionally sold their work for a fee, and/or for the net proceeds from the author's benefit nights to the theatre manager, the Dramatic Copyright Act of 1833 (which meant "to give authors sole rights in any unpublished play and the 'sole liberty' of permitting its representation" [Stephens 91]) and the founding of the Dramatic Authors' Society (with the goal of enforcing playwrights' rights, and collecting royalties and fees), marks a change in the social identity of plays. Rather than supplying the theatre with a commodity, material like feathers for hats and canvas for flats, the playwright now supplied the theatre with the use of his or her work, which was increasingly accorded copyright protection along with other works of literature. Once an artisan, the nineteenth-century playwright is an artist, an Author.[21]

The stage did not compete with literature as an "agential space" until plays were institutionalized within literature, and until literature could be said to vie with the stage for the authentic representation of the English language's now-dominant author, Shakespeare. Much as the late nineteenth century is a period of intensive critical and editorial efforts to recover the authentic texts of Shakespeare, so, too, is it a time when the theatre strives in various ways to mount an authentic Shakespeare on the stage, a Shakespeare whose authenticity is increasingly measured not with regard to contemporary taste, but in reference to the dramatic text. In part, this conflict reflects the general segmentation, professionalization, and bureaucratization of the cultural field, of literature, theatre, and the arts characteristic of Victorian Anglo-North American social and economic life.[22] One sign of this differentiation is the rise of the director in the nineteenth century, a figure whose function measures newly unstable relations between texts and performances, at least in part by seeming both to restate and to rival the work of the author (the late nineteenth century also witnessed the rise of other figures who calibrate the relation between authors, texts, and performances: orchestral conductors, music critics, and theatre critics). The institution of the director arose at the moment when theatrical practice developed both an optional relation to the text and a need to encode its representations in relation to the text and the literary authority it now held. The effort to place the dramatic action of Shakespeare's plays in a densely realized, historically particular "environment" characteristic of actor-managers like Charles Kean and Henry Irving, can be read as an effort to represent the authentic dramatic environment of Shakespeare's plays with the technological resources of the Victorian stage. Historicizing stage productions were conducted in the discourse of authority: using new stage technology and a new respect for Shakespeare's historical imagination, Victorian productions staged the world of Shakespeare's plays in ways that claimed to capture the rich detail of Shakespeare's imagination, a detail everywhere visible in the verbal text of Shakespeare's plays but which unfortunately exceeded the technical capacities of his rude theatre.[23] Similarly, for all his polemical repudiation of Victorian naturalism, William

Poel's summons to return to "Elizabethan" staging practices evinces a cognate urge to restore an authentic Shakespeare, one who inhabits the texts of the plays. Asking whether the "omission of some of the characters in the acting edition of 'Hamlet'" – he might as well have said *Lear*, or *The Merchant of Venice* – "has not impaired Shakespeare's dramatic conception of the play is at least a matter of doubt" (*Shakespeare in the Theatre* 157), Poel's revival of a quasi-Elizabethan production style, though much more heavily inflected by nineteenth-century stage convention than Poel recognized, attempted to recover the now-lost vehicle of Shakespeare's theatre, so that Shakespeare's plays could speak in their proper voice.[24]

The desire to reproduce the authority of the Shakespearean text is especially pointed in the English-speaking theatre, precisely because the verbal text of Shakespearean drama is prized so highly. Productions outside the English-speaking North Atlantic orbit have, on the other hand, long taken the lead in applying innovative scenographic practices to Shakespeare production. Because of Shakespeare's different positioning in the institutions of literature and theatre, these stagings have generally *not* been reduced to simple questions of fidelity or betrayal. The stunning application of expressionist, symbolist, and constructivist staging to Shakespearean drama characteristic of German and Eastern European theatres of the 1920s and 1930s was felt slowly in England and North America, and this dialectic continues to shape the relationship between European (think of Ariane Mnouchkine, Peter Zadek, Peter Stein, Giorgio Strehler) stage production and the critical climate of Shakespeare production in England, the United States, and Canada.[25] In another sense, though, this estimation of the text also raises the stakes, etching in clearer outline the intricate interrelation between the authority of literature and the authority of performance in modern stage discourse.

Despite innovative approaches to Shakespeare performance, the effort to authenticate performance through reference to the text – as though the text were directly accessible, unmediated by its production as reading, in critical discourse – remains a persistent strategy for interpreting and theorizing the work of performance. It is not surprising to find these critical habits in play in journalistic reviewing, or even in many scholarly discussions of Shakespeare production, where an assumed (or desired) homology between stage and page often deflects attention away from the critical, histrionic, or directorial practices that claim this homology, that produce a specific kind of "Shakespeare." The reach of this sensibility is better dramatized by looking for it elsewhere, in productions that appear to deconstruct the lamination of text and performance by situating "the play" in a remote performance idiom. In a fine article on a *kathakali* production of *King Lear*, for example, Phillip Zarrilli describes how Australian playwright David McRuvie and French actor-director Annette Leday collaborated with the Kerala State Arts Academy, using "a group of highly regarded senior *kathakali* artists" to stage a production of Shakespeare's play ("For Whom is the King a King?" 18). This is an important and suggestive piece of work, and Zarrilli both documents and interrogates a range of intercultural issues arising from the production – working arrangements between producers and performers, the play's reception in both European and Malayali press, and the reactions of two institutionalized custodians of canonicity (the Shakespeare industry/press, on the one hand, and the *kathakali* performers and audiences on the other) – that would seem necessarily to challenge a conventional "page to stage" understanding of performance. Both Zarrilli and the producers have a delicate and nuanced sense of how this intercultural performance exchange might work, and of how it actually did work. At the same time, though, the producers saw the interculturalism of the *Kathakali King Lear* to depend on relatively essentialized notions of text and performance: "Leday and McRuvie wanted the production to speak equally to both its original audiences. For Malayalis the production was intended to provide a *kathakali* experience of one of Shakespeare's great plays and roles. Assuming that many in the European audience would know Shakespeare's play, the production was intended as an accessible way of experiencing *kathakali*" (19). And yet it is precisely this notion of origin that is undone – as it must be – by the process of production. Neither *King Lear* nor *kathakali* were produced here/both *King Lear* and *kathakali* were produced here.

Zarrilli notes that McRuvie's "reelaboration of the *King Lear* text to conform with *kathakali's* theatrical criteria . . . radically transformed the original. The typed English adaptation ran barely twenty pages for the two-hour-plus performance. The action focused exclusively on Lear and his three daughters. The Gloucester subplot was completely cut, as were Kent, Cornwall, and Albany" (19–20). Similarly, as Suresh Awashti argues ("The Intercultural Experience"), by working with a script, rehearsing, and by adding characters outside the *kathakali* repertoire, the *Kathakali King Lear* directly violated the traditions of *kathakali* performance. The narrative, sung-dialogue, and gestural passages that structure *kathakali* performance had to be simplified, while the roles of *King Lear* needed to be adapted to the conventional types of *kathakali* characterization, exerting a certain pressure on each.

Describing the British response to the play, Zarrilli notes that one review saw it as having " 'little to do with Shakespeare' "; it also clearly had little to do with *kathakali* (27). What is surprising, then, is that given the extraordinary reelaboration of *both* textual modes, the producers claim to be trying to reproduce some authentic "experience" via the intercultural discourse of *Kathakali King Lear*. The fissuring of the text is not really at issue: the work for this production was in many senses not unlike the cutting and reelaborating necessary for any production, even those that work to encode themselves as "faithful" to the text. In some essentials, this *King Lear* lies on a familiar continuum of modern *Lears*, no less and no more "Shakespeare's" *King Lear* than Peter Brook's famous *Endgame*-inspired production, Kurosawa's *Ran*, or the plays produced by Edward Bond or Howard Barker under different titles. Yet while McRuvie and Leday scorn "some hypothetically universal realm of communication" (Zarrilli, "For Whom" 36), their test of intercultural performance finally rests on the belief that performance will communicate a stable, universally recognized *something*: *kathakali* and *Lear*. *King Lear* remains, even with the cast cut, the plot changed, the language changed, and so on; *kathakali* can be experienced in some essential manner, even when the formal and cultural traditions of the performance have been drastically altered.

What makes this ambitious and exciting project finally disappointing is that the experiment, far from *testing* the condition of performance (intercultural or otherwise), merely confirms it; or, to be more precise, it confirms the extent to which a discourse of authority informs the critical tools for describing, analyzing, and understanding stage performance in the West. McRuvie and Leday rewrite, transgress the written text, but texts are always a field of transgression. At the same time, they see their activity as authorized by its fidelity to the *work*, Shakespeare's work and the *kathakali* tradition. Much as texts always point to an absent origin, so the *Kathakali King Lear* points to an absence as well: *kathakali*, *King Lear*. Una Chaudhuri remarks that a *"practical* interculturalism would not simply reproduce already established (and hence already politically coded) images of cultural difference; instead it would *produce* the *experience* of difference. It would stage the detailed processes of differentiation which are the as-yet unrepresented realities of modern life" ("Future of the Hyphen" 196). To say that the *Kathakali King Lear* rewrites but preserves Shakespeare's play is to understand performance in fundamentally conservative terms, underwritten less by the "text" than by the phantom author who haunts and exceeds it. How the "author" is said to fill that absence is, I would argue, where the politics of performance, and the hegemony of literature, begin.

Although the *Kathakali King Lear* may seem a special case, the dynamics of authority animating Leday and McRuvie's understanding of performative meaning are representative. For in contemporary accounts of Shakespearean performance – and, I would argue, of dramatic performance in general – the apparent gap between text and performance is explicitly filled by the fiction of the author, a point of privileged meaning to which both frames of interpretation finally appeal. Although the desire to reproduce either the dramatic or the theatrical circumstances of Shakespeare's plays has perhaps waned in the past century, contemporary discussions of Shakespeare and performance have in many ways not surmounted this turn-of-the-century problematic: the desire to authenticate performance as a reproduction of the text, of "Shakespeare." Editorial theory has trained attention to the kinds of meaning attributed to texts as material objects in history, recognizing that the authority of any one version of the text – even a manuscript – is largely a cultural construction, a way of governing the potential meanings of texts-in-culture with the imprimatur of the always-absent author. In this book, I consider one aspect of this historically contingent relationship between readings and stagings, texts and performances: how people interested in this problem talk about it. In a startling effort to discern the generic location of drama, Terence Hawkes argues that dramatic texts "constitute, after all, something that our available textual categories currently require us to think of as hybrid," something that resists the conventional assignment of "play-texts" to conventional genres, as novels, as plays, and as poems. Each of these models is, Hawkes suggests, unduly limiting: a novelistic model of play-texts conceives them in realistic terms, in terms of their representation of the "reality" privileged by novelistic narrative; the "play" model reduces the play-text to a mere score consumed in the process of theatrical representation; the sense of play-text as poem conceives of it merely as a "self referring verbal structure" (*Shakespeherian Rag* 76–77). But as Hawkes argues, none of these generic models "takes account of the degree of unclassifiable – and so threatening – productivity which the play-text disconcertingly offers to release, as a result of the tension it maintains between the various modes of reading" – production – "that aim to process it" (77).

But if play-texts summon this disconcerting and transgressive possibility into being, they do so within the determinate constraints of history, within the institutions provided for representing – reading, producing – plays. In the twentieth century, the "literarization" of Shakespearean drama has placed performance in an apparently "ministerial status" relative to the text, much as any produced text was once said to have a ministerial relation to the ideal, coherent, intended Shakespearean work (see Bristol, *Shakespeare's America* 105). Despite the sense that Shakespeare's plays were "written for" the stage, or that the theatre has ways of producing plays that are distinct from the practices of reading, much writing about Shakespearean production, and about drama in general, continues to set the stage in this ministerial, one might even say parasitic, relationship: the value of theatrical representation is measured not by the productive meanings it releases or puts into play, but by the "proximity" it claims to some sense of authorized meaning, to something located in the text or, magically, in "Shakespeare."

Who speaks for "Shakespeare"? In *Shakespeare and the authority of performance* I begin a critique of contemporary understanding of the relationship between dramatic texts and stage performances by considering three places where the authority of Shakespearean performance has been negotiated in the twentieth century: directing, acting, and scholarship. Shakespearean drama may seem an odd choice for this discussion. It might be thought that Brecht, or Beckett, or Müller, or Shange could provide a clearer example of the relationship between textual and performative authority in the modern era. But the questions posed by Shakespearean drama are distinctive. Given the literary and cultural status of Shakespearean drama, the production of a Shakespeare play generates intense and informed debate about the relationship between texts and stage production, a debate that usually centers on issues of legitimacy, power, tradition, and cultural hegemony. Shakespearean dramatic texts are positioned in English-speaking culture in such a way as to inspire the kinds of questions – of the regulatory use of "authority" in performance – that I want to raise here.

Much of the burden of my argument runs counter to the claims of contemporary performance criticism: I regard the stage, and stage practices like acting and directing, not as the natural venue where Shakespeare's imagined meanings become realized, but as one site among many where "Shakespearean" meanings are produced in contemporary culture. Arguing that the modern stage invokes a "Shakespeare" as the authorizing ground of its practice, I attempt to precipitate the critical and interpretive assumptions underlying both theatre practice and the practice of performance criticism. This is the kind of theoretically inflected discussion usually repudiated by theatre practitioners and performance scholars as foreign to the practical immediacy of performance. Part of my concern, however, is to outline the ideological character of this immediacy, how what "works" in the theatre emerges from interlocking assumptions about the text, its legitimate interpretation, and the kinds of performance that are properly Shakespearean, the ways, in short, in which modern performance claims its authority.

In the three chapters that follow, I trace some of the ways that modern Shakespearean performance becomes authorized, and the critical problems arising from these ways of conceiving texts and performances. First, I turn to the work of several significant directors – mainly, prominent directors of the 1960s, 1970s, 1980s, and 1990s. The director is sometimes described as an ineluctable consequence of the increasing complexity of nineteenth-century stage production, and it's certainly true that there are important material reasons for the rise and persistence of the director as *régisseur*. But the director also has an ideological function in understanding the work of the stage. I argue that directors, far from liberating an authentic Shakespeare, consistently work to authorize their own efforts by locating them under the sign of "Shakespeare." This is not, though, merely to take up the tired complaints against "director's theatre." Since part of my argument is that modern Shakespearean theatre is invariably involved with questions of authority, the "director" is necessarily one place where questions of transgression or fidelity come into focus. In addition to the director's managerial function, the director negotiates the production's relation to "Shakespeare," its regulatory invocation of Shakespearean authority. Although specific productions might provide a kind of evidence here, the "director's" relation to the production onstage – from the point of view of the critic or spectator – is much like that of the "author": a principle of attribution, a finally mystified ground of interpretation, a place to locate a reading of the performance *as* a reading of the text. The chapter considers how directors describe their work, how they interpret texts and see their reading as the framework for their work on the production. My intention here is not to provide a history of modern directing, nor a new reading of landmark productions, but to consider the role that "Shakespeare" plays in modern directors' understanding and imagination of the stage.

The third chapter looks at the ways that actors represent their reading of Shakespeare's plays, and how they relate the meanings they derive from reading to their practical training as performers. Although we might expect actors – whose practice is often described as innate, intuitive, physical, naturally reactive – to develop strategies of reading that privilege the independent authority of performance, actors' accounts of their work are insistently informed by notions of fidelity to Shakespeare. Moreover, the disciplines of the body characteristic of modern actor training are troped by notions of the body and its "nature" that reciprocate beliefs about the dramatic value of Shakespeare's plays. In their evocation of the actor's natural physical instrument, acting and voice training express a sense of corporeal nature fully inscribed by what is "natural" to the contemporary theatre: not surprisingly, perhaps, "Shakespeare's" body stalks the modern stage.

The final chapter inspects the formation of performance-oriented criticism of Shakespeare since the 1960s, both in the groundbreaking work of John Russell Brown, Bernard Beckerman, J. L. Styan, and others, and in some current forms. I argue that performance criticism tends to assimilate "Shakespeare" to a universalized sense of theatrical practice, practice which is founded on modern notions of identity and the subject. In so doing, performance criticism both suspends analysis of the interpretive agendas locked in contemporary theatre practice, and evokes a surprisingly belated model of theatrical signification, in which stage practice merely restates meanings located ineffably in the text – the authorized Shakespearean text – itself. One consequence of performance criticism, then, is the unintended marginalization of theatre as a form of contemporary culture. In the end, this critical practice tends to imagine a stage so fully regulated by "Shakespeare" that it is not merely a residual form of cultural production, but a largely redundant one.

Clifford Geertz remarks that "The great virtue of the extension of the notion of text beyond things written on paper or carved into stone is that it trains attention on precisely this phenomenon: on how the inscription of action is brought about, what its vehicles are and how they work, and on what the fixation of meaning from the flow of events – history from what happened, thought from thinking, culture from behavior –

implies for sociological interpretation" ("Blurred Genres" 31). Blurring the boundary between text and performance, Geertz envisions a continuum between texts and the textuality of behavior, one that enables us to ask how this rhetorical "inscription of action" takes place, how texts claim to sustain the embodied discourse of performance, how performances claim to represent the graphic discourse of texts. In this book I am interested in the attitudes – specifically attitudes toward Shakespeare, literature, and theatre– that mediate the inscription of action on the stage. Since this inscription is culturally inflected, I have restricted this discussion mainly to Shakespeare in England, in the United States, and, to a much lesser extent, in Canada. I am certain that asking these questions of other Shakespeares – in Tokyo or Delhi or Johannesburg or Lagos or Buenos Aires, in Paris or Berlin, let alone in Montreal or Belfast or Kingston – would lead to a richer understanding of the regulatory and contestatory uses of Shakespearean authority than I have been able to pursue here. Indeed, given the problematic relationship between Shakespeare production, the Stratford Festival, and the institution of a "national" theatre in Canada, I'm quite certain that "Shakespeare" functions in more diverse ways in postcolonial production – "'Act Elizabethan/Be Canadian'" – *within* this North Atlantic orbit, as well as beyond it.[26]

The "Shakespeare" I am considering – and challenging – here is an explicitly institutionalized Shakespeare. Of course, Shakespeare at the Barbican or on the South Bank, in Central Park, in Stratford, Ontario, and in Ashland, Oregon are not the same thing, the same "Shakespeare." Yet there is a continuity of Shakespeare production in the Anglo-North American orbit that stems from commonalities of history, language, theatrical and theoretical traditions, and even of personnel, as well as from shared – and contested – ideas about the purpose of Shakespeare in the theatre, and in (high) culture more generally, a common "Shakespeare ideology." Attending to institutionalized Shakespeare – to actors and directors working in major subsidy or regional theatres, who have chosen (or been chosen) to publish their reflections about their work, to acting teachers and Shakespeare scholars whose writing and professional visibility reciprocates the

Shakespeare industry they describe – I mean to catch the accents of authority that inform what might be called "dominant Shakespeare," Shakespeare *not* marked as contestatory, or resistant, or experimental, or political, Shakespeare played (with all this implies) "straight." The directors, actors, acting and voice teachers, scholars and critics I discuss here have had their work widely disseminated; many of the texts I discuss here are foundational, "classic" texts in the field. They both reflect and have given shape to a contemporary – often explicitly hegemonic – understanding of the work of dramatic performance. How they claim the authority of Shakespeare as the authority of performance is the substance of this book.

Perhaps one final word of caution: this is not a book about performance itself, but about how a relatively narrow, professionally invested body of people talk about it. By considering how theatre practitioners and theatre scholars imagine the relation between text and performance, I hope to raise some questions about the conceptions and preoccupations brought to bear about drama in the theatre. To do so, however, requires doing something rarely done in literary or theatre scholarship – taking theatre practitioners at their word. Much of the material I work with in this book is "secondary": this is true not only in my comments about performance criticism, but in my presentation of acting and directing as well, where I rely on acting textbooks rather than documenting rehearsal room practices, where I consider how actors and directors have thought about their work in print. In most respects, of course, these accounts are an unreliable and possibly irrelevant index of the performances they describe – as Brecht was fond of saying, the proof is in the pudding. In another sense, though, I am less concerned to interrogate performance *per se* here than to consider the attitudes and assumptions that govern its making and reception. In stage jargon, I'm less concerned with what "works" than with what we think is happening, or how we account for what is happening, when it seems to "work." If the proof is in the pudding, I am more interested here in what we are asking the pudding to prove.

At a recent meeting of the Shakespeare Association of America, a colleague quipped that I put too much weight on what actors have to say about their work; not only is it beside the point (who cares what they thought, it's what they did that counts), but actors are "deceivers ever." While an actor's or a director's work in the theatre speaks for itself, the rich history of commentary about Shakespeare performance suggests that it doesn't clearly or unambiguously speak *of* itself.[27] Much as in the practice of scholarship and criticism, what often remains unsaid by the practice of performance are the things that seem to need no saying, the things taken to be innate to the art itself. Though I share some of my colleague's hesitation, I don't think that the large and impressive body of work about theatre written by its makers is either purely redundant to their work onstage or merely dispensable self-promotion. Taking this work seriously means not merely using it as a mine of anecdote and aphorism, but bringing it into the larger dialogue about theatre and drama; this also means not treating it as a body of mystic, unquestionable lore, but engaging with it critically, taking its blindnesses as seriously as its many forms of insight. For what this literature, like performance criticism, like journalistic reviewing, reveals is the condition of contemporary performance, the attitudes toward, assumptions about, affections for and alienations from Shakespeare that stand at the theoretical center of the theatrical work of the stage.

CHAPTER 2

Shakespeare's auteurs: directing authority

It's not Shakespeare's view of the world, it's something which actually resembles reality. A sign of this is that any single word, line, character or event has not only a large number of interpretations, but an unlimited number. Which is characteristic of reality.... What Shakespeare wrote carries that characteristic. What he wrote is not interpretation: it is the thing itself.

> Peter Brook (quoted in Ralph Berry, *On Directing Shakespeare* 132–33)

The modern director, then, is not simply a person who imposes order upon artistic subordinates in order to express a writer's meaning, but someone who challenges the assumptions of a work of art and uses mise-en-scène actively to pit his or her beliefs against those of the play. Without that confrontation, that sense of challenge, true direction cannot take place, for unless the author's work is engaged on an intellectual level equal to its own, the play is merely transplanted from one medium to another.

> Charles Marowitz (*Prospero's Staff* 6)

I've never stopped in my life to think, "What will the author think?" I feel that what I'm doing is the only authentic production.

> Peter Sellars to the cast of *Ohio Impromptu*, Kennedy Center, 1986 (quoted in Susan Letzler Cole, *Directors in Rehearsal* 189–90)

Orchestrating the verbal, visual, physical, musical, kinetic, and plastic languages of stage production, the modern director plays a critical role in the transmission of Shakespearean authority in the twentieth-century theatre. The director is a distinctly modern

45

figure, arising in the late nineteenth century to impose a newly desired representational unity on stage plays. In earlier eras, of course, many of the tasks now associated with directing a play – rehearsing the cast, for example – were nonetheless part of the process of stage production (playwright/performers like Aeschylus and Molière come to mind), and by the late eighteenth and nine-teenth centuries, actor-managers from David Garrick to Charles Kean to Henry Irving to Beerbohm Tree increasingly composed a consistent visual and conceptual design for stage productions, generally taken to be the hallmark of the modern director. But the necessity for the director as a distinct function in the produc-tion process, and the ways "the director" configures the distinc-tive authority of modern performance, crystallized in the late nineteenth century. In one sense, the director arises as a func-tional necessity of the convergence of two theatrical aesthetics: environmental naturalism and historical picturization. Epitomized by Zola's summons to bring contemporary life into the theatre, naturalism deployed the stage machinery of the nineteenth-century theatre (the design, setting, acting, and dramatic elements of naturalism were common to the romantic and spectacular theatre of the period as well) to assert "verisimilitude" onstage in characteristic ways. The rhetoric of naturalism claimed to trans-form stage space into an "environment," an integrated scene in which all elements were thematically related and appeared to operate under the environmental influences of the absent, mysti-fied, but nonetheless palpable forces of history, society, and guilt.[1] Brecht's call for the epic theatre to emphasize the "radical *separa-tion of the elements*" (*Brecht on Theatre* 37) confirms the conceptual hegemony of naturalistic practice: a concrete and detailed physi-cal milieu signaling the determining forces of social life, acting that revealed an internalized "character" as the effect of a scrupulously imagined personal history, and the invention of a drama at once privileging and problematizing these issues were the signs of modernity in the theatre.

Naturalism created the need for directors like Antoine and Stanislavski, someone to manage the dense scenic detail of natural-istic representation and to calibrate text, acting, and design ele-ments in a consistent, lifelike whole. But the need for a director was also a consequence of the romantic trend of the nineteenth-century theatre, the equally meticulous realization of the "past" in the historicizing productions associated with Charles Kean, the Saxe-Meiningen company, and others. For much as in the theatre of Ibsen and Strindberg (both of whom also wrote sweeping historical romances), Shakespeare production increasingly called for detailed and localized stage settings – medieval Scotland for Charles Kean's *Macbeth,* republican Rome for the Saxe-Meiningen *Julius Caesar,* Saxon England for Irving's *King Lear.* Even the "Elizabethan" innovations of William Poel's Elizabethan Stage Society were deeply entwined with this desire to picture the historical environment of the drama. While Irving recreated the dramatic milieu of Shakespeare's plays, Poel's reconstructed Fortune stage – often set within a proscenium frame – recreated the historical environment of Shakespeare's theatre (as Poel and his contemporaries imagined it) as the proper milieu for the plays.[2]

The representational economy of the nineteenth-century theatre – a materially full scene and psychologically full characters signaling the ideological saturation of the environment – produced a cluttered and overstuffed Shakespeare, soon to be much reviled; it also created the director as a formal and functional necessity. And yet, as the varied work of the first generations of modern directors – directors as diverse as Antoine and Lugné-Poe, Stanislavski and Meyerhold and Vakhtangov, Reinhardt and Piscator and Brecht, Poel and Granville-Barker – suggests, the need for the director was not merely the result of newly visible technological challenges and opportunities. To produce a play in the modern period involves the open assertion of the play as a consistent conceptual, thematic, scenic whole, the assertion of an *interpretation* of the text. The "director" points to a distinctive crisis in modern theatrical performance, a crisis of legitimacy. For the director comes into being at the moment that "drama" gains an independent existence as literature, a mode of being and a cultural authority independent of theatrical production. The director manages the material production, but the function of the "director" is to manage the conceptual, rhetorical, or ideological relationship between the dramatic text – as "literature," inscribed with values of coherence and transcendence – and theatre. The "director" summons the "author" into the discourse of modern performance.

This crisis is immediately visible in the tensions between "fidelity" and "creativity" that stalk efforts to describe the work – or art – of directing. As Harold Clurman writes in John Gassner's widely influential *Producing the Play*, the director's role is to "translate a play text into stage terms: that is, to make the play as written, clear, interesting, enjoyable, by means of living actors, sounds, colors, movement" ("Principles of Interpretation" 272). Although "there can be no binding rules for creative work," in that every "director is a new personality, and his emphasis will vary according to his nature" (275), Clurman's understanding of the work of the director is fully entwined with questions of literary authority. What do directors do? Do they imaginatively/slavishly translate the truth of the text into the alternate languages of stage production? Or are they rival writers in the poetry of the *mise-en-scène*, working the materials of theatre – actors, movement, design, as well as the dramatic text – into a new, original creation, much as the poet works the material of language and poetic form into an original statement? This tension is amplified by the fact that playwright and director, like the text itself, are only virtual figures in the final production. Though the playwright has provided a written text of the play, that text is transformed by its staging, speaks now not as a text, but as acting, movement, spectacle. And while the director may be responsible for orchestrating the production's many languages, it is often difficult to say just where the director's hand has been at work, and where responsibility lies elsewhere, in the specific contribution of playwright, actors, designers, audience, or in the felicitous synergy of their efforts.

The director was both a "godsend" and a necessity of "modernist Shakespearean performance" – a "manager of the formidable possibilities of a text otherwise too distant in time, language, and thought" (Kennedy, Introduction, *Foreign Shakespeare* 13) – and it's not surprising that the imposition of conceptual coherence expected of modern directors brings Shakespearean directors into an explicit dialogue with questions of authority. Relative to stage production, directors and authors share a certain mystery, or mystification: authors and directors resemble one another as abstract principles for the attribution of intention or meaning. And as the weary controversy surrounding modern directors – faithful servants or egomaniacal traducers of the unprotected word – suggests, the desire to fix the authority of performance, is nowhere more visible than in the desire to root the elaborate congeries of theatrical signification in a figure of our own creation: the absent author and his faithful/faithless Horatio/Iago, the absent *auteur*.

"The director is there to attack and yield, provoke and withdraw until the indefinable stuff begins to flow" (Brook, *Empty Space* 109). A director's principal task in the theatre is to rehearse: to bring the diverse yet specific amalgam of personnel (designers, technicians, musicians, dancers, actors, staff) through the trial-and-error process of shaping a dramatic performance, all within the densely particular constraints of budget, location, time, physical resources, and skill. While it is possible to list the chores a director might handle in a production, and even to map an ideal flow chart for play production, in general directing involves a creative engagement with a formalized but relatively open process. Like playwriting, acting, criticism, even teaching, directing is a "continual preparation for the shock of freedom" (Brook, *Empty Space* 57).[3] When directors describe the significance of their work, though, they tend to touch lightly on the nitty-gritty process of getting the play on its feet, emphasizing instead their impressions of the play, their research, the ways in which their plans were challenged, frustrated, or fulfilled in the practical working-out of the play.[4] Peter Brook is perhaps representative when he remarks "There's a formless hunch that is my relationship with the play. It's my conviction that this play must be done today, and without that conviction I can't do it. I have no technique. If I had to go in for a competition where I'd be given a scene and told to stage it, I'd have nowhere to start" (*Shifting Point* 3). Some directors are notoriously open in rehearsal, using rehearsal as a workshop to explore the performance possibility of the play; others take a more formal approach, using rehearsals to develop a preconceived understanding of the play's dynamics.[5] This dichotomy underlies director training as well, to judge by the major textbooks in the field. Some, like Robert L. Benedetti's *The Director at Work*, for instance, take the fledgling director through one production, as a way of illustrating typical problems and ways of solving them.[6] Others – textbooks by Alexander Dean and Lawrence Carra, or by Francis Hodge, for example – formalize and structure the creative and organizational process of directing, devoting separate units to textual analysis, casting, working with designers, blocking, and general stage management, culminating in devising a detailed production notebook in rehearsal. In either case, it is fundamental to the training of the modern director that the preparatory work be open to the process of rehearsal itself, however much that "openness" has already been hedged by the material and ideological structures of theatre production itself.[7] As Charles Marowitz remarked describing Brook's rehearsal of *King Lear* for the Royal Shakespeare Company in 1962: "Every rehearsal dictates its own rhythm and its own state of completion. If what is wrong today is wrong tomorrow, tomorrow will reveal it, and it is through the constant elimination of possibilities that Brook finally arrives at an interpretation" ("Lear Log" 10).

Directors read, reread, and analyze the script of a play throughout the long process of a play's production. Regardless of whether the director begins the process with fixed meanings or goals in mind, these are necessarily and repeatedly negotiated, often on fronts that (while they have critical bearing on the final production) have little direct relation to intrinsic features of "the text." The meanings of a production arise from a process that is sometimes routine but never predictable (casting call, tech rehearsals), often absorbed by intractably local matters (funding, competing obligations of the cast, material costs and supply, the theatre's technical resources, design problems, rehearsal space and scheduling) and that frequently operates in the register of discovery, as the director and the cast find what they can do with and through the play – what Brook calls the "secret play" that surfaces through rehearsal (quoted in David Williams, *Casebook* 149).

Despite the emergent and collaborative process with which a stage production – and so the interpretation it may appear to express – takes shape, the meaning of a production is often described in terms of the director's "authorial" translation of the text's innate meanings or intentions. To think of the director as a version of the author is to map the signification of stage perform-ance on the paradigms of literature, to evoke the "director" as a way to stabilize and restrict the proliferation of meanings any stage production generates. In *The Director at Work*, for example, Robert L. Benedetti outlines three ways of understanding the work of directing:

> One major distinction among the conservative, liberal, and radical points of view centres on the degree of transparency of the director's work. The conservative would insist that the production of a play be as transparent as possible, its function being to transmit the text directly, completely, faithfully – and therefore anonymously – with a minimum of "distortion" caused by the director's personal point of view. In this effort to "conserve" the play, the conservative director adheres strictly to the text as written, accepting it as the best form through which the "timeless" beauty of the play may be communicated.... By contrast, the liberal point of view holds that the value of a play lies in the way it lives relative to the present moment, and that a successful production results when the essential spirit of the play, transmitted by but not entirely bound in the text, is happily married to the specifics of a given cast, theatre, and audience, even if this requires some adjustments in the play's form such as changes in period, language, or even structure.... The radical esthetic eschews the forms of the past altogether and returns to the *radix* or *source* of a play in order to generate new forms inspired by the original; thus the text may, for the radical director, be only a source of inspiration for a new, intuitive creative process. (13–15)

Benedetti's three directorial modes all enact a single function: to transmit the authority of the text – its timeless beauty, its innate spirit, or its originating meanings – to the audience. In all three versions Benedetti's "director *translates* the play from its literary form into its new manifestation as a living theatrical event. Like any translator, the director is responsible for both an accurate interpretation of the original and an effective translation which makes its essential meaning and style available to a particular audience within particular theatrical circumstances" (17). Stage meanings, however, are not "translatable" from the text, because meaning in the theatre arises from the application of productive practices *to* the text – behavior, scenic design, lighting, movement, the full panoply of institutionalized theatre practice – that stand outside and beyond the text. Benedetti's sense that the director "translates" the play into a theatrical form attempts to guarantee a reciprocal possibility: that audiences can translate the stage production (through the mediating figure of the author/director) back to stable meanings located in the text.[8]

This desire to authenticate the stage animates the discourse of modern stage production, and also surfaces in the ways that directors describe their own work in the theatre. Asking whether the director has "any creative identity of his own," for example, William Gaskill finds the purpose and meaning of directing in the record of the author's intention inscribed in the text. Gaskill's director "is not creating something new," but is instead "on the quest of creating an experience for an audience of something that has already existed in the writer's mind" (*Sense of Direction* 139, 140). Although some directors think "it is impossible to know a writer's intentions and that it is not the director's business to try," Gaskill finds this to be "plainly untrue": "Shakespeare means the ghost of Hamlet's father to be in full armour, wearing the visor of his helmet up, with a silvery grey beard and walking slowly." When "fashionable" productions alter this intent – the ghost as "a misty figure in the film speaking with Olivier's voice, something in Jonathan Pryce's stomach, a swirling curtain for Yuri Lyubimov" – the production verges on inauthenticity, un-Shakespeare: "Something of the writer's intention has been changed. That is, the image has been changed but not the text so one contradicts the other. The question is, 'Do I find the director's imagination as powerful as Shakespeare's?' The answer is 'No'" (139–40).

To Jonathan Miller, the director's task is to find an animate, modern version of the author's meaning, a "version of what he actually did write down." In a well-known article, Miller argued that Peter Brook's white-box-circus-gymnasium *A Midsummer Night's Dream* (Royal Shakespeare Company, 1970) had found an "objective correlative" for the play's "supernatural world that lies beyond the reach of common sense," an image which, "while it may have violated Shakespeare's unstated thought upon the matter, fulfilled a version of what he did actually write down." Brook's direction recapitulated the conversation with antiquity characteristic of Shakespeare's practice as a playwright: "Shakespeare himself wrought the same changes upon antiquity, not because he arrogantly supposed their stories to be smaller or thinner than his own imagination but because he realised that one of the tasks of art is to overthrow the tyranny of time and to recreate a universe within which the dead converse at ease with the living" (*The Times* 13 October 1971; quoted in Ralph Berry, *On Directing Shakespeare* 2–3). Brook's inventive staging of *A Midsummer Night's Dream* is, Miller suggests, doubly authorized: Brook not only images "Shakespeare's" vision in a readably modern stage practice, but in doing so he recapitulates the process – and spirit – of Shakespeare's creation.

Charles Marowitz more closely approximates Benedetti's "radical" view. To Marowitz, "the only way to express an author's meaning is to filter it through the sensibility of those artists charged with communicating it." Marowitz's director is "a man [*sic*] who insists on reading his own thoughts into those traditionally associated with the author whose work he is communicating"; the director is "the master of the subtext as surely as the author is of the text, and his dominion includes every nuance and allusion transmitted in each moment of performance" (*Prospero's Staff* 3–4). Marowitz (whose collage versions of *Hamlet*, *Macbeth*, and *Othello* speak eloquently to his sense of the director's collaboration with the playwright) sees the director as co-creator rather than as mere interpreter. And yet Marowitz's director, for all his in(ter)vention, works "to fulfill the cycle of creativity begun by the author" (6). Indeed, Marowitz's director even works in the author's medium: his director "*is* writing, even if he never puts down a single word. The impulse to cut, to change, to transpose, or to expand belongs to the craft of writing" (8). Like Miller and Gaskill, Marowitz is engaged in a writerly colloquy with the dead, for "the modern director appropriates to himself those intellectual ingredients usually reserved for the playwright – using the tangible instruments of the stage as a kind of penmanship with which he alters or gives personal connotation to the text of writers both living and dead" (*Recycling Shakespeare* 2).

As their work in the theatre attests, these directors have very different perspectives on their craft and on the work they mean to accomplish on the stage. Though it is an oversimplification to identify Gaskill, Miller and Brook, and Marowitz with Benedetti's "conservative," "liberal," and "radical" perspectives, each claims a distinct, and apparently different version of the director's work. Yet by seeing the director to reproduce meanings manifest on the surface of the text, or in its spirit, or in the "cycle of creativity begun by the author," each frames the aleatory possibilities of the stage in the register of authority. Not surprisingly, a theatre in search of an author finds one in "Shakespeare." To the extent that Shakespeare is accorded a kind of transcendent genius (Shakespearean drama is coexistent with "reality" itself in Peter Brook's view), the director's interpretive role is not constrained by the limits of a merely human author, whose chosen style and range of reference make his or her plays seem more local, temporally bound. Shakespeare is in this regard unlike Jonson or Marlowe, Behn, Racine and Molière, or even perhaps Ibsen, "authors" who seem not so readily to license the "universal" for modern tastes. Shakespeare is at once Elizabethan and always our contemporary – "Any time the Shakespearean meaning is caught, it is 'real' and so contemporary" (Brook, *Shifting Point* 85).[9] Michael Kahn's sense that "an interpretation given to Shakespeare reduces Shakespeare; and what is extraordinary about Shakespeare is that he is in a sense irreducible, that he is bigger and beyond," or Giorgio Strehler's view that "of all the great dramatic poets," Shakespeare "had the largest, most universal vision," a vision that enables "the possibility of speaking to contemporary audiences of problems which pierce us today through something that Shakespeare has written," perform a fascinating gesture, at once divesting Shakespeare of specific meaning, and recuperating all contemporary meanings to Shakespeare (quoted in Ralph Berry, *On Directing Shakespeare* 90, 128–29). The interpretive crisis of the modern theatre, the crisis that summons the director into being, is nowhere more visible than at this point. Despite theradical discontinuities between Shakespeare, his theatre, his culture, and the circumstances of the modern stage, the modern director stages an authentic encounter with Shakespeare, transcending the differences of history, culture, language, theatre. The "director" creates a modern, timeless "Shakespeare."

That plays can be produced to have new meanings for new audiences is not at issue here. What *is* claimed for plays of genius is a special property, the ability to *contain* such new meanings. Historical change is anticipated by such plays, and theatrical practice succeeds in "making it new" largely by claiming to find a new language to preserve this mysterious essence. Charles Marowitz argues that "A classic that says one thing can, by dint of reinterpretation, mean something entirely different. To call that *mis*interpretation is to deny the ability of living things to change their nature with the passage of time" (*Prospero's Staff* 33). Yet at the same time, it seems to be *only* the "classic," the masterpiece that continues to "live" in this way: "The magical property of a masterpiece [but only of a masterpiece] is that it can be made to *mean* again even when a society no longer thinks the way its author did at the time of writing" (*Prospero's Staff* 120). This property of the Shakespearean masterpiece – to be everything and nothing – marks the ideological work of "Shakespeare" in much writing about stage performance. Fidelity to Shakespeare, to his genius, to his masterpieces, is a way of positioning authority in a field of activity where such authority is continually challenged by historical change, let alone by the collaborative character of theatrical production. Critics like Terence Hawkes have "questioned whether we could have any genuine access to final, authoritative or essential meanings in respect of Shakespeare's plays," to the effect that "like it or not, all we can ever do is use Shakespeare as a powerful element in specific ideological strategies" (*Meaning by Shakespeare* 3). Though Hawkes is writing about the situation of literary criticism, his remarks characterize the situation of theatrical production as well, for the stage necessarily speaks through modern actors to modern audiences. Fidelity to Shakespeare clearly marks the theatre's participation in the reproduction of hegemony: the theatre's strategies for producing Shakespeare's plays are inflected by the necessity of producing visibly "Shakespearean" meanings.

The normative work of "Shakespeare" is most clearly marked when a specific kind of stage practice is disqualified as un-Shakespearean, despite the sense that Shakespeare expresses the essence of theatre. Jonathan Miller, for example, carefully

disclaims an interest in "what the author intended," yet understands that "there are extremes when one knows that the text
has been denatured": although productions are infinite in their
variety, the principle of "congruence" is nonetheless exclusive.
Peter Hall believes that the text determines the kind of staging
that is the most satisfying: "I don't like chamber Shakespeare and
I don't think you can mutter Shakespeare in little rooms. For that
matter, I don't think you can mutter Shakespeare on television
either. It is a rhetorical form to wrap the tongue around; it was
meant to be relished." Talking about Isabella's mystifying silence
in the finale of *Measure for Measure* – an absence of spoken "text"
that leads inevitably to a crucial moment in any staging of the
play – Robin Phillips suggests that the appropriate stage image
can be "the embodiment of what the text (or the lack of text for
her) is saying. If it's the right image, it will also be finally the text
that you're remembering" (quoted in Ralph Berry, *On Directing
Shakespeare* 28, 215, 118–19).

   Nevertheless, Miller also remarks that the text of any play is
always "surprisingly short on the instructions required to bring a
performance into existence" (*Subsequent Performances* 34). To the
extent that the rules for bringing a text into existence lie outside
the text in theatre practice, we might think that the text provides
no such instructions.[10] A production's claim to "congruence" –
what Gary Taylor might call "proximity" – reveals the rhetoric of
its realization. For the text of a play is produced through a variety
of stage practices which more or less systematically reframe the
text on the page as action and behavior. One sign of a production's relation to Shakespearean authority is the way the "text" is
said to dictate aspects of the performance. Miller, for example,
sees the play's genre as one of the inhering features of the text
that constrains directorial practice. Arguing that a *Hamlet* that
"turned Claudius into a shining hero, and Hamlet into a treach-
erous villain" would have "violated the genre within which the
playwright was working," Miller goes on to suggest that while a
play's meanings are historically contingent, emerging in an "evol-
ution, during which meanings and emphases develop that might
not have been apparent at the time of writing, even to the
author," it is nonetheless "usually easy to identify a performance

in which the deep structure of its inherent meanings has been dislocated" (*Subsequent Performances* 35). "There *must* be a notion of constraint," he remarks later, "and this is introduced by the language and by the notion of genre. If a genre within which the playwright is working is not recognized as a constraint it is possible to misidentify the play and to start to stage it in ways that denature the work" (85). In locating genre as a fixed point of repair, Miller employs what is both a traditional literary and a traditional directorial interpretive procedure: the play's text stands in a fixed relation to fixed genres.[11]

But genre is a tricky business, confirmed by Miller's effort to stabilize interpretation by replacing authorial intention with another point of authorized closure, the choice of a determinate genre. For much as genres themselves are neither timeless nor immutable – would anyone today write a "revenge tragedy"? in what sense do *Philoctetes* and *Richard III* and *Bérénice* belong to the same genre? what about *Rosmersholm*? or *Endgame*? – so too plays often seem to migrate within genres. *The Merchant of Venice*, *Titus Andronicus*, and *Troilus and Cressida* are only three plays whose genre, or whose relation to genre, has altered markedly within the past forty years or so. The assertion of genre is an effort to stabilize the text in relation to the fluid values of its ambient culture. Miller's fascinating production of *The Taming of the Shrew* for the BBC-TV Shakespeare Plays series (1980) makes just this point. Attracted to John Cleese's "irritability" in the role of Basil Fawlty in the *Fawlty Towers* series, Miller also noted "strange sympathetic depths in the man that I thought could be usefully applied to the character of Petruchio"; no doubt Cleese's talent for both verbal and physical comedy (and his *Monty Python* cachet) were not lost on Miller either. But Miller's reading of *Shrew* as a template for production strikingly resists assimilating the play to any recognizable Renaissance genre:

The attention that Petruchio pays to the tuition of Katharina can be portrayed much more sympathetically than it is in most productions. Unlike so many of the other suitors, he is not put off by her tantrums and there is a sense in which he is seen as a more caring character. He identifies Kate as someone worth spending time with, and sees that much of her difficulty is due to her self-image – she thinks of herself as unloved and unlovable, rejected by her father and not so favourably regarded as her sister. By suddenly becoming the subject of such detailed and apparently bullying tuition, Kate realizes that somebody has bothered to look beyond her unruly appearance and see her for the first time. It is as though she has become spiritually and morally visible in a way that she was not when simply perceived as a scold. Petruchio has recognized in her shrewish behaviour symptoms of unhappiness and, by behaving badly himself, he gives Kate back an image of herself. (*Subsequent Performances* 121–22)

This is a brilliant and productive reading of the play, and led to a fascinating configuration of relationships in Miller's production. Miller's *Shrew* sought – as all stage production must seek – a modern idiom for the play. This is not a special case: it is the only case. But why *should* Petruchio's actions be portrayed more sympathetically? We might think that Miller labors so mightily here to redefine the action of the play in psychological terms precisely because the Elizabethan genre of the play – scold-comedy, I suppose – is fugitive; the pleasure of publicly watching a man abuse a sharp-tongued and intelligent woman for several hours in order to make her submit willingly to his rule is perhaps not the same entertainment for modern audiences that it was for Shakespeare's contemporaries.[12] Regardless of the play's original generic affiliations, the dominant mode in which Miller and Shakespeare are now working is a purely modern one, the "what-do-we-do-about-*The Shrew*?" genre.

Attributing the "meaning" of stage production to intrinsic features of the text, to its intentions, its genre, its origins, necessarily involves the invention of an "author," a Shakespeare of our own making. Although Charles Marowitz charts a more confrontational relationship between director and author/text, Marowitz's director is also constrained, not by the play's genre, but by its intrinsic, structuring myths.

The core of *Hamlet* is not to be found in the *Historica Danica* or the *Histoires Tragiques* of François de Belleforest or Kyd's *Spanish Tragedy*, but in myths so embedded in human consciousness that no one can trace them to any one source. It is because *Hamlet* is essentially *mythic* that one can weave endless variations on its theme. Shakespeare's play is itself a variation of one or several of those legends that swirl around in every country's subculture. (*Prospero's Staff* 133–34)

Like Miller, who sees the director's task as both limited by the fixity (and enabled by unacknowledged malleability) of genre, Marowitz takes the sign of the masterpiece to be its limitless *re*interpretability. And again like Miller, Marowitz replaces the author with another, less "intentional" category. Instead of restricting a play's meaning to those inherent in its original genre, Marowitz locates it in the play's plot, its (unchanging) representation of the (unchanging) mythological structure of human consciousness. While Miller transforms *Shrew* from scold-comedy to an uplifting new-age parable of personal worth, Marowitz admits elsewhere that the mythic deep structures he finds "in" the plays are in fact the reflections of his own preoccupations: "Throughout much of my work in the theatre, I have found there is often a correspondence between my own psychological state and the material with which it happens to connect at any time. In that sense, 'interpretation' has often meant transferring a personal paradigm into the classical work and using the objective work of art as the carrier for a thoroughly subjective preoccupation" (*Recycling Shakespeare* 51–52). This admission is hardly shocking: all participants in a production are trying to make it speak, which means that they must speak for it, by it, and that it will speak in their present voices. As Peter Brook remarks, "When we perform the classics, we know that their deepest reality will never speak for itself. Our efforts and our technique are to make them speak clearly through us" (*Shifting Point* 85–86).

Directors claim to make their productions speak Shakespeare's meanings, but they finally speak only their own; with Foucault, we might wonder "What difference does it make who is speaking?" ("What Is an Author?" 160). Gay Gibson Cima suggests that "in the mainstream theater the director frequently now seems to fulfill what Foucault calls the 'author function,' the agent within the theater apparatus who delimits the meaning of the work" ("Strategies" 103). But rather than delimiting meaning, the "director" more accurately recapitulates Foucault's authorial function as a site for the ascription of meaning, a zone of ideological activity where institutionalized systems of interpretation come into conflict. "/Director/," John Rouse argues, "has become the sign we use to inscribe that connotational consistency and interpretational purpose we propose to glimpse within and behind a 'weaving together' of the strands of the dramatic with those of the performance text" ("Textuality and Authority" 147). Both Miller and Marowitz rightly respond to the fact that dramatic texts are objects in history, whose interpretation responds to the moment of their representation, the moment of reading or of onstage enactment. What is striking is the difficulty of seeing that moment of production as complete in itself, a moment that makes meaning rather than reiterating it, reproducing the voice of the absent author or his many stand-ins: the text, genre, myth, essence, spirit, "director." Peter Brook remarked in 1968 that at Stratford, "about five years, we agree, is the most a particular staging can live." It's not merely that theatrical style, "the hair-styles, costumes and make-ups look dated. All the different elements of staging – the shorthands of behavior that stand for certain emotions; gestures, gesticulations and tones of voice – are all fluctuating on an invisible stock exchange all the time" (*Empty Space* 16). Much as the Shakespearean text is peppered with words that are now archaic and with familiar words whose original meanings have changed, so too the means of stage representation also undergo constant change, change inflected by the shifting behaviors animating the social world outside the theatre. Stage performance not only takes place in the present, but can only speak in the idiom of the present.

"What the poet" – or the text – "can never provide is the social and historical ambience in which his work is being revived. As much as he may understand human nature and the complexities of the human soul, he cannot foresee the priorities and preoccupations of future generations" (Marowitz, *Prospero's Staff* 5). The modern director's task is to make the play speak in a theatre and a world unimagined by the play's author. David Bradby and David Williams argue that the modern "directors' theatre" forcibly intertwines the roles of author and director: "It is a distinguishing feature of directors' theatre that here the director claims the authorial function even though he has not written the original play. Where he is working with a classic text, he will rearrange, cut and rewrite to fit his production concept" (*Directors' Theatre* 1). Yet the function of the "author" is perhaps nowhere more visible than in directors' relation to the text of a play. Merely using the full or original or authentic text of a play is in itself no guarantee of fidelity; many "experimental" productions – such as Peter Sellars's 1994 *Merchant of Venice*, which I discuss later in this chapter – have used a relatively uncut and unrevised text, developing other ways to challenge the play's discourse in performance. In most conventional productions, on the other hand, the text of the play is considerably altered. Inasmuch as standard play-production practice involves selectively cutting material to achieve a two-to-three-hour running time, clarifying apparent redundancies or opacities in the action, and moderniz-ing at least a few words (let alone silently eliminating characters, redistributing lines between characters, or shifting the order of scenes), even the most "traditional" Shakespeare productions often take an eclectic approach to Shakespeare's text. With the possible exception of directors working with First-Folio-based productions (who often use several texts as well), contemporary directors are not (unlike their literary colleagues) especially anx-ious about the ontological or even authorial status of the material text. As Mark Lamos remarks, "Shakespeare and his actors edited his texts.... The plays are living, breathing vessels of communication. Words must be changed if they are to be com-prehensible for a modern audience. There is nothing as im-portant as understanding what each moment is about" (quoted in Bartow, *The Director's Voice* 180). The reason for this nonchalance is plain: despite the rhetoric of fidelity that undergirds modern directing, that fidelity is to "Shakespeare," a sense of the spirit or meaning of the play that transcends the concrete accidents of any particular version of the text.

"If you just let a play speak, it may not make a sound. If what you want is for the play to be heard, then you must conjure its sound from it" (Brook, *Empty Space* 38). Working on a new play, the director often "creates bits of dialogue or adds to the action and movement of a play in such a way as to influence its final, printed outcome" (Marowitz, *Prospero's Staff* 17), and Shakespeare's plays are conjured in much the same way. Few productions of a Shakespeare play scrupulously follow *any* single text of the play without emendation, adaptation, elimination, substitution, or addition of text; in many cases, actors and directors will clear up a problem in the script by referring to another edition of the play, without much regard to arcane editorial controversies. Trevor Nunn notes that cutting is both necessary and enjoyable: "the study exercise of making a slightly different scene from the one that exists on the page by linking certain speeches together or leaving a section out is most seductive. Occasionally what is required is a line here or two lines there, in order to make sense of a passage. So one has to write the line or two. That too is a wickedly enjoyable exercise. And nobody ever, ever notices" (quoted in Ralph Berry, *On Directing Shakespeare* 79–80). Of course, since the play – or many *documents* of the play – remain for future productions, the interventions of any one production don't really cost anything. Shakespeare, in the late twentieth century, resides between the pages, taking an occasional turn on the stage; this seems to be the burden of Brook's sense that "after all, the texts do not get burned – each person can do what he thinks necessary with a text and still no one suffers" (*Empty Space* 82).

Revising, rewriting, adapting, modernizing the text – or translating the mechanics of the quarto and Folio printing (punctuation, capitalization, line length, speech prefixes) into signs of "the conflict within each character" (Freeman, *Shakespeare's First Texts* 4) – is simply a non-problem in contemporary theatre practice.[13] Stage production does more than merely evoke, enunciate, or complete the text; it re-presents the text in a variety of incommensurable visual, embodied, kinetic discourses. In this sense, the meaning of any stage production is (at least) as involved in the use and implication of these practices as it is in any intrinsic features of the text (even if we accept, in other words, that the text's "intrinsic features" are palpable without some kind of interpretive technology that produces them). At the same time, though, directors tend to regard the material text from a distinctly non-Barthesian perspective. The material details of the text – extending from spelling and punctuation to word choice, syntax, length and organization of speeches, roles, scenes – are to some degree always accidental distractions from the intentional "work" immanent in them, a work unified by a shared conception of properly Shakespearean meaning, and properly Shakespearean – whether conservative, liberal, or radical – theatre. Most directors share the rough-and-ready sense of the relationship between text and work sketched by Martin Mueller in his critique of contemporary textual theory: "the identity of such large-scale intentional structures like *King Lear*, Mozart's *Don Giovanni*, Verdi's *Don Carlos* or the Bruckner Eighth, is a viscous and globby kind of thing rather than a glassy essence." Although we now recognize that there "is no Ur- or final text" of any of these works, "their stability has cheerfully survived authorial indecision and editorial interference. To say so is not to invoke metaphysical essences but to recognize phenomena that for all their contingency are gradual and stable" ("Redrawing the Boundaries?" 614).

My point here is not that directors should be more careful, consistent, or scholarly in their use of texts; far from it. Instead, I mean to dramatize how a theatrical practice that necessarily works to displace, disrupt, or disintegrate the Shakespearean text is sustained by a constant assertion of fidelity to the globby essence of "Shakespeare." Indeed, given the fungibility of any "text" in the theatre, directors most clearly seem to confront Shakespearean authority not in their choice of the words they stage but in setting and scenography, in producing the written text in the visual discourse of the spectacle. Setting the play – determining the visual and even gestural environment in which the dramatic action will take place – is at once the most visible dimension of the director's work and a mark of how the "director" becomes a functional site for the attribution of meaning (after all, most of the visual elements of a production are developed in negotiation with designers, and directors sometimes must work with design ideas determined in advance of the production). Ralph Berry handily charts four dominant approaches to setting Shakespearean drama: Renaissance, modern, period analogue, and eclectic staging (see *On Directing Shakespeare* 14–23). Renaissance, which now includes "mediaeval for the histories and Roman for the Roman plays," echoes what we know of Elizabethan staging, with a tang of the pictorial tradition: "The central idea is that the period of composition, or the period to which the author alludes, should be directly reflected in costumes and settings." Renaissance is the "immediate possibility for most of Shakespeare's plays," and because it avoids apparent interference with the text – the characters logically wear rapiers, points, codpieces and the like – Renaissance is the approach most readily recognized as the sign of authentic Shakespeare. Although Berry suggests that this approach "can tolerate *pourparlers* with eclecticism" (such as the 1972 RSC *Julius Caesar*, which was staged in black-leather Roman costume, "suggesting strongly the aura of Fascism"), in another sense, Renaissance staging is always silently eclectic: using modern materials, modern technology, modern theatres, and modern acting to stage a Renaissance Shakespeare to modern audiences. The strength and simplicity of Renaissance staging arises from this openly rhetorical gesture of fidelity to the text, from this encoding of what we now imagine to be the historical circumstances of Shakespeare's stage through modern means: "The simple, powerful strategy of the historical approach is never likely to be discredited" (14). Of course, as the "historical" approaches of Poel or Irving suggest, the power of this mode lies in its ideological redundancy, its ability to naturalize a modern system of theatrical signification as a transparent instrument, one that appears to disclose the original practice of Shakespeare's theatre and so the original meanings of Shakespeare's plays.

Although Restoration and eighteenth-century productions of Shakespearean drama were conventionally in "modern dress," the contemporary notion of "modern-dress" staging is clearly a consequence of Victorian historicism, a *decision* to extract the play from the location of its setting or the period of its composition and place it in a more urgent dialogue with contemporary social life. Modern-dress production in this sense dates from the post-World-War-I period. Although there are earlier European examples, Barry Jackson inaugurated modern-dress Shakespeare in England with a landmark production of *Cymbeline*, a controversial *Macbeth*, and a brilliant *Hamlet* in the 1920s. He also inaugurated the terms with which modern-dress production is usually criticized. While Ivor Brown praised the "gabbling cynical world-hatred" of Jackson's 1925 *Hamlet*, finding in "its fiery mood of relentless railery... a perfect expression of a shell-shocked world," Harley Granville-Barker was more reserved, and voiced a critique of modern-dress production which has now become perennial: "A joke's a joke," he remarked, "and, our medicine taken, it can go back to its cupboard till next time" (quoted in Kennedy, *Looking at Shakespeare* 110, 112–13).

The principal advantage of modern-dress production is that it "undoubtedly communicates rapidly and directly to a large portion of the audience" (Berry, *On Directing Shakespeare* 15).[14] Modern-dress has the advantage of immediacy, but also consti- tutes a "brusque attack upon the relevance of the text," not merely in the inevitable anachronisms between text and costume, but in the larger resituation of the dramatic action in the ideo- logical context of the present time. "Much has to be denied in the text to shape up the present-day analogies," Berry suggests, "and this denial may be altogether too sweeping," damaging "the fabric of the text, which is sustained by a web of assumptions and attitudes confined to Renaissance thinking," attitudes which are undamaged by Renaissance staging, even when it merely signals the period, or uses modern technology – music, sound, lighting, makeup, fabric, climate control, set and costume construction, wigs (to say nothing of acting style) – to represent it. The "danger" of modern-dress production arises precisely from the reason for doing it, to bring elements of the play into more immediate dialogue with the present: "The danger is always that an immediate point can be made vividly and tellingly, but that it relies on a set of assumptions about our own society that the remainder of the text cannot sustain." Yet while modern-dress potentially narrows the play's frame of reference, it also univer- salizes it: Shakespeare was really writing about *us* all along. Modern-dress production makes explicit the fact that all stage productions – hose-and-doublet or jeans-and-T-shirt – represent Shakespeare through the discourse of contemporary social atti- tudes, behaviors, and "assumptions," which may be why Berry and others see modern-dress as the least attractive alternative: while modern-dress may be "best adapted to the comedies,"

Berry suggests that the "mode is out of favour for staging the tragedies," where the stakes for fidelity are presumably higher (*On Directing Shakespeare* 14–16).[15] Modern-dress productions universalize Shakespeare by claiming the plays' relevance to contemporary life, yet they also appear to distort or even "damage" the text – since Shakespearean meaning is universal, all parts of the text must be universalized at all times.

Staging the play in a period other than the present, the Renaissance, or the period of the dramatic setting is a third tactic. Berry describes period production as ranging along a spectrum: at one extreme, period setting is merely *décor*; at the other, period setting provides the leverage of a "non-decorative" act of "criticism" about the play that can "impose a permanent layer over the text in the minds of the audience" (17). While a merely decorative setting is "innocent of genuine reflection upon the text" (16), a critical period setting reframes the play's meanings. Peter Brook's Watteau *Love's Labour's Lost* (1946) is the now-classic example of period setting becoming "an act of criticism of a very high order," and gave rise to a series of similar productions on both sides of the Atlantic.[16] Although modern-dress seems like a version of period production, period setting appears to preserve the "historical" character of the Shakespearean original. Productions like Jonathan Miller's *Measure for Measure* (1975), set in Freud's Vienna, highlighted "the play's unquestionable concern with sexual repression." And while one "consequence of this approach is that strong light implies shadow, that certain aspects of the text can expect at best a neutral exposition," Berry finds this not to be a "major drawback. The fact is that a Shakespeare text is so large and comprehends so many possibilities that a metaphor which illuminates a single major aspect within the two hours of playing time is fully self-justified" (18). Moreover, "it is undeniable that separate metaphors can coexist peacefully within the same text. The Miller post-colonial *Tempest* and the Hall Renaissance *Tempest* are incompatible with each other, but perfectly congruent with the text: and that is all that matters" (19).[17]

While Berry sees modern-dress production as invasive, period settings provide a range of imagery ultimately authorized by the richness of Shakespeare's metaphor-stuffed text, an infinite variety that can, apparently, only accommodate the present when it has, like Antony, ebbed into the past. Shakespearean history is even amenable to period-treatments claiming to depict "a dialectic of historical forces," the "territory claimed if not owned by the Marxists." Again, though, "Marxist" treatments of Shakespearean history – the approach "works best for *Coriolanus*," but is also effective for *The Merchant of Venice, King John*, and the history cycles – are appropriate precisely because the Marxist preoccupation with class struggle finds its precursor in the terms of Shakespearean dramaturgy itself, in that Shakespearean history tends to deal with individuals as "representatives of social groups, or classes, in conflict." Since "the early histories are fairly Brechtian" and "Brecht, be it added, was profoundly influenced by Shakespeare," it is possible to locate "Marxist" preoccupations in Shakespearean texts themselves (19).

Period productions, on the other hand, use history as a metaphor for the recovery of authentically Shakespearean meanings. Recognizing that the texture of Renaissance social life may be too remote for contemporary audiences, period productions set the play in a still remote, "historical," but nonetheless familiar context of costume, setting, and gesture. Renaissance staging asserts the production's fidelity to Shakespeare's original meanings by identifying modern stage practices with those of Shakespeare's theatre. Modern-dress production claims the relevance of Shakespearean insights to contemporary life, and/or suggests that the forms of modern living can still provide access to Shakespearean meanings. On the other hand, modern-dress staging sometimes appears to remind audiences of the remoteness of the Shakespearean original, foisting a discomfiting dissonance between the performance and Shakespeare. Period production appears to transform "history" into a metaphor for meanings latent in the text. While modern-dress staging opens up the possibility of historical rupture between the Shakespearean original and its contemporary production, period staging implies that the dynamics of Shakespeare's plays represent the fundamental forms of human relations, individual and collective action. The apparent changes of history are, in this sense, merely metaphorical – Shakespeare in different clothes.[18]

The dominant mode of contemporary staging is the "eclectic" alternative, reflecting a desire to "keep the options open" that Berry finds "characteristic of today" (20). Citing the "indeterminate period" of Ingmar Bergman's *Hamlet* (1987), the intermingling of Crimean and American Civil War costumes and settings in Howard Davies's *Troilus and Cressida* (1985), and David William's Stratford, Ontario *All's Well That Ends Well* (1988), Berry concludes that "there was modest historical licence, but nothing to make the average theatregoer feel that any violation of decorum was taking place" (21). Eclectic production has the advantage of enabling the director to key various aspects of the production – different scenes, the costuming of different characters, even different physical actions such as combat – to different historical periods, geographical locations, social classes, and so on, enabling the production to construct the text's contemporary meaning through a much wider range of reference. Eclectic staging also has obvious affinities both with Elizabethan theatre practice and with postmodern pastiche. While it tends on the one hand to blur the production's historical frame of reference, this is not taken as a sign of the play's fragmented or disconnected discourse, or of an intermittent relation to contemporary modes of understanding. Instead, the broken images of eclectic staging signal the universality and coherence of the play's basic "myth," or, more accurately, are said to succeed when they appear to do so. Although Berry concludes that eclectic "production itself cannot be judged on its supposed fidelity to the *Ur*-text of the myth, the words of the Folio," the decorum of eclectic production rests on its ability to "harness the myth's energies to a new pattern that holds meaning for us" (23). In this sense, eclectic performance literalizes the practice of other modes of production, declaring openly what Renaissance, modern-dress, and period practices conceal behind the metaphor of historical consistency: the rhetoric of contemporary Shakespeare production subordinates the signs of history to the authority of the text. While Renaissance staging claims to place its audience in the presence of the play's original meanings, modern-dress and period stagings "work" in Berry's view when they show the application of Shakespearean meanings to other moments in history. The decorum of eclectic staging lies in the sense that "Shakespeare" reveals a "new pattern" to us, the pattern of history itself.

These efforts to consider a production's meaning in terms of its scenography point to the difficulty of preserving the historicity of Shakespearean meanings while at the same time recognizing that such meanings must speak in a contemporary register. Whether using Renaissance, modern-dress, period, or eclectic staging, the stage works to speak Shakespearean meanings; the work of directing, the work of performance, is to stage an ongoing dialogue with authority. To see directing, and theatre practice generally, in this manner is to qualify the fundamentally romantic sense of the creative independence of the theatre and its artists. More precisely, we might take the difficulty of describing the relationship between author, text, director, and performance to arise from the contradictory imperatives of modernist theatre aesthetics: to preserve the authority of the text, and yet to make it new. One place where this tension surfaces is in books by directors themselves, especially books in which directors attempt to precipitate a theoretical account of theatre practice. Two contemporary directors – Charles Marowitz and Jonathan Miller – have engaged this question, and although Marowitz and Miller are markedly different in temperament, in their orientation to theatre, and in the kind of Shakespeare they produce onstage, books like *Recycling Shakespeare*, *Prospero's Staff*, and *Subsequent Performances* dramatize the constitutive function of the "author" in the work of the contemporary director.

Charles Marowitz's *Recycling Shakespeare* is, as he declares in the preface, "directed at two enemies – the academics and the traditionalists," who believe "that 'a classic' is an entity fixed in time and bounded by text," rather than "a prism in which I discern innumerable reflections of myself and my society and, like a prism, it refracts many pinpoints of colour, rather than transmitting one unbroken light" (ix). In chapters headed "Harlotry in Bardolatry," "How to Rape Shakespeare," and "Free Shakespeare! Jail Scholars!" Marowitz derides the ways in which academic scholarship and teaching, and traditionalist directors have constituted Shakespeare as the deadliest of icons: "the bastions that protect William Shakespeare have been established by scholars, critics and teachers – people with a vested interest in language and the furtherance of a literary tradition. It is in their interests that the texts remain sacrosanct, that they are handed down from generation to generation, each providing new insights and new refinements, like so many new glosses on an old painting" (4). Since, in Marowitz's view, scholarship is largely a matter of careerist ambition and institutionalized pedantry – "wanking is a full-time job, and teaching others how to wank, a sign of intellectual respectability" (73) – it's not surprising that he takes academic work on Shakespeare "to examine the most abstruse aspects of scholarly questions in a spirit of audacious inquiry, without realising that they are splitting hairs and vivisecting follicles" (73). Precisely because their "theories, suppositions and speculations are ends in themselves," academics are able to ignore "what in the theatre are called 'playable values' – that is, ideas capable of being translated into concrete dramatic terms" (1). While the professors never "get on their feet and demonstrate their ideas," an "actor or a direc- tor, on the other hand, tests his theories before audiences, and they not only can be proven, they are *obliged* to be" (72).[19]

Marowitz articulates the familiar opposition between scholar- ship and the stage: preoccupied with reading, and with the strat- egies of meaning-making common to scholarly argument and demonstration, scholarship produces only abstract and specu- lative results; theatre practice, if it can sidestep the essentially "scholarly" trap of "fidelity," restores Shakespeare to his medium, the flexible medium of the stage. I will consider how this ener- vating opposition infects performance criticism in a later chapter; here, however, I want to explore what Marowitz hopes to gain by freeing directors from such triviality. Marowitz is refreshingly straightforward about the self-reflective quality of directing. While scholars are narcissistic pedants, Marowitz confesses that "What I love best in Shakespeare are the facets of myself and my world that I find there" (ix). What's needed today "is not the routine repetition of his words and imagery, but the *Shakespearian Experience*, and, ironically, that can come only from dissolving the works into a new compound – that is, creating the sense of vicissitude, variety and intellectual vigour with which the author himself confronted his own time" (31).

Much as Marowitz works to compromise Shakespearean authority in order to value the director's creative collaboration, his understanding of the director's role is complicated by the same issues of evidence and authority that afflict the scholars and teachers.[20] Despite his huffiness about scholars, Marowitz's view of the director's craft is ultimately a readerly, critical, interpretive one; the director's "main concern is reconstituting Shakespeare's ideas and finding new ways dramatically to extrapolate them" (*Recycling Shakespeare* 5). Marowitz suggests that the "only fidelity that cuts any ice in the theatre is a director's fidelity to his personal perceptions about a classic; how well and how truly he can put on stage the visions the play has evoked in his imagination" (7). This sense of the director-as-collaborator leads Marowitz to argue for the kind of collage-productions that have been his most innovative contribution to the contemporary theatre:

And, by insisting on the preservation of the Shakespearian language, as if the greatness of the plays were memorialised only there, the theatre is denying itself a whole slew of new experiences and new artefacts which can be spawned from the original sources, in exactly the same way that Shakespeare spawned his works from Holinshed, Boccaccio, Kyd, and Belleforest. The future of Shakespearian production lies in abandoning the written works of William Shakespeare and devising new works which are tangential to them, and the stronger and more obsessive the Shakespeare Establishment becomes, the more it will hold back the flow of new dramatic possibilities which transcend what we call, with a deplorable anal-retentiveness, the canon. (15)

Marowitz gestures toward a de-authorized theatre, one that *uses* Shakespearean texts to discover new meanings.[21] At the same time, though, Marowitz evokes a palpable anxiety about the prospect of a purely theatrical Shakespeare. Much as the intervening director recapitulates Shakespeare's dramatic procedures, so by cutting and rearranging lines from Shakespeare's *Hamlet*, Marowitz's collage version claimed to "convey the essence of the play without relying on narrative"; "the ideas, attitudes, and characters of the collage were in every particular related to, or made comment upon, Shakespeare's original" (*Prospero's Staff* 36).

Although the radical director works to express a unique,

romantic subjectivity through theatrical production, that vision is finally troped by Shakespeare. The "validity or nullity" of a director's work "depends on the consistency of a director's *mise-en-scène*: how much of a piece he can make of that vision which he sees staring back at him when he gazes into the ruffled pool of Shakespeare's play." In that reflection, the director sees both himself and something of the Shakespearean original: "there is some unmistakable line, which, stretched as it may be to breaking-point, still connects up to the themes and ideas contained in the original material" (*Recycling Shakespeare* 11). This "line" seems finally to originate in "Shakespeare," something outside the writing itself, an enabling directorial fiction: "a kind of imagery-cum-mythology which has separated itself from the written word and can be dealt with by artists in isolation from the plays that gave it birth" (15). While the scholars stroke their hermetic theories, Marowitz's director conjures up the figure of the author to underwrite *his* own creative efforts, an author who lives not in the text but around it in the vague web of myth. Scholars construct a "Shakespeare" amenable to their theatrically irrelevant careerism; Marowitz appears to construct a "Shakespeare" amenable to his own reflection, a vehicle that stimulates – and authorizes – his imaginative work on the play, but which relates to any other Shakespeare only in the mysterious world of myth and dream. Between the wankers and the narcissists, Marowitz doesn't offer much choice.

Jonathan Miller's measured commentary on directing and on his own productions in *Subsequent Performances* is some remove from Marowitz's rebarbative prose. And yet like Marowitz, Miller is interested in defining and preserving the sphere of directorial activity as a distinctive mode of authorship, an independent creation underwritten by "Shakespeare." Like Marowitz, too, Miller has a keen sense of the work of Shakespeare in contemporary culture; where he begins to differ from Marowitz is in his unwillingness to establish fixed boundaries between different modes of Shakespearean representation. While Marowitz, for instance, sees reading/scholarship and performance as fixed polarities, Miller – who concedes that "plays can be said to exist without being theatrically performed" – suggests that plays can have a complex and multiple "afterlife":

As long as we recognize and accept the argument that performance is, necessarily, a limitation, then the destiny of a great play is to undergo a series of performances each of which is incomplete, and in some cases may prove misleading and perverse. By submitting itself to the possibility of successive re-creation, however, the play passes through the development that is its birthright, and its meaning begins to be fully appreciated only when it enters a period that I shall call its *afterlife*. (*Subsequent Performances* 23)

In a subtle reading of how various artworks have changed in the kinds of meaning they have had throughout history, Miller invokes the notion of an afterlife as a means of bridging the gap between the "original" significance of an artwork and the meanings it has in the present. Artworks of the past are invariably disjoined from their original context – medieval paintings originally designed for altarpieces are one example here – and gain apparently intrinsic meanings and values that were nonetheless not part of their creators' intentions nor of the context of signification in which they first appeared. Miller's "afterlife," then, is an attempt to forge a pragmatic heuristic for the tension between the text as origin, and the practices and significance of modern theatrical behavior. Miller approaches this "afterlife" through a variety of metaphors and comparisons – with the historical transmission of European painting, with the relationship between score and performance in music, with the projection of the Earth's curved surface onto a flat plane in mapmaking – which attempt to grasp the difference between texts and performances, and to account for their changing relations over time. Comparing the staging of plays and opera throughout history with models drawn from evolutionary biology, for example, Miller remarks,

Each performance is constrained by the script but in the process of being brought to life as a living production it acquires characteristics that are due to the interpretive efforts of the performers and producers, not to mention those brought about by staging it in different formats. Once the production has died with its final performance it sheds its acquired characteristics and theoretically reverts to the condition of the script or score from which a new production can be revived. (68)

Yet "this is where the comparison between plays and living organisms breaks down": for although the acquired characteristics and skills of an organism are not transmitted genetically, the "acquired characteristics" a play develops in its production history "are often to be found in subsequent productions" (68). The play text brings an intrinsic and an historical "genetic" inheritance to bear on stage production, no matter how divergent the producers' understanding of action, character, behavior, morality, might be. For the afterlife of plays requires of directors a "conscious effort to reconcile what is foreign and incomprehensible with what is permanent and readily intelligible" (69).

Miller's "afterlife" is a flexible means for attempting to claim contact with origin – author, text – while at the same time recognizing that any production necessarily speaks in the present tense, since even those moments in which Shakespeare's historical difference is being emphasized are fashioned from the present's perspective on the past. Yet much as Poel's productions now look to us like Edwardian Elizabethanism, Miller remarks that they "were considerably less *inauthentic* than the ones that had been staged throughout the preceding century"; "Ironically, by stripping away the picturesque and releasing the plays into a dramatic rather than a pictorial space, Poel revealed their essentially literary character, making them increasingly susceptible to the sort of 'conceptual' interpretations that critics so often deplore" (57). Miller rightly seizes on the turn of the century as the moment when the "essentially literary character" of plays marked a shifting institutional balance between theatre and literature. We can no longer read medieval altarpieces in the manner of their original audiences, decoding their symbolism as part of a sustained structure of feeling and being in the world; Miller's "afterlife" is a way to preserve the authority of the original in a mode of transmission – theatre – that now stands apart from the "literary" ontology of plays.[22]

Marowitz's "recycled" Shakespeare and Miller's Shakespearean "afterlife" are expressions of – and hard-won efforts to come to grips with – a theoretical crisis characteristic of the modern Anglo-North American theatre: how to legitimate the critical work of theatre, when theatre is understood, despite frequent claims to the contrary, as an essentially *re*productive art. This sense of afterlife and authenticity is most called into question today by productions in which Shakespeare's implication in cultural and political history is figured as part of the production of his plays: in aggressively postmodern performances, in intercultural performance, and in various kinds of production undertaken in post-, neo-, and still-colonial contexts. As Patrice Pavis remarks, such productions "no longer ask to be accepted as authentic (re)readings of Shakespeare's text" ("Wilson, Brook, Zadek" 271). Nonetheless, this sense of liberation seems somewhat premature, especially given the complexity of intercultural and postcolonial encounters with Shakespeare. As Pavis suggests of Peter Brook's 1990 *Tempest*, "Brook's relationship to the Shakespearean tradition is highly ambiguous: according to his conception of transcultural communication, Brook relativizes all Eurocentric claim to release the enigma of the text. At the same time, Shakespeare is for him so mysterious and complex that one cannot interpret him with words and ideas; at best, his potential force can be unleashed thanks to the presence and vivacity of actors: 'even though Shakespeare's words are inevitably coloured by their period, the true richness of this writing lies at a deeper level, beneath the words, where there is no form, nothing but the vibration of a great potential force'" (280–81). In this sense, the force of Shakespeare's shadowing of the work of direction may be more plain, and more consequential, not in productions that invoke the modern rhetoric of Shakespearean fidelity – Renaissance style, conservation of the text, psychological consistency – but in those that appear to resist it. How does the "director's" transmission of Shakespearean authority contain such productions, and provide interpretive closure – or the illusion of interpretive closure – to performances that seem otherwise invested in revising or resisting Shakespeare? And how does the "director" – both in his/her imagining of the production, and as a functional site for the attribution of meaning by the play's audiences and critics – participate in this transmission? To consider these questions, I want to turn now to Peter Sellars's 1994 staging of *The Merchant of Venice*.

I want to describe an unusually interesting performance, one that raises a range of questions about how producing dramatic "subjects" – characters – onstage, and how "character," registers the production's – and the director's – relation to Shakespeare. The dominant image of the work is the Los Angeles uprising of 1992, and the racial and political dynamics surrounding the apprehension and beating of Rodney King, its global videotape transmission, and the rioting and police action that took place in the city after the acquittal of several Los Angeles Police Department officers. Yet in many respects, this image remains in the background; the dramatic narrative is an interracial romantic comedy involving a shady young man – vaguely but distinctly involved in illegal or at least illicit business – and a more respectable young woman from another part of town. Perhaps the most striking feature of the performance, though, is the way the technological reproduction of performance – video "experience" – complicates the enactment of the "characters" and a sense of their integrity and coherence. An interrogation of the "subject," that is, provides a formal and ideological linkage between the closure of the romantic plot and the unstable texture of social life, the multiplication of pseudo-agents, perhaps even the frightening erasure of agency.

I am thinking here about Peter Sellars's 1994 production of *The Merchant of Venice*; or at least, I was thinking about *Merchant* until my thinking about it was infected by striking similarities with the 1995 film, *Strange Days*.[23] For all its high-tech fantasy of the multiplication and dispersion of identity, *Strange Days* enacts a deep nostalgia for the centered, individual, self-present subject, a nostalgia enacted before the canvas of Los Angeles, 1999, a city on the brink of riot, celebration, anarchy. Sellars's *Merchant* – set in Venice Beach, deploying a racialized casting pattern and a variety of "mechanical" means for interrupting and reproducing "acting" – connects this nostalgia to a more locally theatrical crisis, a crisis of authority. The production proved controversial on several fronts, not least for violating acceptable canons of Shakespeare production. And yet Shakespeare is everywhere visible in criticism of the production, from Sellars's remarks about his own intentions as a director to the commentaries (positive and negative) by theatre reviewers. Here, I want to assess the work that Shakespeare performs in Sellars's mapping out of the work of his production, and in critical efforts to assess the meaning of this baffling *Merchant of Venice*. For in many respects, the work of Sellars's *Merchant of Venice* began, as the work of all theatrical production begins, at the moment it resisted this bondage, this captivity to the sign of the author, to "Shakespeare."

Peter Sellars's production of *The Merchant of Venice* opened at Chicago's Goodman Theatre in October, 1994. Sellars's notoriety and the production's explicit engagement with the racially charged themes of the Los Angeles uprising of 1992 drew national media coverage (it was reviewed not only in the Chicago papers, but also in the *New York Times, Time, Newsweek, The Los Angeles Times,* and elsewhere); the production then toured to England, Germany, and France. Sellars's *Merchant* received other kinds of attention – or inattention – as well. While the Chicago papers were divided over whether Sellars's exploration of American culture and of Shakespeare was profound or pretentious, Goodman audiences voted with their feet: most evenings saw the audience depleted by as much as 60 per cent after the intermission. *Merchant* was routinely described as slow, tendentious, unfunny, and un-Shakespearean. Sellars's ambition, however, was not merely to offer a new, postmodern reframing of the play. Instead, he proposed to "touch the texture of life in contemporary America," using *The Merchant of Venice* to reflect, represent, and analyze contemporary social conditions.

Four centuries ago, at the moment that modern capitalism was being invented, Shakespeare wrote a play that remains the most astute and shockingly frank analysis of the economic roots of racism that we have. He called it, not insignificantly, *The Merchant of Venice.* Shakespeare's Venice is an international city whose trading partners include China, Africa, the Americas and the Arab world. The Venice that I live in is Venice, California. By inviting African-American actors to take the roles of the Jews, Asian actors to play Portia and her court, and Latino actors to play the Venetians, I can begin to touch the texture of life in contemporary America; the metaphor and the reality of anti-Semitism is extended to include parallel struggles and their related issues. (Sellars, Untitled Commentary 4)

On the one hand, Sellars's *Merchant* appeared to deflect a traditional sense that an authentic performance is immanent in the
text. Staging *The Merchant of Venice* today, Sellars implies, seems to
require the discovery of a contemporary stage idiom, in which
the play's specific representation of antisemitism "is extended to
include parallel struggles and their related issues," struggles and
issues that necessarily conflict with the specifics of the text itself.
At the same time, though, the desire for authentication is difficult
to displace: Shakespeare's Venice must somehow anticipate
Sellars's Venice Beach. Sellars's production captures the dialectical crisis of contemporary dramatic performance, or more precisely, of the critical discourse describing the role of the director
in the production of plays. For much as Sellars wanted to use *The
Merchant of Venice* to explore the dynamics of contemporary
society, he appeared wary of *confronting* the play, of posing a gap
between the play's ways of interlacing race, social privilege, economic power, and dramatic action and contemporary American
attitudes. Instead, a gesture of fidelity to Shakespeare haunts his
sense of the work of performance, much as it haunted the production's critical reception. Using *The Merchant* to read America
Sellars was frustrated precisely by his – and his critics' – desire to
shape this reading under the sign of "Shakespeare."

Sellars's account of his *Merchant* dramatizes the conditions of
authority framing contemporary Anglo-North American Shakespearean production. "Shakespeare" is often invoked at moments
of ideological strain, summoned as ground for interpreting or
evaluating refractory events, elements in a stage production that
resist assimilation to the dominant aesthetic practices of the
theatre and the cultural investments they represent. In commentary on Sellars's *Merchant*, "Shakespeare" appeared when the production put pressure on two familiar interpretive paradigms:
"theme" and "character." Sellars's casting raised questions of thematic relevance, of the ways this staging traduced/reproduced
the Shakespearean original in order to comment on racial and
economic tensions in American life. Although this thematic tran-
scription was provocative, Sellars's innovation of performance
practice proved more controversial. Videotaping the actors with
hand-held cameras and broadcasting their images on TV moni-

tors during the production, using sound and video environments as a critical part of the *mise-en-scène*, and miking the actors and repeatedly distorting their delivery, the production called into question not only the staging of the text, but the ways acting evokes relations of authority, impersonates "Shakespeare" so to speak. In this sense, the production urged a dialectical engagement between the discourse of *The Merchant of Venice* and racial and economic aspects of contemporary American society, a confrontation registered paradoxically less in Sellars's racialized casting than in the strategic subversion of "character" itself.

Sellars's casting exploited and modernized the play's thematic texture of social relations, and capitalized on the conventions of modern-dress Shakespeare: because the play's meanings are already universal, modern-dress production doesn't so much "translate" the play into contemporary terms as reveal Shakespeare's uncanny anticipation of modern social and ethical life. Sellars claimed a symmetry between contemporary American society and Shakespeare's London, arguing that the seventeenth century was a pivotal moment in the development of modern social and economic relations: "We go from a random exploitation and some of the unhappy encounters of the first century of exploration, into, finally in the seventeenth century, an extremely organized system of capital and profit." In the play, Antonio represents this transformation, the archetype of "this new middle class." Yet to see the characteristic forms of seventeenth-century social injustice only as analogies of twentieth-century oppression made Sellars uneasy. With some urgency, he places Shakespeare, "writing at the time of the invention of states, colonialism, and capitalism," at the origin of modern culture: "Literally in his generation it is being created." Though Sellars is clearly impatient with the play's exclusive focus on antisemitism, the warrant of the production demands that this moment in the play's theatrical afterlife be an extension of its animating intentions: "This is the modern capitalist state. Shakespeare is present at the creation of the kind of hideous karma that we're living with: the Gulf War, Rwanda, Bosnia. All of these borderlines were drawn by colonial powers" ("Peter Sellars Interview" 13).

Despite Sellars's notoriety as the *enfant terrible* of American theatre, this sense of direction is profoundly conservative: the meanings produced on the stage must appear to arise from "the text," as the sign of the author's animating intention. Assuming that the play's ability to speak to modern audiences rests on its internal anticipation of modern values and ideologies, Sellars must take *The Merchant* not merely to participate in, say, the exploitative dimension of capitalist economic and social production, but to adopt a thematic perspective consistent with the values of his audience. To forge this thematic identity between the play's "meanings" and modern social liberalism, Sellars drafts Shakespeare as his critical ally. Sharer in the company, servant at court, real estate investor, armigerous landholder, Shakespeare epitomizes the moment of nascent capitalism in his participation in both emergent and residual modes of social life. Sellars's "Shakespeare" – the sign of the author – assimilates the play's internal meanings to modern liberalism by identifying Shakespeare's situation as continuous with our own. Sellars figures this continuity by insisting that "The man who called his theater 'The Globe' wrote about a multi-cultural society in which institutionalized racism permitted the subversion of justice for short term financial advantage" (Sellars, Untitled Commentary 4). Shakespeare's purposes are also confirmed by the audiences that he and Sellars address: "Shakespeare is writing to an audience which is basically like most people in America today, like the Simi Valley jury, who just really weren't aware that black people were that angry" ("Peter Sellars Interview" 14). Of course, in reclaiming "Shakespeare" for the present, Sellars overplays not only the diversity of Shakespeare's London, but of Shylock's Venice as well, which – for all the play's allusion to distant trading connections – is basically a monocultural city, in which a dominant Christian mercantile class exploits and oppresses a small and ghettoized Jewish community (the princes of Morocco and Arragon, we might recall, are only visitors at Belmont). Yet whether Sellars is right or wrong in his reading of Shakespearean biography, of Elizabethan social and theatrical history, or even of *The Merchant of Venice* is beside the point. What is to the point is the fact that Sellars must elaborate these parallels – between Venice and Venice Beach – in order to clear a conceptual space for his work as a director. Placing Shakespeare at the origin of modern economic relations, writing about modern social injustice, to a modern audience, Sellars locates the production's progressive social agenda not so much in its engagement with contemporary American social concerns, or even in *The Merchant of Venice*, as in a mystified, expansive principle of interpretation, ideology, value, what you will, that governs the potential meanings of the play. The name of that principle is "Shakespeare."

Sellars's Shakespeare enacts a traditional authorial function, guaranteeing closure between text and interpretation; "Shakespeare" not only substantiated Sellars's reading of the text, but his imaginative work as director as well. Attempting to preserve Shakespeare's critique of racial injustice and economic exploitation (rather than, for instance, seeing the play and perhaps even his own production as conditioned by or invested in them), Sellars used casting to suggest thematically "parallel struggles and their related issues." Producing a play – as reading, as stage performance – transforms it into a new product "which cannot be mechanically extrapolated from an inspection of the text itself" (Eagleton, *Criticism and Ideology* 65). Putting *The Merchant of Venice* into practice necessarily inflects its racialized discourse in new and unanticipated ways, ways which distort a simple parallelism between Shakespearean and modern ideologies. Sellars's casting gave a contemporary, accessible shape to the visceral hostilities animating *The Merchant of Venice*. Casting Antonio, Bassanio, Salerio, Solanio, and Gratiano as Latinos, and Portia and Nerissa as suburban Asian Americans, Sellars's *Merchant* concretized the play's tribal loyalties – blacks (or Jews), Latinos, Asians, men, women – and showed how they prevent community from coming about. Sellars also wanted to accentuate the privileged domain of Shakespearean theatre on the horizon of contemporary performance, not only by choosing a diverse cast of performers, but by choosing performers whose careers are institutionally framed outside Shakespearean precincts: "they mostly get to play gang members, drug dealers, and cops" (*Shakespeare Laboratory*). Yet analogy is a two-way street. Although contemporary forms of social identification were applied to explain, sharpen, and motivate the play's roles, the play's forms of social identification also exerted a reciprocal interpretive leverage on contemporary models of racial, ethnic, gender, and economic relationships. In performance, Sellars's *Merchant* seemed to resist a simple parallelism between Venice and Venice Beach. Shylock, for example, was a business-suited, dominating, bankerly figure, more a part of the play's economic power elite than its exploited casualty; as one reviewer noted, Paul Butler's Shylock was more reminiscent of Clarence Thomas than of Rodney King (Albert Williams 34). Much as Sellars's casting repositioned Shylock in the play's social structure, the production also represented the social and racial dynamics of contemporary Los Angeles from an oblique angle. The production showed Asian Americans and Latinos forming a united front against Shylock (at least before the unraveling of the romance plot in Sellars's final act), and although the Duke and the Gobbos were played by Anglo actors, the action of the play represented the racial dynamics of contemporary America as taking place somewhere beyond the frame of Anglo culture and its institutions. Even the Duke, in the trial scene, seemed less the agent of dominant culture than a bored and frazzled bureaucrat, dispensing rote "justice."[24]

The production's "parallel" between American race relations and antisemitism proved particularly opaque, neither a rendering of Shakespeare nor a cogent representation of contemporary history.[25] On the one hand, by casting African Americans as Jews, the specificity of antisemitism was blunted. As Michael C. Kotzin remarked in his review, by rendering Jewishness "only as some sort of figure of speech," antisemitism was also registered as an abstraction (77). At the same time, keying the play's social groupings to American ethnic identifications bore its own confusions. While treating Jews as figures of speech refined antisemitism out of history, mapping American race relations on the paradigm of *The Merchant of Venice* proved a confusing way to read contemporary racial strife, in part because "the persecutors of these blacks are not whites but Latinos" (78). Sellars's casting of Portia and Nerissa as Asian Americans (their African American servants, Shannon Steen points out, were marked *as* African Americans by their gospel singing) proved similarly unstable; though wealthy and powerful, Asian Americans were both exoticized and "feminized" relative to the play's other social groups, an orientalizing gesture apparently at odds with Sellars's intentions. Despite the "profound universalism of the English language's greatest writer," Sellars's production seemed at once to muddy the dynamics of Shakespeare's narrative, and to muddy the play's relevance "to the contemporary moment" (Kotzin 79).

"We're testing Shakespeare against our lives, we're testing our lives against Shakespeare," Sellars remarked in a film made of the production's rehearsals (*Shakespeare Laboratory*). What this production dramatizes, though, is the failure of such a "test," of the idea of such a "test." The play confronts audiences with its remoteness, and seduces them with its familiarity. Sellars's parallel between antisemitism and racism marks the ideologically mobile relation between texts and performances and the way "Shakespeare" is summoned to mask, euphemize, and contain this slippage. By treating the signifiers of race and ethnicity as "signs," however, Sellars's *Merchant* opens a more productive line of thinking about the relationship between texts and performances. *The Merchant of Venice* seemed to render two conventional strategies for reading text-and-performance untenable. On the one hand, the production's casting seemed finally to obviate any clear sense of fidelity to Shakespeare. Rather than expressing ideas about race and power unambiguously present in the play, Sellars's *Merchant* seemed to put a new, surprising, and sometimes frustrating spin on the play's articulations of ethnicity and society. At the same time, however, the production seemed not to offer a readily legible account of contemporary Los Angeles or of American race and ethnicity more generally; despite Sellars's fashioning of "parallel struggles," this Shakespeare did not seem to be our contemporary. Instead, *The Merchant of Venice* staged an unresolved confrontation between Shakespeare's Venice and Sellars's Venice Beach. Refusing to frame a transparent opening between "Shakespeare" and "America," the performance clouded the exchange between the play's formal categories of identity and action and those of contemporary social life. It resisted, in other words, a simple allegorizing of modern racism on the paradigm of Shakespeare's play. Working as much against Sellars's intentions as "Shakespeare's," *The Merchant of Venice* seemed to dramatize an asymmetry between the ways in which race, ethnicity, and power were mapped in 1594 and 1994.[26] The production marked the "alien" quality of early modern culture, while at the same time "alienating" – de-naturalizing, marking as historical in a specifically Brechtian way – modern social relations, confirming, in a sense, Alan Sinfield's notion that Shakespeare's characters (and the "people" they represent) "were very different from us, but not totally different" (*Faultlines* 62).

In various commentaries on *The Merchant of Venice*, Sellars models his thematic use of casting as an act of recovery, a directorial dialogue with Shakespeare. Yet other aspects of his work on *The Merchant of Venice*, particularly the production's distorting interplay between live and taped performance, reveal a different, more disruptive directorial agenda. The set was unusually bleak – a bare stage with a few scattered pieces of office furniture – and the television monitors hung above the stage and positioned along the sides of the auditorium played a prominent and powerful role in the performance. Antonio, for example, spoke his opening monologue into a standing microphone while Salerio and Solanio videotaped him, projecting his face on the screens; video loops of water and flowers decorated the Belmont scenes; the "news of the Rialto" was delivered as a news report, and so on. Moreover, the characters frequently spoke into the microphones strewn around the stage: their speeches swung wildly from near inaudibility to loud amplification, and they frequently repeated lines in different registers. Two uses of video were particularly effective: in some scenes, important speeches (Shylock's "Hath not a Jew...," for example) were delivered upstage, shutting out the audience from the "live" performance, while the monitors projected the actor's image and multiplied it throughout the house. And footage of the Rodney King beating and the Los Angeles uprising played in video counterpoint to the trial scene onstage.

Sellars's technological dispersion of stage "character" explicitly drew *The Merchant of Venice* into dialogue with the ways other media – particularly television – represent modern subjects, and so into conflict with a conventional channel of transmission for Shakespearean authority, the live enactment of (realistic, psychological) "character." Rather than the psychological depth-effect associated with Shakespearean acting, Sellars's production also staged the superficial-effect associated with TV. Though not a "high-tech lynching," Sellars's "C-SPAN Shakespeare" (Albert Williams) reminded critics of Court TV (Zoglin 78), of the "documentary talking-head close-ups and reaction shots" familiar from TV news (Swed F5), of "tabloid news" (Christiansen), and of the O. J. Simpson criminal trial (Henning). Such comments restate the reservations typically directed to modern-dress Shakespeare: that by insisting on contemporary relevance, modern-dress productions omit or trivialize what's truly Shakespearean. Furthermore, Sellars's use of video was taken as an assault on the essence of Shakespeare, and so of theatre itself – the revelation of character through the present, emotionally sincere performance of the live actor. David Richards's *New York Times* review emphasized the dissemination of character, describing the production as "dismantling characters' psyches and spreading out all the pieces for us to examine":

Much of the production is relayed over nine television monitors, positioned onstage and in the auditorium. Just as Shylock prepares to deliver his celebrated speech, "Hath not a Jew eyes?" he deliberately turns his back on the audience. Only because a supernumerary is focusing a hand-held video camera on the actor's face, do we see it – larger than life, but also stripped of any visceral immediacy – on the monitors. Similarly, rather than address each other, the characters often talk into the microphones that stand at either side of the stage and sit on various tables.

What Mr. Sellars sees happening to society at large – a pulling apart of the races and a general breakdown of humanity – happens to his performers as well, who become less than the sum of their parts. Frequently, a conscious effort is required to match voice and body, face and feeling. ("Sellars Moves the Merchant" B2)

Arguing that "Emotions, thus fragmented, lose their power to move us," Richards concludes by asking whether "Mr. Sellars might be a more potent force in the theatre if he felt more and actually thought less?" To Richards, Shakespeare is signified by the working of the dominant mode of modern acting – psychological realism – and other critics similarly saw Sellars's production as most un-Shakespearean in those moments when it departed from this convention, and the "visceral immediacy" it projects. One reviewer specifically faulted Sellars for failing to "engage our emotions" in the manner of Chicago native David Mamet: "Chicago theater, like the city itself, may lack refinement, but it does not lack heart. Performance here demands to be judged in terms not just of craft but of relevance, honesty and immediacy. If it doesn't hurt, it doesn't matter" – and it's not Shakespeare (Iglarsh 5).

It is possible, of course, that the kind of acting that Sellars developed for *The Merchant of Venice* was just plain bad.[27] But it is also worth asking whether Sellars's *Merchant* challenged contemporary social attitudes – regarding, say, the role of the individual subject in the discourse of American racial and ethnic diversity – at just the point in which the cultural authority of Shakespeare was most clearly challenged: in the play's rhetoric of characterization, its ways of producing "character" onstage.[28] One way to gauge the politics of characterization Sellars staged in *Merchant* is to turn for a moment to another work that involves the replaying of the Los Angeles riots through a blend of live and "recorded" performance – Anna Deavere Smith's *Twilight: Los Angeles, 1992*. Like Sellars's *Merchant*, *Twilight* foregrounded Smith's live "performance" of her interview subjects against a backdrop of shifting images of Los Angeles, including images of the King beating and the subsequent uprising.[29] Sellars's decision to represent Shylock's Venice as divided among three (or four) distinct, hostile, noncommunicating groups – Jews/African Americans, Latinos, Asian Americans – replicates the gesture of *Twilight*, examining the events of April 1992 and their repercussions through the separate voices of members of distinct communities held in the sprawling embrace of LA. Indeed, one way to grasp the work of Sellars's *Merchant* is to note that it disoriented audiences in ways that echoed the reception of *Twilight*; in both cases, discovering the "author" – "Sellars," "Shakespeare," "Smith" – seemed both essential to an account of the work's significance, and to be frustrated by the complex ways in which "subjects" are recorded and represented onstage.

The question of authority in Smith's work is focused largely on her work as a performer, and reflects the distinctive virtuosity of her approach to acting. *Twilight* is part of a series of works – collectively called *On the Road: A Search for American Character* – that Smith initiated as a way to explore alternatives to the psychological realism dominant in American acting.[30] Acting in the "Method" mode works to vivify the actor's performance by training her to feel her way into the life of the part. Method training produces a realistic performance by forging an emotional and psychological identification between actor and character, a single, affective subject in which actor and character appear to be powerfully unified (as they are in the best performances of, say, Marlon Brando, or Meryl Streep, or Al Pacino). Smith, however, works for a realism that is aggressively externalized. Interviewing her subjects with a tape recorder, Smith's "work on the role" consists not of trying to find the emotional "spine" of the "character" she will perform, the mystified Stanislavskian "I am," but of exactly reproducing the posture, gestures, verbal tone and vocal inflection of her subjects, the socially encoded signs of identity. Rather than penetrating the subject's ineffable "self," Smith's deft mimicry registers identity as a public, discursive event. In an interview with Carol Martin, Smith characterizes her work by imagining how she would approach enacting the "character" of Leonard Jeffries, the controversial chair of the City College of New York's Black Studies department:

Psychological realism is about – this is a real oversimplification of Stanislavsky – saying: Here's Leonard Jeffries. You have to play Leonard Jeffries now. Let's look at Leonard. Let's look at his circumstances. Let's look at your circumstances. How are you two alike? How can you draw from your own experience? Contrary to that, I say this is what Leonard Jeffries said. Don't even write it down. Put on your headphones, repeat what he said. That's all. That's it. (Carol Martin, "Anna Deavere Smith" 56)

Smith doesn't "want to own the character and endow the character with my own experience. It's the opposite of that. What has to exist in order to try to allow the other to be is separation between the actor's self and the other" (52).

Twilight in performance presents a reading of modern social conflict that at once summons the power of the individual subject

(Smith's virtuoso performance) and displaces it as the ground of meaning or interpretation, in much the way Sellars's *Merchant* both asserts the "presence" of its characters through the conventions of live performance while at key moments withdrawing that aura, by displacing the representation of "character" into the register of video. The characters of *Twilight*, even in their most intimate moments, are rendered in an essentially public manner. In her rigorously externalized performance, Smith refuses the emotional identification that would claim to provide audiences with a privileged access to the characters' interiority: she becomes "the 'them' that they present to the world" (Carol Martin 57). Refusing to "act" (in the Method sense), to use her own emotional and psychological delicacy to "open up" her subjects to the theatre audience, Smith herself recedes into the "palimpsest" of others she performs.[31]

Or does she? For while this rigorously theoretical dimension of Smith's performance work is often noted by the press, the figure of the author/performer is everywhere displayed in efforts to assess the meaning of *Twilight*.[32] In part because of the formal elegance of her acting, and in large part because "her own presence – and our recognition that Anna Deavere Smith is the ground of the performance – provides the dominant signified within the *performance* text" (Lyons and Lyons, "Anna Deavere Smith" 46), Smith's critical reception, and the reception of *Twilight* as a work of social reflection, is grooved in the discourse of Smith's personal authority. Understanding *Twilight*, that is, means finding Smith at its authorial center, not only its central intelligence, but a site for the ascription of (Method-based) values of sympathy and identification. Judith Hamera cannily questions Smith's disappearing act as the mystification of a governing ideological "matrix": "What controlling intelligence, what politics has decided which voices, and which shards of which voices, to leave in and which to leave out? Or are we simply to pretend that *these* voices, like those on the evening news, exist somehow outside of an organizing ideology?" (Review 116). But other reviewers directly assimilate Smith's performance to the familiar conventions of American realism and the rhetoric of individual agency they articulate. Martin Hernandez cites "Smith's vast emotional range," used "to

successfully convince us of the psychic pain of the subject"
(Review 114); Susan Suntree remarks that "Smith's ability to capture the body language as well as the words of Blacks, Asians,
Anglos, and Hispanics told the deepest tale. From within one
woman arose all the 'others'" (Review 114); and Sae Lee suggests
that Smith's work is in this respect the "antithesis" of Brecht:
"Smith uses this medium to become, as it were, the incarnation
of the souls of the twenty-seven characters. She continually
engages the audience in conversation, speaking with the different
voices. She is persuasive yet not overbearing, and shows the audience they are one of the twenty-seven souls. Through that realization the audience then becomes one with Smith" (Review 118).

The 1996 version of *Twilight* staged at the Berkeley Repertory
Theatre appeared to signal an intervention in this controversy.
First, in what may be a response to the Pulitzer Prize committee's
sense that Smith is not the "author" of *Twilight*, Smith performed
"Anna Deavere Smith, Playwright," her name and profession
projected above the stage, much as other "characters" she performs are supertitled as "Twilight Bey, Organizer, Gang Truce"
or "Cornel West, Scholar." When this title was projected above
Smith on a screen, however, Smith did not speak. Instead, she
arranged a table, chairs, and microphones for the next segment
of the performance – "*a conversation about race that never happened but
was created from fragments of interviews collected for this play* (These
words were said but these people have not, to date, been in such
a room together)" (*Twilight* Program). This image cannily figures
Smith's work as the author of *Twilight*, the way her selection and
arrangement of the monologues of various speakers – the implicit
dialogue that structures the performance as a whole, and the
actual dialogue she stages between Paul Parker, Elaine Brown,
Gladis Sibrian, Judith Tur, Jin Ho Lee, Bill Bradley, and Theresa
Allison – is predicated on her own silence, and frames her characteristically displaced way of speaking. Another aspect of this
production was more striking. At the opening of the performance, Smith entered wearing a leather jacket over her usual white
blouse and black pants; she carried a large duffel bag, crossed the
stage, and carefully hung up her jacket and removed her wristwatch and shoes before assuming her first "character," "Jessye

Norman, Opera Singer." Smith closed the performance with the
speech of Twilight Bey, but during Twilight's speech, Smith
removed "Twilight's" jacket, and paused in her speaking to put
her own jacket, shoes, and wristwatch back on. She delivered the
last few words of "Twilight's" monologue – "I can't forever dwell
in the idea / of just identifying with people like me and understanding me / and mine" (Smith, *Twilight* 255) – in her own voice.
The force of this moment is hard to recapture, but it seemed to
me that Smith's framing of the performance, and the gentle
sound of her own voice, still speaking another's words at the
close, was a way of asserting the work of her performance, which
is precisely involved in *not* speaking for all the others, but in the
elegant, dialectical effort to represent them speaking for themselves.

The "neo-individualism" of Smith's audiences implies a linger-
ing nostalgia, a desire to locate social ills – and, presumably, the
possibility of social healing, social reform – in the agency of a
myriad-minded artist, a Shakespeare for our times.[33] Smith's performance distinctively "alienates" the "characters" she portrays;
meticulously demonstrating the various speakers of *Twilight*,
Smith systematically refuses to locate the meaning of the performance – or, presumably, of the Los Angeles uprising, or of racial
tension in the US – in the agency of an individual subject,
author, actor, or character. "The premise of the performance,"
Janelle Reinelt argues, "is that a dialogic engagement is put into
play among the characters, Smith, and the audience" ("Tracking
Twilight" 54), a dialogue that seems more pronounced, more in
the foreground in the current incarnation of the work.[34] Yet the
reception of Smith's performance is traced by the desire to find
just this subject, this point of interpretive, explanatory repair.
Despite Smith's efforts to displace her "personality" or "charisma"
from the production, to refuse the illusion of authorial insight
into Daryl Gates or Reginald Denny or Twilight Bey enunciated
by Method identification, critics describe her alienated portrayal
in accents reminiscent of more conventional performances,
inventing an "Anna Deavere Smith" whose values, agency, responsibility underwrite and contextualize the performance. And like
"Shakespeare," this ghostly "Smith" – containing multitudes, the

point at which the audience "becomes one" – performs a critical role in how works like *Fires in the Mirror* or *Twilight: Los Angeles, 1992* are positioned in relation to the social world they represent. "Smith" is the site at which the individual and the universal are identified, transcending the immediately local, historical, discursive problems that *Twilight: Los Angeles, 1992* seems so urgently to place in the foreground.[35]

Twilight – a work which disperses the voice of the author in the precisely mimed, urgently alienated voices of "othered" subjects – provides a critical index of dynamics of authority which continue to animate both journalistic and academic analysis of performance in the United States. It points not only to the poverty of critical instruments trained on dramatic performance, but to the persistence – despite the supposed inroads of deconstruction, multiculturalism, poststructuralism, and other demons of the New Right – of the unified subject (and its various avatars/ epigones/guises, the author, the individual, character) as a paradigm for cultural analysis and interpretation. Acting can, of course, express a subject, but as Smith's performances demonstrate, it can also indicate a subject, even appropriate a subject. An African American woman engaged in a kind of non-ironic, alienated demonstration of various social "characters," Smith troubles the ways that identity, representation, and the "subject" come into play in the mutual discourses of theatre and society. Refusing to play identity, Smith signals its making; refusing to take sides, Smith demonstrates identity politics without producing them; staging "characters" in the elegant immediacy of her bodily enactment, Smith refuses an unmediated identification – with the character, with her – as a mode of analysis.

Much as *Twilight*'s critics struggle to locate the meaning of the production in "Smith," so too Sellars and his critics readily assimilated the distinctively American casting pattern to the paradigm of Shakespeare's intentions, and worked valiantly to read *The Merchant of Venice* in those terms: is it or is it not Shakespeare? Sellars's work as a director seemed particularly frustrating in his staging of racial and ethnic tension in a mode of performance that refused to privilege the present subject as the point of contact, the place where the audience should look to seize the meaning of the drama and its relation to social life. Sellars's distribution of the audience's means of access to "character" did not, of course, entirely displace the subject: to move from the stagey intimacy of realistic acting to the intimate voyeurism of a televised talking head is not to eliminate the individual but to imply its constitution in different means of production. In this sense, Sellars's *Merchant of Venice* complicated the theatre's emphasis on presence, *aura* in ways that recall "the very crisis in which we see the theater," a crisis in the representation of subjects dating (at least) to Walter Benjamin's remarks on Pirandello in "The Work of Art in the Age of Mechanical Reproduction" in 1936 (229). To read the discourse of racial and economic interaction in Sellars's *Merchant of Venice* was to approach those interactions not at the level of "character" – good and bad, sincere and deceptive – but at the level of cultural production, the ways in which identities are produced not only as individual expression, but as moments in the working of the public machinery of social representation, as mediated and mediatized performance. Rather than refusing identity, Sellars's production interrogates the ways that identity is claimed, asserted in contemporary culture, and the kinds of work that identity can be made to do. Like modern society, perhaps, *The Merchant of Venice* is haunted by the "subject" it seems so earnestly to disrupt.

Although Sellars's use of racial casting was perhaps the most visible confrontation with his Shakespearean original, where Sellars seems to have careened in a more dangerous direction is in the decision to decenter the production of "character," removing the self-present, affective subject as the center of judgment and evaluation in the play, as the play's vehicle of the truth of the individual, the truth of Shakespeare. As a director, Sellars seems to have disrupted the spatial "focus" conventionally sought by modern directors, a "focus" which reciprocates the "astonishingly linear, prescriptive, and logocentric approach to dramatic character and human subjectivity" characteristic of acting in the realistic mode (Knowles, "Frankie Goes" 6).[36] Reading Sellars's staging in the light of Anna Deavere Smith's *Twilight*, we can see it as part of a much broader effort to chart the work of stage performance in general, and the performance of the classics in particular, in the space of American culture today. In part, of course, this crisis is one consequence of the post-structuralist dispersion of a traditional understanding of "literature," with its attendant dissemination of the literary work and its author into the field of textuality, and a complex sensitivity to the ideologically overdetermined work of literary production. This crisis responds to the shifting boundaries not only between theatre and literature, but between theatre and other performative instruments of culture. The theatre's crisis of authority has become more pronounced as other media (film, television, video art), forms of performance (happenings, performance art), and ways of understanding performance (the impact of performance studies) have threatened to transform dramatic theatre into a merely residual mode of cultural production, what Richard Schechner has described as "the string quartet of the 21st century: a beloved but extremely limited genre, a subdivision of performance" ("New Paradigm" 8). Despite Sellars's attempts to authorize the production in "Shakespeare," his *Merchant of Venice* might be understood as a challenge to traditional ways of authorizing dramatic performance as dependent, even parasitic, on literary authority, a challenge signaled by his directorial multiplication of "focus," a disruption of the audience's privileged access to internalized Shakespearean "character." Onstage, the production seems to transcend Sellars's intentions to restate Shakespeare to the extent this *Merchant* interrogates "other agencies of public meaning" (Bennett, *Performing Nostalgia* 23). Sellars stages the play in an explicit relation to the ways that contemporary culture reproduces itself, and reproduces its institutions, its values, its ideologies. At the same time, both the press and Sellars himself represent the work of the production as succeeding or failing to the extent that the director has been able to recapture authentically Shakespearean meanings. Despite Sellars's efforts to think through the play's material inscription of contemporary American social realities in performance, both Sellars and his reviewers finally epitomize "the universalist urge to treat all productions of Shakespeare as somehow comparable theatrical realizations or interpretations of what is 'in' the scripts" (Knowles, "Shakespeare, 1993" 225).[37] Sellars's *Merchant of Venice* illustrates the liabilities of this kind of critical myopia, how assimilating the work of the stage to the sign of the author/director can prevent us – audiences of dramatic performance, whoever "we" may be – from grasping the work of stage production, from using it to "generate meaning" rather than repeat it, from using the theatre to "mean *by* Shakespeare" (Hawkes, *Meaning by Shakespeare* 3). To think about the meaning of Sellars's *The Merchant of Venice* is to try to think how the stage might mean *by* it, how Shakespeare, *The Merchant of Venice*, and Sellars's production of the play speak to the Los Angeles riots, the technological subversion of the subject, a nostalgia for authority – and perhaps even to *Strange Days* – through a rich, and troubling, abeyance of authority.

CHAPTER 3

Shakespeare's body: acting and the designs of authority

In the world, Barthes seeks a political change that would cede power from a certain kind of critic to a certain kind of reader. On the stage, however, a proclamation of the author's death asks no change at all, but merely accepts what has always been. The deceased is no loss here, having never made his presence felt. This fabled hero, rumors of whose death Barthes has exaggerated, is that author who (I assure you) turns over in his grave when *you* act in a way that *I* don't like. Appeals to authors were already false on the drama's first day, for when vegetables begin to fly, no bard takes them in the face. The only authors who ever ruled the stage were also actors.

Hollis Huston, *The Actor's Instrument: Body, Theory, Stage*
(162)

Whatever kind of play, whatever "style" of theatre you are engaged in, your work must be *authentic*. This word literally means *self-authorship*, or *to be the author of yourself*, and this is a beautiful summation of the actor's creative purpose. Your deepest task is to be *trans-formed*, to allow your total personal energies to flow into a new form, to *re-define* or *re-author* yourself so as to serve a precise and meaningful artistic function within the demands of your play.

Robert L. Benedetti, *The Actor at Work*, 2nd ed. (23)[1]

Unlike many Asian theatres, in which actor training has been regarded as a discipline for centuries, in Western theatre, training has traditionally been pursued on the job. Yet while actor training was not "schooled" in Europe until the late nineteenth century, acting had long been the subject of moralizing polemic, theoretical and philosophical speculation, and practical advice: in

95

the rhetorical manuals of the seventeenth and eighteenth centuries; in the more theoretical "painting-the-passions" inquiries of Aaron Hill, John Hill, Henry Siddons, Denis Diderot, and others; in the innumerable guides to the stage of the nineteenth century. In the twentieth century, as the theatre has migrated toward the sphere of "high culture," acting training (like literary study in this respect) has been institutionalized, in conservatories and studios, in drama schools, and in the formal curricula of secondary and higher education.

The recognition that learning to act for the stage, film, and television is not just learning the tricks of the trade, but demands the refinement of specific talents – voice, movement, diction, characterization, emotional expressiveness – has led to a large, rather inchoate literature-of-practice. The most influential writers/ teachers/directors consider actor training within a palpable, if sometimes vaguely defined, commitment to reform the aesthetic and ideological mission of the stage. Their written and practical work has framed the sustaining paradigms of theatrical and dramatic representation in the twentieth century, and informs the training and practice of actors and directors today. I'm thinking here not only of Stanislavski's work, but also of Meyerhold and Vakhtangov, as well as the impact of Richard Boleslavsky on the Group Theatre of the 1930s and the rise of Lee Strasberg's "Method"; of Brecht's theoretical/polemical writings; of Artaud and Grotowski, of the experiments of The Living Theatre, The Performance Group, and the Open Theater, and the books by Julian Beck and Judith Malina, Richard Schechner, and Joe Chaikin which they inspired; of Peter Brook's *The Empty Space*; of Augusto Boal.[2]

A second genre – typified by Peter Barkworth, Robert L. Benedetti, Cicely Berry, Robert Cohen, Mira Felner, Uta Hagen, Kristin Linklater, Charles McGaw, Sanford Meisner, Sonia Moore, and Patsy Rodenburg, among many others – is more directly and extensively concerned with training the actor's "instrument" for the professional theatre. These books, only the tip of a massive literature devoted to actor training, auditioning, and career development, take a narrower mission: training actors for the contemporary stage. Of course, nobody ever learned to act from reading a book. Theatre practitioners learn their craft through practice, through the concentrated physical, intellectual, imaginative, sensory, affective work of training, rehearsal, and performance. And yet these manuals are particularly revealing about the commitments of theatre practice today. Acting manuals and handbooks offer a gradual and systematic regime for making stage behavior significant in the contemporary theatre. In their conception of the nature and purpose of performance, and in the significant activities their exercises train actors to perform, these books *discipline* their subjects, and in that discipline we can read the traces of a more pervasively ideological subjection.[3]

A third kind of writing about acting has come to bear directly on discussion of Shakespearean performance: books and essays written by actors. Unlike the occasional remarks on a given role that might be gleaned from an actor's memoirs or journalistic reviews of a given performance, books like the *Players of Shakespeare* series, Carol Rutter's collection *Clamorous Voices*, Antony Sher's *Year of the King*, and Simon Callow's *Being an Actor*, among others, have enabled actors to describe the specific challenges posed by Shakespearean acting, to relate those challenges to their own training and performance preparation, and to position their process within the entire ensemble of a production's work. Such writing provides at best only indirect evidence about performance itself. Written after the fact, sometimes dictated, occasionally written to order, it testifies instead to how actors conceptualize their work, and represent it to an audience of readers. Written with an eye to changing how Shakespearean drama is taught and understood, such books often speak to a still-embattled sense of the authority of performance, as interpretation, as criticism, and as a site for the cultural production of Shakespeare. Surprisingly enough, this anxiety about the location of a legitimate Shakespeare – in the words on the page or in their embodiment on the stage – persists in an academic climate in which the "poetic" Shakespeare of the New Criticism has been largely displaced by the "theatre poet" of performance criticism, indeed by a writer whose fullest reach extends beyond both textual and theatrical poetics, to the larger stage of the poetics of culture.[4]

In this chapter, I consider the role of Shakespeare in this body of literature, how relations of authority – between "author" and actor – inform the training and practice of contemporary acting. Naturally, in retaining a sense of what is, of what is right, and of what is possible in the theatre today, this literature – and the classes, rehearsal rooms, and stage productions from which it arose and in which its teachings are engaged – marks an important ideological dimension of performance practice. Actor training teaches performers how to represent the "subjects" of the drama, and subjects the performers themselves to a way of interpreting, inhabiting, and acting in the world of the theatre. Describing their complex and imaginative encounters with playing Shakespeare, actors reinforce this closure, for their apparently personal and idiosyncratic engagements with Shakespearean roles express a clear sense of the parameters of possibility in contemporary Shakespearean performance.[5]

Moreover, actor training texts and actors' accounts rehearse a surprising gesture, one that links the propriety of performance to the right expression of Shakespearean authority. This investment in "Shakespeare" involves a more complex act of inscription. On one level, invoking the author is a manifestly rhetorical move, a way to claim that Shakespeare somehow stands behind the meanings we now find stageable. More significantly, however, "Shakespeare" becomes a powerfully naturalizing trope, used to justify the battery of techniques applied to the performer's body to make its performance readable in the theatre. Actor training doesn't merely produce a well-tuned instrument for the playwright and director to play; training produces agents, whose behavior is fully involved in representing and reproducing the ideology of the subject. Acting evokes deep, even invisible commitments to the fictions of nature, origin, and identity, fictions sustained by the ghostly hand of "Shakespeare," writing the body of the modern performer. In his influential essay, "Bodies and Texts," Harry Berger, Jr. argues that the body is a "*naturalizing* symbol," conferring "the appearance of inevitability, inalienability, and transcendent reality inscribed in it by 'nature'" (147). In one sense, actor training can hardly be expected to be a mode of ideological critique; as Brecht argued, conventional stage practice is definitively a mode of ideological redundancy. But stage acting, and especially the acting of classic drama, articulates and reproduces hegemony in particular ways. Contemporary actor training provides a means of rendering the "natural" signifying capabilities of the body explicit and articulate as theatre, freeing the performer from the bogeys of inauthentic acting: interpreting, indicating, intellectualizing. At the same time, however, the disciplined body incorporates the necessarily distant, recondite prescriptions of the text, a text already freighted with meaning and history. While Shakespeare – that remote, verbally dense, intellectually imposing figure of cultural authority – might be expected to represent the otherness of texts, their irreducible distance from the discursive "naturalness" of the body, actor training works to close or occlude that gap. The complicity of actor training in ideological formation is nowhere more visible than at this point: "Shakespeare" becomes a naturalizing metaphor on the order of the body itself, representing the universal, transcendent, and natural in ways that both legitimate and render unquestionable the dominant discourse of the stage. As the actors I discuss in the second half of this chapter testify, "Shakespeare" appears to enable the body to recapture itself.

Actor training is training of the body, and it is not surprising that the body becomes the vehicle for the transmission of Shakespeare. Indeed, the author might be registered in the body in various ways, and Shakespeare participates in naturalizing the body of the actor to the conventions of stage practice, in framing the meanings of "character," and in structuring a relationship between performer and text. Anglo-American actor training is hardly monolithic, and draws eclectically on various theatre traditions: the realistic mode of Stanislavski and the American Method; the improvisational theatre games of Viola Spolin and Keith Johnstone; the traditions of movement training associated with F. M. Alexander, Rudolf Laban, Etienne Decroux, Moshe Feldenkrais, and more recently on various Asian acting and martial-arts disciplines; several approaches to vocal training; and a mixed bag of theatrical, physiological, psychological, and therapeutic writings.[6] Yet as John Harrop notes, while most "actors work eclectically, using whatever elements of process seem to have worked for them over the years," probably "the most fundamental and commonly acknowledged, if not agreed upon, basic process is that of Stanislavski" (*Acting* 52). Stanislavski's goals and practices developed and changed over his long career, and have been misread, mistranslated, and misappropriated by later acolytes. Nonetheless, Stanislavski stands behind many of the values of contemporary Anglo-North American actor training: a commitment to living in the moment, the need for actors to bring physical and psychological preparation ("the actor's work on himself") into equipoise with the analysis of character ("the actor's work on the role"), the sense that subtextual meanings are evoked clearly and convincingly through the trained responses of the body itself.[7] These are, in a sense, the values common to actor training, the values that – as John Gronbeck-Tedesco demonstrates – are readily assimilable to the "new voices and ideas" of "Grotowski, Schechner, Chaikin, Barba, Marowitz, Brook, Feldenkrais, and Alexander" (*Acting Through Exercises* xxvii).[8]

Lauren Love remarks that it is now "in vogue, in fact, to refer to Stanislavsky's system not as 'the method' but as the 'organic approach'" ("Resisting" 276), and this organicism marks the ideological affiliations of actor training. The "organic" approach centers theatre in the "experience" of its participants – actors and audiences – and "organic" training represents the experiencing body in two ways: as a pre-cultural, pre-ideological "nature," and as the ground of an organic wholeness, the self, identity, or presence of the performer. Experience is the actor's basic tool; only when "the actor has been trained to respond and to experience" can he or she enter "the realm of what the play deals with" (Strasberg, *Dream of Passion* 78). To Robert Benedetti, the "theatre is uniquely organismic in nature," because "the 'instrument' that creates the experiences – the actor's total self – is identical with the 'instrument' that receives the experience – the spectator's self. It is this organismic identity between actor and spectator that makes the theatrical experience feelingful as well as comprehensible. The biological identity is expressed primarily in the nonverbal aspects of theatrical (as well as everyday) communication"

(*Actor at Work* 7). Benedetti's sense that theatrical communication depends on the shared experience of actor, character, and audience has a long history in dramatic theory and criticism, yet in many ways points to the hegemony of modern individualism and its related emphasis on a bounded, autonomous identity. As Brecht's interest in the demonstrative aspect of performance – or the divergent affects of pity and fear in Aristotle's description of catharsis, for that matter – suggests, Western drama tends to frame a more complex and contradictory performance for its audience, in which psychological (or social, or economic) identification is dialectically marked, as identification is always marked, by distance, by the difference it claims to elide. Ritual performance represents its communicants as participants, inside the action, transformed by it. Western dramatic theatre represents its audience as active, live observers. The *point* of plays like *Othello* or *Twelfth Night* or *The Winter's Tale* is not to make the audience want to *be* Othello, Viola, Malvolio, Leontes, or even Perdita, but to stimulate and render meaningful the desire to *watch* them, and (in the best theatre) to engage the consequences of this act of involved, disengaged, seeing.[9] That theatre works – aesthetically, politically, ideologically – by framing the audience's distance and channeling what and how it sees is pretty obvious, I admit. The obviousness of this fact is what renders Benedetti's conventional sense of an "identity" between actor and audience so striking, such plain evidence for the working of ideology itself: "the imaginary relationship of individuals to their real conditions of existence," as Althusser has it ("Ideology" 162). Forging an identity between the experience of the actor and that of the audience, Benedetti reifies the body as the ground of self-presence, an apparently prediscursive identity. Because the "freedom to act is born in the union of feeling, thought, and action," teachers work to present "an integrated approach to acting that links understanding with experiencial knowledge," through exercises that train "students to relate physical, psychological, and analytical techniques' in "a personal and organic creative process" (Felner, *Free to Act* vi).

Phillip B. Zarrilli points out that "experientially saturated approaches to acting where 'being in the moment' is emphasized" tend to reinscribe a Cartesian dualism "in the form of an overly simplistic and monolithic subjectivity often described as the actor's 'presence,' or as an 'organic' or 'natural' state of being" (Introduction 15). In an important sense, however, this presence – the presence of the individual subject – arises from an "instrumental" rhetoric, understanding the actor mainly as an instrument of expression, rather than as an agent of signification. Training stressing a unified sensibility, an organic instrument, positions the body as the sign of the natural, in opposition to the cultural, the learned, the conventional; the actor's immersion in the local, in history, is cast as a sociocultural limitation to effective performance. Denis Salter remarks, for instance, that the Method preempts Canadian actors from developing a "personally enabling politics of location": "Method acting takes it for granted that ideology and the social order that it interpellates *do not exist.* 'I act, therefore I am': beyond this self-referential and self-generating, deliberately apolitical proposition, Method acting has refused to let the postcolonial actor go" ("Acting Shakespeare" 128).[10] Much as "experience" elides the possibility of a "negotiable dialectic" between the various forms, positions, and possibilities of theatrical "identification" (Zarrilli, Introduction 21), instrumentalizing the actor not only unifies the subject, but universalizes it as well, laminating it to the timeless vehicle of *the* body.

John Harrop clarifies how this instrumentalizing rhetoric positions the actor as an uninflected nature given meaning by the playwright:

After all the playwright writes for an instrument – just as Mozart wrote for the Stradivarius – the actor's body, voice, legs, arms, torso, hair, hands, feet, etc. These have their own physical vocabulary of potentiality. The way in which they are used will of course differ in different times and according to the demands of different styles; but the instrument hasn't changed, and we can look at the technical vocabulary, and examine the sliding scale of values and techniques along which acting is practised. (*Acting* 6–7)

Harrop views the body as the playwright's grammar, as though the body's potentiality were in some way inherent in its biological structure. Yet as recent studies of medical history – such as Thomas

Laqueur's *Making Sex* – have demonstrated, the understanding of the material body, even the ability to see its physiological organization, is shaped ideologically. Judith Butler puts a finer point on the body's "potentiality" for performance, arguing that the performing body "cannot be theorized apart from the forcible and reiterative practice" of regulatory regimes. Focusing her critique of bodily representation on the relationship between gender and sexuality (that is, on a relationship that seems to oppose the merely "ideological" – gender – to the absolute "materiality" of sexuality and sexual difference), Butler argues that the category of the material is itself ideologically constituted: "the regime of heterosexuality operates to circumscribe and contour the 'materiality' of sex, and that 'materiality' is formed and sustained through and as a materialization of regulatory norms that are in part those of heterosexual hegemony" (*Bodies that Matter* 15). Though it is inviting to view the body as the actor's instrument – Harrop's analogy recalls Laurie Anderson's simultaneous distortion of her violin and her own voice in *Home of the Brave*, refunctioning both "instruments" through a denaturing technology – to do so is to ignore how the meanings of the body, and of individual bodies, are ascribed meanings, how the body's "potentiality" for signification is constituted by its implication in the behavioral, social, medical, literary, theatrical discourses that represent it.[11]

Instrumentalizing the actor works a complex duplicity into the sign of the performing body. On the one hand, the body becomes the register of nature; stigmatized behavior – "indicating," in Method acting, for instance – is an obstacle to be overcome, eliminated, purged, so that the natural expressiveness of the body can be released. Actors must be trained to penetrate beneath language and cultural cognition to reclaim and amplify the "full use of sense perception" that has been subverted by the "cultural tyrannies" of their socialization (Gronbeck-Tedesco, *Acting Through Exercises* 70). At the same time, that absent nature is also the vehicle of the playwright's work. Authors don't write for the discursively limited bodies of their own era, but for the universal body beneath. History, language, and culture change, but the author's transcendent message still appeals through the unchanging and natural discourse of *the* body, shaped and configured by the interesting accidents of dramatic style. Of course, actor training must take into account these stylistic differences, given the recondite nature of the classical repertory: not only the alien rhetorical richness of classical language (the verse of Elizabethan drama, the witty balance of Restoration comic prose), but also the alien social and cultural attitudes that inform the language and the action of classic plays. Yet if a playwright like Shakespeare is seen to speak universally, then his plays must be susceptible to a variety of stylistic experimentation; as Michael Schulman remarks, "It's clear that Shakespeare wanted real and organic emotions from his actors, so we handle the emotional work in his plays the same way we do in contemporary plays, finding personal and character stimuli to arouse real feelings." Molière, on the other hand, is taken to be rooted in the moral and social milieu of seventeenth-century France; as a result, "Molière is played in very stylized ways today" (quoted in Mekler, *New Generation* 65).

Even at those moments when training works to preserve historical difference, the body/author exerts this naturalizing effect. In *Freeing Shakespeare's Voice: The Actor's Guide to Talking the Text*, Kristin Linklater encourages performers to attend closely to the markedly different milieu in which Shakespeare's plays were crafted, in order to train their attention to the specifics of the text. Linklater reminds her students that much as they no longer share Shakespeare's culture, they no longer inhabit the bodies of Shakespeare's original performers:

Classical music is played on instruments that bear a distinct resemblance to their ancestors, but classical drama has to be played on a human instrument that experiences and expresses life in a manner radically altered even from a hundred years ago. The Western human behaves, thinks and speaks quite differently now from the days four hundred years ago when Shakespeare's classics were contemporary. (3)

Although the "human instrument" experiences and expresses differently than it did in the seventeenth century, it remains nonetheless a seductively "human instrument," Shakespeare's instrument. For this reason, though the manner of experience and expression has altered, the content of "Shakespeare" remains available. Culture passes through the body and into history. Shakespeare, however, remains present in the body, speaks most directly through the body.

Time and again I have seen, heard and felt Shakespeare's words enter and restore power to a boy or a girl, a woman or a man, whose sense of worth has been obliterated by childhood abuse, social inequality or racial bigotry. This happens *not when they read Shakespeare, not when they hear Shakespeare, but when they speak the words themselves.* (195)

This effect takes place not only because by speaking the words and hearing "their stories told," people recognize "that their experiences are part of the fabric of human experience," but because "Speaking Shakespeare leads us to the sources of our own power because we find a language which expresses the depths of our experience more fully, more richly, more completely than our own words can" (195).

Linklater's characteristically therapeutic rhetoric may not be representative of all actor training, but the way the body becomes the vehicle for the transmission of dominant ideology – speaking the name of "Shakespeare" – is typical of much actor training today.[12] The "natural" instrument of the actor's and the author's work, the body is encrypted with meanings and possibilities dramatized by the kinds of work it is given to perform. Training is geared to producing a unified subject, in which the recovery of a precultural identity rooted in the body legitimates not only a system of training exercises, but an entire conception of theatrical meaning. Benedetti suggests that while "Our bodies seem complex when we think of all the organs and systems operating in a delicate balance and cooperation," there is nonetheless "a way in which our whole organism, body as well as consciousness, can be experienced as a unified whole with each part, each sensation, fully integrated. The actor strives for such a sense of wholeness because the stage demands total responsiveness simultaneously from all the aspects of his organism; only an integrated, 'together' organism can supply such responses" (*Actor at Work* 20). While this wholeness requires analysis and preparation, it is in an important sense a pre-ideational, pre-ideological, unthinking moment: Sanford Meisner looks for exercises "where there is no intellectuality," exercises that "eliminate all that 'head' work," and "take away all the mental manipulation and get to where the impulses come from" (*On Acting* 36); another handbook recommends, "If you've taken the time to intellectualize what is happening in any way, the impulse will be lost" (Bruder et al., *A Practical Handbook* 43). This phrasing of the actor's organic experience is reminiscent of the sociologist Mihaly Csikszentmihalyi's description of "flow," the particular pleasure that arises from the dynamic relationship between ability, concentration, challenge, and opportunity associated with pastimes, games, sports – what tennis players call "playing in the zone." But Benedetti, Meisner, and others are not merely describing the sensation of masterful acting, the feeling of impulses meeting and overcoming significant obstacles. They see successful performance as the property of the body, something that arises beyond, below, beneath socialized identity.

Actor training takes this readiness as the native state of the pre-ideological body; discovering – or inventing – this "nature" is the common work of actor training. Peter Brook remarks of Cicely Berry's voice training that it is based "on the conviction that while all is present in nature our natural instincts have been crippled from birth by many processes – by the conditioning, in fact, of a warped society" (Foreword 3). This primitivizing gesture is common in voice training. Kristin Linklater sees vocal and emotional expression to be inhibited by social life, arguing "that the tensions acquired through living in this world, as well as defenses, inhibitions and negative reactions to environmental influences, often diminish the efficiency of the natural voice to the point of distorted communication." Her emphasis, then, "is on the removal of the blocks that inhibit the human instrument" (*Freeing the Natural Voice* 1). In *The Need for Words*, Patsy Rodenburg locates a similar attitude within a larger project of cultural nostalgia. Taking a "'post-modernist' age of 'deconstruction'" to have "cut us off from the fount of language" (18), Rodenburg elaborates an opposition between "language" and "media culture." Living "in an age of cacophony, of dissonance and discord" produced by the media saturation of modern industrial culture, "we have ceased to speak and be aurally stimulated (except, perhaps, by music)" (37). Rodenburg contrasts this apparently unnatural state with the more actively oral culture of a village she visited in Portugal in the late 1970s. As Rodenburg sees it, modern indus-trial living has reduced both the opportunity and the "need" for complex, public oral exchange (such as sitting around the village café gossiping), and in the process has depressed the "need" for great literature, for texts that inform and sustain this "need" to speak. This is brought home to Rodenburg when advertising uses "literature" for sloganeering, as when Elizabeth Taylor echoes a line from *Julius Caesar* ("I see that passion is catching") to push per-fume. "Language associated with human passion used to promote hair sprays, cars, beer or candy bars steals trust from words. As we search for truth and seek words that will help us communicate a higher need through those words we suddenly find the words have become bankrupt" (66). Rodenburg's sense that literature retains an essential relation to speech enables her to position the literary as a distinct category, in opposition to other modes of verbal production. To speak literature, to discover the "need for words" that have not yet been debased, is to recover preindustrial modes of expression, "natural" performance.

In a theatre which values (the appearance of) spontaneity as the sign of the natural (duplicating the representation of identity in culture at large), training must find ways to betray the body into its "nature."[13] John Harrop points out that improvisation exercises and games can "release the body's spontaneous response," and through "the physicality of the game, the emo-tional content of the action can also be released. Searching for inner feeling through intellectual understanding can often pro-duce a self-involved and static result. Attacking a role physically can break down inhibitions, release energy and reveal the para-meters of the action" (*Acting* 60). The body is returned to nature for a paradoxical purpose: to render its expression of dramatic action more volatile, more lifelike, more like the socialized and repressed body it has been trained to un-become: "In order to represent the human community, the actor attempts to free him-self or herself from the very inhibitions the community imposes as the price of membership – a price that makes its members

predictable and less powerful in the course of their daily lives"
(Gronbeck-Tedesco, *Acting Through Exercises* 44). Rather than
making stage performance critically different from social behavior, though, this sense of an evanescent nature mystified
behind the knowable limits of social organization duplicates the
paradigms of modern social subjection. To adapt Terry Eagleton's
sense of literature's ideological positioning between the "distancing rigour of scientific knowledge and the vivid but loose
contingencies of the 'lived' itself," we might say that theatrical
performance appropriates "the real as it is given in ideological
forms, but does so in a way which produces an illusion of the
spontaneously, unmediatedly real" (*Criticism and Ideology* 101).
While literature and theatrical performance may work to mystify
the "spontaneous presence of the work," actor training is nakedly
the means by which "literature" claims the "real" onstage.

   Actor training produces a performance that attempts to elide
body, text, and author. History, indeed "difference" of any kind,
disappears into the absent nature of the body itself: the natural
body speaks the author's voice. One place where literary authority is most explicitly reproduced in training is in the relationship
between "author," "character," and "actor," Not surprisingly,
training in a Stanislavskian lineage takes the "Creation of an
imaginary character behaving logically in circumstances given by
the playwright" to be "the primary task of the actor" (McGaw,
Acting Is Believing 10). Stanislavski's coordination of the "actor's
work on himself" with a series of character "objectives" directed
toward the play's organic "super-objective" is manifestly a way to
recode literary authority in performance. Character becomes a
joint product of author and actor, lying on the frontier between
the actor's natural body and the spectral voice of the absent
author.

   Although in its most extreme forms – Lee Strasberg's work at
the Actors Studio, for example – the actor's physical and psychological "work on himself" might seem to interfere with the production of the dramatic character, modern acting's emphasis on
the actor's integrated and authentic experience onstage generally
serves a single goal: to substantiate the dramatic character as a
unified, fully realistic subject – the actor/character.

To a very considerable degree the actor must always "play himself." He can create another person only by drawing upon his own experiences, actual or vicarious. No matter how he may alter his outward appearance, no matter how he may change the sound of his voice (and this outer form is necessary to complete characterization), his ability to communicate the essential truth of his role – which is, after all, the core of any performance – is dependent on what he is able to bring to it from his inner resources. Even though study and observation in the preparation of a specific part may greatly enlarge these resources, they remain essentially the same as the actor attempts one character after another. The way to get to any character is through yourself.

So the final performance is "the actor in the part." It is a unique creation because no one else can duplicate it. (McGaw, *Acting Is Believing* 112)

The "core of any performance" is the communication of "the essential truth" of the role, a truth that is finally discovered within the actor her/himself. Although acting in an explicitly Stanislavskian tradition identifies the actor's and the character's objectives – so that, as in the title of McGaw's book, "acting is believing" – other less-explicitly Stanislavskian approaches nonetheless understand character in a similar way: character is the means to the actor's self-discovery. This is, I think, what acting teacher Michael Howard means when he says that an "actor illuminates the material, reveals the playwright by revealing some aspect of him or herself; often something private" ("A Method of One's Own" 24). It is also probably what Morris Carnovsky has in mind when he feels he has not yet finished his work on a role, like Falstaff: "If I am impatient with myself as Falstaff, it is because now, even in performance, he is not enough Morris. I know what there is in me which refuses as yet to come out into the character" (*The Actor's Eye* 27). John Harrop, who disowns the focus on the "feeling of the actor" associated with American Method training (*Acting* 41), nonetheless sees characterization as the "*Ding an sich*" of theatrical performance (4). Moreover, citing a history connecting Moshe Feldenkrais and William James to Meyerhold, Artaud, and Grotowski, Harrop argues that character is finally the expression of the body: placing "character" *in* the body is "the principle upon which rehearsal is based: the incarnation in body memory of the choices the actor makes. Through the actor's process, the text becomes a score of physical actions inspired by and attached to impulses. While the score is fixed, it is not without spontaneity because the body, in revealing its encoded signs, is at the same time responding to the stimulus of the moment" (77).[14] Cicely Berry also sees the connection between actor and character to be physiological, located in their shared "breath." The current of the actor's breathing animates the "elemental nature" of the dramatic character: "there is a parallel between the actor reaching down for that breath, and Othello reaching for that thought." Here and in other roles, "The breath needed in this passage is deep and needs preparation as does the thought, for you have to reach down within yourself to find the image of the sea, the current within yourself. And Othello is moved by the current of his own passion" (*Actor and His Text* 27).

The actor releases his/her body into its organic nature, but this freedom turns out to be surprisingly narrow, the freedom to play a similarly totalized "self," that of the dramatic character. Actor training assumes an integrated and organic "subject" which can be discovered through the body, beneath the blockages and obstructions of culture. The theatre requires this body, though, in part because it regards the production of character as the actor's principal task, and takes "character" as the transparent mimesis of human being in the world, rather than, say, as an interested, rhetorical representation of subjectivity, a limited model of agency. The body is freed into its nature only to have the more deeply ideological version of identity inscribed within it. This sense of character-in-the-body arises as well in the notion of the bodily center of an actor's performance. On the one hand, associating different aspects of characterization with different styles of bodily display has a manifestly heuristic purpose: it helps the actor to bring the character to the body, enables the actor to experiment with different ways of carrying the body, different styles of inhabiting it. Mira Felner, for example, describes the actor/character's "center" as a fusion of physiology and character: "Head centers seem to be cerebral and controlled, whereas pelvic centers sensual and erotic," she remarks, urging actors to "Note how your center moves down when you are sexually aroused, or up when you are tense or frightened" (*Free to Act* 16). Similarly, Robert Benedetti suggests "five primary character centers" that are the result of both "bodily logic" and "cultural tradition": "head (the cerebral and/or sexually repressed person), chest (the sentimental, or even the 'militaristic' person), stomach (the indulgent person), genitals (the libidinous, or perhaps the naive person), and anus (the sexually withdrawn, 'constipated' person)" (*Actor at Work* 79).[15] The body center is, of course, useful to the actor in physicalizing the role; as Morris Carnovsky remarks, "an actor playing a person who is given to thinking a great deal might place his center automatically in the center of his head, and everything about his body would follow suit; the head would take sovereignty over everything else in his body" (*The Actor's Eye* 157). The language of body centers as expressed in manuals like Benedetti's and Felner's, though, is the language of character in nature: the "body center" locates the formal devices of character in the body's natural means of expression.

In its emphasis on developing a natural instrument for acting, training produces a body inscribed with various values: the actor's body is feelingful, expressive, gendered, unthinking, re-active, humane. Moreover, the prevailing typology of human character can also be found in the body as well, for the function of various organs – heart, brain, genitals – appears to exert a kind of behavioral power over identity. Beyond that, however, training uses a variety of exercises to develop the body's expres-siveness, exercises that also determine how the authority of the text will be mapped onto, and naturalized by, the expressive body. In most approaches to acting, the first series of exercises develop a sense of sensory and physical responsiveness. Acting exercises encode the text's designs on the body; the text of the social – behavior, language – is registered as bodily nature. In the fifth (1990) edition of *The Actor at Work*, Robert L. Benedetti describes an exercise for "rhythm analysis and embodiment" (206). After analyzing the poetic elements of a scene's language, and consid-ering its breathing and dialogue cadences, Benedetti urges the actor to "embody" it:

Using your analysis as a basis, create a dance-like version of the speech which exaggerates its rhythms. Move from your center; involve the deep muscles, not just the arms and legs. Speak the speech as you move, and allow your voice to be freely influenced by your movement. Give your entire body a chance to participate; do not limit yourself to "realistic" movement, or even to the way you might do the speech in performance. (207)

"The body will 'remember' these experiences far better than the mind," Benedetti suggests, while locating the exercise in its Stanislavskian tradition: as a way to create "*sense memories* based upon the qualities of the text." The bodily rhetoric applied to the text – the idiom of modern dance, of physical gesture from social life – is taken to be transparent, as the body restores the text to nature with a nearly Wordsworthian spontaneity: "these bodily memories will automatically enrich your performance without conscious effort. Trust your body to remember the really important things, and let the rest fall away!" (207).[16] "Working with the process of Authentic Movement" (a physical training regime derived from dance, particularly from Mary Wigman and Martha Graham), Judith Koltai has "been able to witness how words can flow effortlessly, simply and directly from a kind of rootedness in the body: speaking from recalled experience rather than about it" ("Authentic Movement" 21); the actor, in consequence, "is *affected* and *moved* to action and speech through the total engagement of his organism" (24). In one of Cicely Berry's exercises, the actors link arms in a circle, and each half of the circle pulls in opposite directions while everyone speaks the text. Such training enables modern performers to discover "the physical weight of the words," "to feel your whole body become part of the words you speak" (*Actor and His Text* 186, 187).[17] The text haunts the body, while the body corporealizes the natural meanings of the text.

That such exercises "work" is not in question here; indeed, my point is that they so fully duplicate the captivating ideology of modern capital (individual subjects whose conscious agency is troped on a bodily nature unquestioned in terms of spontaneity, gender, etc.) that they could do little else.[18] What is striking is the way that the body is not so much a *tabula rasa*, but a script itself, the repository of apparently "natural" physiological, psychological, and gender attributes, attributes which training brings into a significant dialogue with the dramatic text. Jacqueline Martin, for example, argues that "Normal barriers, such as those to do with sexual differentiations and social behaviour, must be broken down if the individual is to realize his full potential through the human voice." Martin regards the "barriers" to communication as cultural, yet the body is already traced by the marks of gender: "In practice this means that females are encouraged to explore the deeper, masculine voices normally associated with aggression, while on the other hand, males are encouraged to confront within themselves the softer, more feminine and traditionally vulnerable sides of their personalities" (*Voice in the Modern Theatre* 66).

In some respects, voice training – the point at which text and body meet most directly – provides the clearest example of the mutual investment of text and body in the discourse of authority. As a means to naturalizing scripted speech in performance, voice training often works not only to find means to inscribe language and character in the body, but to situate language and proper speech as prior to culture. Cicely Berry strives to bring "our physical self" into an expressive relationship with the "physical nature" of words (*Actor and His Text* 19). Although Berry recognizes that contemporary language is deeply implicated in its manifold social and cultural functions (she mentions "technological jargon of every kind," "legal language, language of sensibility and emotion allied to literature and art," "the bloated language of the media and of much political speaking," "sophisticated slang which communicates social patterns and change"), language is finally "primitive in essence" (19): "words evolved out of noises which were first made to communicate basic needs; they were in fact signals. And we still have that sense memory within us – that resonance if you like. For they still act as signals and can arouse quite basic and primitive responses in us" (19–20).

The actor's task, then, is to recover the primitive, to be "less consciously organized, and less culturally based" (19) in approaching the text, and in approaching performance. The means, strikingly enough, to this penetration of precultural identity, is the inscription of the Shakespearean text on the body, or, perhaps more accurately, the unwriting of the constrained modern body to discover the Shakespearean language, the Shakespearean body, lurking within. Characteristically, this unwriting remaps the relationship between bodies and texts, as Linklater suggests in a typical exercise:

To allow this first slow process you can follow this simple procedure: Go through the relaxation exercises described earlier. Then, lying on the floor with the text beside you, explore, phrase by phrase, sentence by sentence, sometimes word by word, the images and ideas that are contained in the text. The steps might be:

1. Look at the page and find a phrase (not necessarily the first).

2. Close your eyes.

3. Without speaking, allow the phrase to swim behind your eyes and then drop it down to your breathing center.

4. Let pictures attach themselves to the words.

5. Free associate.

6. Let feelings generate round the pictures and associations.

7. Sigh out what you feel.

8. Whisper the words with the feelings they have aroused.

9. Let the words and the feelings find your voice.

(*Freeing the Natural Voice* 188)

This exercise trains actors to possess dramatic language by imagining that it possesses them, largely by reconfiguring the relationship between mental imagery, breathing, and vocalization. As Linklater continues, "In this process words are given a solid physical home, become sensorily familiar and create their own harmonic reservoir of association, memory, music and rhythm. This reservoir serves to give life, character and independence to the words which make up the overall sense" (188). Moreover, Linklater takes the meanings solicited through this process to be located in the text itself. Through such procedures, "the sense of the text will be revealed, along with a much deeper meaning than

can be arrived at by purely mental effort." Though Linklater recognizes that such exercises need to be coordinated with whole-play
concerns ("Obviously if the 'text' is part of a scene in a play, the
final sense will depend on interplay with other characters" [188]),
the use of exercises to break down habits of reading through the
interposition of the physical body results in the discovery of meanings latent in the text itself. The body is now free, Linklater's
second volume makes clear, to speak with "Shakespeare's Voice."

In the theatre, Patsy Rodenburg remarks, "every speaker
becomes the new 'author' of a text," in that "the author's meaning will always be overlaid with your meanings" (*Need for Words*
154). But this dynamic relationship of difference, in which the
stage necessarily produces the text's contemporaneity, runs
counter to the figuration of the body in actor training. For the
actor's recovery of "Shakespeare" in the text of the body has a
variety of consequences. It appears, surprisingly to derive from a
relatively New Critical sense of the organization of the dramatic
text: the play is an organic, ambiguous, yet totalized expression of
an individual vision, and the performer's job is both to recover
that vision and register its universal appeal. Though Robert
Benedetti uses "polarization exercises" to create "an extended
visceral experience that renders the rhythm, tone, imagery or configuration of your character's language into *real* bodily experiences" (*Actor at Work* 153), these exercises are in the service of a
relatively narrow understanding of the relationship between the
originary text and contemporary production:

The playwright begins by developing a living experience or idea, which
we will call his *vision*. It is this vision that moves him to create a specific
play, and each character in that play comes to life in the writer's consciousness as part of a whole mechanism that expresses the central
vision or purpose of the play.

Unlike the novelist, the playwright cannot usually speak directly to us
to describe or qualify a character; the character must speak for himself.
Ultimately, the words spoken by the character will be all that is left
(except for a few stage directions) of the fullness of the author's visual-
ization. For you as an actor, then, the text is the *residue* of a much larger
conception of the character. It is your job to give life to this residue in
your own way. (*Actor at Work* 125)

Benedetti here negotiates the central issue in most actor training books: the desire to free the performer while preserving the authority of the text.

This "ability to penetrate a script's inner meaning and make a visceral connection with the text is vital to successful perform-ance" (Felner, *Free to Act* 157): actor training works to legitimize the "text" by signifying it viscerally. What is more interesting, though, is how the massive effort of training programs to free and release actors from intellectual and social constraints is grooved on the recovery of authorial intention. In one sense, this recovery of "Shakespeare" serves as a kind of pragmatic shorthand, a way to strike "a practical partnership between you and the writer of the text" as a way to "collaborate with Shakespeare when you speak his texts" (Rodenburg, *Need for Words* 96). The British actress Prunella Scales understandably feels that "After reading the play I always want to talk to the author. Often an author can tell you where a character was born, and when, what her child-hood was like, even what she looks or sounds like" (quoted in Barkworth, *More About Acting* 163). But beyond that, the agency attributed to the author derives from an organicizing habit of reading the text, derived from Stanislavski and New Criticism. It is a small step from Cicely Berry's sense that "there is in Shakespeare an energy which runs through the text which is not a naturalistic one; an energy which impels one word to the next, one line to the next, one thought to the next, one speech to the next, and one scene to the next" (*Actor and His Text* 82), to John Harrop's sense that a "play text is the reduction into words, ciphers and signs on paper of the flesh-and-blood inspirations of the author in his or her creative state. Actors need to discover the organic pulse behind the printed page" (*Acting* 62).

By placing the actor in touch with the author, training con-strains performance in specific ways: the author becomes the sign of the universal and transcendent, a register of meaning strangely at odds with the local immediacy of performance itself. Although this authorizing gesture is common throughout actor training, it is especially well developed in voice training. Shakespeare plays a special part in voice training, in large measure because Shakespearean drama is the classic that Anglo-American actors are most likely to encounter in the original, in a verse and in an English that remains in some respects untranslated, unmodern. But while actors must be trained to meet this densely other language, they are urged to do so not by making the difference between Shakespearean language, thematics, and ideology their own, nor by finding discrete points of identification in a sea of strangeness. In her first book, *Freeing the Natural Voice* (1976), Kristin Linklater raises this question in terms of accent, how actors should consider the contemporary marks of class, region, and education traced in their voices when performing Shakespeare. Insofar as Shakespeare's "plays are universal and reflect life, they should reflect the diversity of life and there is no standardization of speech in life. Nor is it likely that the actors in Shakespeare's companies spoke alike, coming as they did from all parts of England." At the same time, however, while Linklater admits that it may be "distracting to hear a strong New York accent next to a Southern and a Midwestern one," she believes that "any accent will be modified by freeing the voice," and suggests that "the actor who allows Shakespeare's text to influence and shape him as any good actor must, will be fulfilling the rich variety of sounds that great poetry demands, and will naturally remove the limiting stamp of regionality" (191). While Linklater recognizes the artificiality of working to remove accent, the proper approach to speaking the poetry will inevitably produce a natural, nonregional speaking voice, because Shakespeare is the voice of human nature.

In *Freeing Shakespeare's Voice* (1992), Linklater modifies this position to take into account both the changing demographics of theatre and the cultural politics of contemporary stage production, especially surrounding race and ethnicity in casting. While she had earlier argued that Shakespearean language pulls class and regional difference toward its own norms of right speaking, here she carves a space for identity politics within Shakespearean performance. Recognizing that "the deification of Shakespeare as the genius of the English language bolsters a conscious or unconscious Western, white, cultural-supremacist attitude" (194), Linklater nonetheless considers ways to preserve Shakespeare's ability to "illuminate our time as thoroughly as he did his own" (193).

Believing that a "large part of the power of Shakespeare's writing lies in his archetypal stories and characters" (194), Linklater argues that Shakespearean archetypes have a therapeutic value, and that such archetypes provide a platform for the examination of racial and ethnic difference in a context of multicultural pluralism.

In part because Shakespeare's stories are "archetypal," they "tell the stories of the everyday lives of millions of people who suffer painfully the effects of an unequal society, people who feel powerless in the face of the random cruelty of poverty" (195). Shakespeare therapy takes place, then, because "Speaking Shakespeare leads us to the sources of our own power because we find a language which expresses the depths of our experience more fully, more richly, more completely than our own words can" (195). This therapeutic aspect of Shakespearean performance blends into Linklater's "multicultural" agenda through her sense of how the categories of Shakespeare's social representation – rank, for example – find analogies in contemporary culture. For although contemporary behavior provides a distant analogy of the behavioral codes and meanings of Shakespeare's era – as Linklater demonstrates when she compares the inequality of wealth in contemporary America to class and status difference in the Renaissance – the meaning of contemporary experience is nonetheless more fully expressed by Shakespeare: "One must not diminish the size of Shakespeare's expression in order to accommodate contemporary truth, but rather must allow personal and contemporary truth to expand to be given the fullest life in Shakespeare's expression" (201).

Linklater has a worthwhile end in mind here. For although she doesn't return to the issue of regional accent, it seems implicit in her sense that "cultural diversity on the stage is a good thing" (201) that "Shakespeare" will be registered in a more differential way, that actors of various racial/ethnic origins and affiliations will speak the text in their own free, natural, and accentuated voices. But while we may now think that "Mono-cultural Shakespearean productions are not only false but dull," Linklater is at pains to show that this is not merely a reworking of Shakespearean texts to engage with contemporary social realities.

Instead, while such production values reflect "on stage the racial and ethnic riches of the world we live in," they do so with a singular purpose: "Theoretically, right-minded people know that the classics should reveal to the audience a universal message plumbed from depths reverberating deep below national or racial distinctions" (201). As Richard Paul Knowles remarks, "Linklater's formula for the redress of inequalities begins to sound very like a recipe for cultural imperialism, or what I think of as the 'we-are-the-world' school of interculturalism" ("Shakespeare, Voice, and Ideology" 103). Rather than regarding the text as a field of production, a field of appropriation, a site where meanings are made, rather than taking a contestatory attitude toward the cultural politics represented both by the Shakespearean original and by contemporary culture, theatrical performance remains captive to notions of authenticity, most captive at precisely those moments in which it seems most faithless.

The way that "Shakespeare" is made to ground personal, and ultimately political choice, is revealed in the final chapters of *Freeing Shakespeare's Voice*. In "Which Voice? *The Texts*," Linklater conducts a brief overview of editions of Shakespearean drama currently available, recognizing that renewed interest in Shakespearean editing has produced many new editions and a series of controversies regarding Shakespearean editing itself. Like many actors, Linklater tends to regard editorial controversies as a distraction from the real business of coming up with line readings that make sense: "While the scholars come up with intriguing alternatives for this word or that word, the actor must not be lightly seduced away from her/his choice, whose study should be the clarification and development of character" (204). Yet while she appears to place the performance text firmly in the hands of the actor, Linklater nonetheless pays obeisance to the authority of the Folio, "venerated by actors because legend has it that the secrets of the actual performance readings of Shakespeare's actors are encoded in the punctuation, the spellings and the capitalizations of the Folio script" (204–5). Indeed, one of the most striking conjunctions of literary and performed authority comes about in the work of directors and teachers who use the 1623 Folio text and earlier quarto texts to articulate a system for training and rehearsing actors for the Shakespearean stage. Although actor and voice training work to recover Shakespeare's words in the natural body of the modern performer, Folio-based training works to recover the signs of the modern body in the authentic Shakespearean text.

Although techniques based on old texts are enunciated somewhat differently by Patrick Tucker in the UK, Barbara Gaines in Chicago, and Neil Freeman in Canada, Freeman's book, *Shakespeare's First Texts*, and the extensive series of "folio scripts" he has made available in both hard-copy and electronic form, have made his practice the most widely disseminated. Like modern editors, Freeman is interested in the materiality of early printed texts of Shakespeare plays. In "The Materiality of the Shakespearean Text," Margreta de Grazia and Peter Stallybrass argue that the materiality of Renaissance texts – the "old typefaces and spellings, irregular line and scene divisions, title pages and other paratextual matter" – insist "upon being looked *at*, not seen *through*. Their refusal to yield to modern norms bears witness to the specific history of the texts they make up, a history so specific that it cannot comply with modern notions of correctness and intelligibility" (256–57). Folio-based actor training similarly attends to the "accidentals" of Renaissance publishing, looking *at* them rather than seeing *through* them. Yet while de Grazia and Stallybrass and others see the materiality of the text to disperse the field of individual authority, Freeman takes the anomalies of early texts as the register of authoritatively "Shakespearean" attitudes, thinking, intentions.

Freeman's goal is to train and rehearse actors to perform Shakespearean drama, and in practice, his use of early printed texts is focused almost entirely on "character." Freeman takes the formalities of early printed texts – line-breaks, punctuation, spelling, capitalization, regular and irregular speech-prefixes – to record an essentially "rhetorical" conception of character and of public discourse. Regarding "the first printed texts of the Shakespeare plays" as "products of a speaking-hearing society," Freeman suggests that "What was set on paper was not just a silent debate. It was at the same time a visual reminder of how the human voice might be heard both logically and passionately in that debate" (2).[19] Modern edited texts, which regularize spelling, punctuation, and so on, obscure this rhetorical dimension of the Shakespearean originals, and "remove the Elizabethan flavour or argument and character development (especially in the areas of character stress and the resulting textual irregularities), thus watering down and removing literally thousands of rhetorical and theatrical clues that those first performance scripts contained" (3). By providing his actors with a systematic means of reading those accidentals as signs of character development, Freeman provides not only a way to produce the plays, but a way to produce them *authentically*, tracing through the printed page to Shakespeare's original design.[20]

Freeman argues that the Elizabethan conception of the rhetoric of character is lost when Elizabethan means of representing it in print are altered. While Freeman appears to locate Shakespearean character in historical terms, however, constituted at the intersection of theatrical and social practice, the "character" that Freeman discovers by reading the material page seems distinctly modern. Characters' emotional turbulence (what is valuable in performance) appears at moments of "dysfunction," moments reflected in irregularities on the printed page, "the all-important unbalanced dramatic viewpoint, the human values, the stepping-stones of argument and especially the moments of irrationality and swamping emotions" (5). Modern Shakespeare editions may make it easy to assimilate the plot and gross outlines of a play, but they "cannot give you the conflict within each character, the very essence for the fullest understanding of the development and resolution of any Shakespeare play" (4). What Freeman supplies is a technology for reading these irregularities as signs of character change, of the kind of subtextual movement which modern actors are trained to produce as the sign of "character" itself.

Although Freeman takes the printed texts to offer "information" particularly useful to the actor, what the printed texts provide is a field of interpretation; Freeman offers a systematic way of making the forms of the printed page translatable into a certain conception of character, acting, and theatrical value. Believing that it is the actor's job to excavate (or discover) emotional contradiction, Freeman provides a way of reading old texts as indications of "many more inner switches between the two sides" of a character's "nature" (9). Noticing, for example, that "Lady Capulet" is indicated by several different speech prefixes in *Romeo and Juliet,* Freeman shows how thinking about the prefix – *Wife, Old Lady, Lady, Mother* – as a guide to the character's function in the scene can "give wonderful acting dimensions to a character that is often played quite colourlessly. The four different prefixes seem to specify quite precisely the different obligations she is expected to fulfill and thus what 'social' role she is expected to play and when, even to the extent of requiring her to change her status several times within a single scene" (8). Freeman makes a similar point about Puck, noting that in *A Midsummer Night's Dream*, the role is prefixed as both *Puck* and *Robin*. Here, Freeman detects a different function in these alternating prefixes; while Robin is gentle and generally benevolent, Puck is more of a trickster, and "the actor's ability to play both aspects and to switch back and forth between them is fundamental to the character's growth throughout the play" (9).

Freeman's technique can have powerful results. What seems disputable is Freeman's sense that these distinctions arise *within* the text, rather than as part of a more general strategy for interpreting the text, a way of making it conform to beliefs about Shakespeare, acting, and theatre that are already in hand. This sense is particularly visible in Freeman's use of line-breaks, punctuation, and capitalization, all of which he reads not in purely formal or rhetorical terms, nor as a record of compositorial inattention, illiteracy, or exigency, but as the material form of the inner conflict of the characters, the signs of emotional stability or unbalance. So, for example, "the colon indicates that, whatever the demand, the speaker can continue with the argument: here matter wins out over manner," while "the semicolon suggests that the demand is so strong that the speaker falters for a moment and is thrown back into her/himself and her/his own personal (emotional) needs" (101). Similarly, "there is mental energy in the capital [letter], suggesting the finding of the right word, thus reflecting logic in the matter of the speech"; "clusters of capital letters" suggest "sudden repeated piercing insights, thus indicating the manner of discovery as well as the matter being discovered"; "if a word is capitalised, and then a moment later not, the character may be deftly moving from an intellectual point to something more reflective and/or personal, just for a moment" (147). Spelling, too, reveals the shifts in character: "where words appear in a more complex ('Schreemes' instead of 'screams') form, the character is moved by the image to release more of a personal reaction than if they were reacting in a harmonic/balanced way"; "where words appear in a more simple form ('honor' rather than 'honour') the character is recoiling from the image, attempting to hold something back the image might otherwise release"; "what appears as conventional spelling to modern eyes suggests that no matter what the character is undergoing, they are capable of handling their emotions and personal reactions of the current moment in a calm manner, even though their private volcano may be bursting all over the place" (168–69).

Freeman teaches actors to read a text closely, and to incorporate its material features into their ways of thinking about performance. What seems questionable is the sense that this kind of interpretation arises immediately from the printed form of the text, that these rules for interpreting the text recover its innate representation of "character." Recognizing that Elizabethan writing was not fully conventionalized in terms of spelling, punctuation, and capitalization, Freeman nonetheless sees the irregularities of printed language as being regularly deployed to signify the drifting passions of Shakespeare's characters. But in what sense is "honor" more *simple* than "honour"? In a system of imperfectly conventionalized rules, Freeman's systematic assignment of character-motive to punctuation, capitalization, and spelling seems almost purely arbitrary. For example, Freeman offers a fascinating reading of *As You Like It* 1.2, centering on Orlando's reply to Duke Frederick.

The pride Orlando takes in being his father's son is clearly shown in his reply
     Orlando my Liege, the yongest sonne of Sir Roland de Boys
with emphasis on "sonne" rather than "son." Unfortunately, this is

exactly the wrong reply for Duke Frederick, since Orlando's father had been a supporter of the rightful Duke Senior (just banished by Duke Frederick), hence Frederick replies using "son" rather than Orlando's image filled "sonne"

> I would thou hadst beene son to some man else,
> The world esteem'd thy father honourable . . .

and the cold reduction of that single word "son" speaks enormous volumes within such a seemingly tiny act. (152)

To read the text in this way is, given a good actor, almost sure to produce an interesting, tiny moment of tension in a production: Freeman's technique – like any hermeneutic, it might be argued – produces "results" consistent with its assumptions and its practice. Yet this moment also reveals the wild semiology of Freeman's technique, for Freeman's privileged signified – emotional tension, complexity, "swamping emotions" – can, finally, be encoded in any signifier. Had Orlando used the spelling "son," and Frederick replied with "sonne," Freeman would have been at no loss for an equally telling reading: Frederick's ironic *expansion* and emphasis of Orlando's merely factual statement of relationship speaks volumes, etc.

Freeman, then, offers a technology of interpretation that claims to elide the process of history and representation, to take actors and audiences back to the moment of "Shakespearean intent or practice" (149). Freeman soft-pedals the complexity of textual transmission, attributing to ambiguous agents – Shakespeare, copyists, typesetters – a continuation of Shakespeare's original intentions. Locating emotionally volatile "character" at the center of those intentions, Freeman enables modern actors to read the modern text as offering insight and instruction in the practices of modern acting. In an odd sense, Freeman is not so much the contemporary of Gary Taylor as the inheritor of A. C. Bradley: we may never know how many children had Lady Macbeth, but if we count the capital letters and multiply the colons, we may be able to anatomize the quantity of her emotions.

The belief that the Folio preserves "Shakespeare's own words, his own punctuation," and other accidentals such as capitalization (Gaines, "Using Shakespeare's First Folio") is widespread among actors and directors, and complements the sense that in returning the body to its nature actors discover the truth of Shakespeare's plays. Using the Folio can have, of course, extraordinary results in performance; in my view, these results have less to do with the dubious claim that the typographic layout of the Folio texts has any source authority in Shakespeare's manuscripts, in Jacobean theatre practice, or even in Jacobean speech habits (as though the compositors may have punctuated or capitalized according to how they would have said the lines), than with providing a systematic way of attending to the text and organizing its expression that speaks to the preoccupations of modern audiences. Attending to the texture of the Folio, actors recode the text in the dynamics of modern performance: the various pauses, "beats," and emphases supposedly indicated by the Folio's typography are interpreted through the lens of realistic performance in the Stanislavskian tradition, as ways to articulate a clear, consistent, and emotionally complex character through subtextual intention. Freeman's technique, like the discourse of "body centers" or the efforts to restore the body to its "natural" expressiveness, testifies to a vexed desire to ground what "works" – what speaks to contemporary audiences in the idiom of contemporary performance – in a deeper authority, to inscribe the body of performance with the authority of Shakespeare.

What is the impact of this rhetoric on actors themselves? Before returning to actors' sense of authorized embodiment, it may be useful to reflect on some of the differences between how actors and scholars understand Shakespearean characters. The widespread popularity of actors' accounts of Shakespearean performance is part of a larger crisis of legitimacy, one that is in many ways the inevitable outcome of conceiving the meanings generated by stage production as *opposed* to those generated when the text is produced in other ways – as reading or criticism, for example. For neither *text* nor *performance* point to a stable identity; each term marks out an arena of shifting practices of production and reception, where signification is imbricated in a close-grained fabric of values, attitudes, identities, and desires. The intensity of the "text vs. performance" skirmishing suggests that the stakes have less to do with Shakespearean drama than with how competing visions of culture are sustained by a "legitimate" vision of "Shakespeare."[21] When Robert Smallwood introduces the third volume of the *Players of Shakespeare* series by citing A. C. Bradley's introduction to *Shakespearean Tragedy* as a decisive "stage in the educational establishment's appropriation for the class-room and lecture hall of Shakespeare the writer for the popular theatre" (Jackson and Smallwood, *Players 3* 1), we can see claims about an essential Shakespeare (popular and theatrical, not effete and literary) being used to mark stage production as the natural venue of authentic "Shakespearean" meaning. In this view, "the actor's professional disciplines" provide insight not only into the acting process itself, but also into the innate and timeless features of Shakespearean drama, the vision of ethics, morality, and behavior – the "properties of being human" – that lie at the heart of Shakespeare's greatness as a playwright (Brockbank, Foreword ix; Introduction 1). To read the *Players of Shakespeare* volumes is to enter a zone of "purely" theatrical interpretation, where de-cisions are held to be "instinctively made, perceptions uncon-sciously arrived at, fine discriminations mysteriously achieved" (Brockbank, Introduction 3).

Despite repeated efforts to distinguish their process from criti-cism as such, the actors' readings help us to locate the interface between the interpretive priorities of scholarship and those of the stage, and the strategies of authorization informing the actors' sense of performance. At first glance, the essays in *Players of Shakespeare* seem remarkably insulated from the concerns driving much of Shakespeare studies today. While the actors variously allude to Coleridge and the Lambs, Muriel Bradbrook, Nevill Coghill, Wilson Knight, Jan Kott, F. R. Leavis, Kenneth Muir, Marvin Rosenberg, Edith Sitwell, and Dover Wilson, other names more representative of the state of contemporary critical thinking about Shakespeare – say, Catherine Belsey, Lynda Boose, Jonathan Dollimore, Stephen Greenblatt, Stephen Orgel – are absent.[22] To be sure, citation of scholarly authority is precisely beside the point in a series of essays devoted to the pragmatic ways and means of acting. What this metonymy reveals, though, is a particular kind of rupture between the actors' sense of the purpose of scholarship and the issues and practices animating academic Shakespeare studies today. This has less to do with the innate propriety of either old or new critical approaches, or with the inherent adequacy of either theatrical or scholarly conceptions of Shakespeare. Read as a whole, these essays reveal a consistent body of interpretive practice, strategies for reading Shakespearean drama that produce a palpable vision of what counts as Shakespeare, in the theatre and in modern culture. Actorly reading is notably trained on questions of character, the integrated, self-present, internalized, psychologically motivated "character" of the dominant mode of modern theatrical representation, stage realism. And although recent stagings of Shakespearean drama have often engaged the themes of gender, class, race, and empire, such thematics are conceived as ways of exploring – rather than unseating – conventional conceptions of character. Where scholars and performers seem at the moment most opposed is in their understanding of character, of what and how the roles of Shakespeare's plays signify. These brief essays on Shakespearean performance are evidence of the different strategies of reading practiced in the institutions of the academy and the theatre. They record the shifting ways that Shakespeare is made to mean, and the different visions of culture that Shakespeare appears to authorize.

One of the challenges shared by both actors and scholars has to do with the historical remoteness of Shakespearean drama. The plays arose in circumstances quite different from our own, and those differences must be acknowledged; at the same time, both performance and scholarship are involved in making the plays speak to audiences today. This engagement with history provides one way to mark the interpretive work of performance, and the way it both invokes and produces a particular vision of Shakespeare. In the *Players of Shakespeare* series, the politics of interpretation emerge in the ways performers understand and represent character. Despite the British theatre's reputation for being less involved in an explicitly Stanislavskian tradition than the American stage, the *Players of Shakespeare* essays are informed by notions of a coherent and internalized characterization fully consistent with Stanislavskian mimesis. Granted, Gregory Doran, describing his preparation for Solanio in Bill Alexander's 1987

production of *The Merchant of Venice*, is one of the few actors to
allude directly to a "Stanislavskian search for detail," "the tenta-
tive extrapolation of arguable subtextual hints into quintessential
radix traits" (Jackson and Smallwood, *Players 3* 72). Nonetheless,
throughout *Players of Shakespeare*, actors conceive of "character" as
an entity whose "radix traits" can be discovered in the text and
used to motivate a single spine of action, the actor/character's
"journey" through the play. Philip Brockbank attributes the "journey" metaphor to Peter Hall's influence (Introduction 2), and its
effects are apparently pervasive: actors learn to resolve the fragmentary and inconsistent signals of the role into the continuous
experience of a discrete, individual subject. As Roger Rees discovered working on Posthumus in *Cymbeline*, the "journey" and
the centered "self" are reciprocally defining terms: he attributes
his difficulty seizing on Posthumus's "journey" to an inability to
find "Posthumus's true centre" (Brockbank, *Players* 142, 147).[23]

   Meredith Anne Skura remarks that in "an era mistrustful
of 'presence,' drama maintains a convincing illusion of immediacy, resistant to postmodern technology and fragmentation"
(*Shakespeare the Actor* 29). The actors' essays suggest that this "presence" is implicit not in the drama but in the actors' ways of
reading it, their trained approach to translating the text into embodied action. In some respects, the actors' performance occu-
pies a familiar postmodern position, the unstable terrain where
personal and cultural history and identity meet in the register
of representation: the terrain of *pastiche*.[24] Translating the
Stanislavskian super-objective into the metaphorical "journey"
involves the actors in a dual engagement with history: with the
past traced in the text – the play's given circumstances, the eccen-
tricities of character drawn from an era so removed from our own,
their necessary effort to write a motivating personal history for the
role – and with the present, the moment of performance, which
necessarily decenters or displaces the authority of the text. What is
surprising is that the actors understand their interpretive practice
less as a mode of self-authorized creation than as a mode of
fidelity to Shakespeare. Conceiving Shakespearean character as
an organic whole, the actors stage a Shakespeare closer to Ibsen
or O'Neill than to Heiner Müller or Anna Deavere Smith.

The actors often use history to open and sustain their readings of Shakespearean character. On the one hand, the actors use historical research to help them enter the imaginative space of the role, to identify and particularize the odd quirks and edges of a dramatic style and sensibility so removed from a contemporary idiom. The ultimate purpose of this historical inquiry is usually to deny history, to achieve an interpretation that *is* properly Shakespearean precisely because it denies the difference of the past. The actors' principal mode of engagement with the past concerns the need to develop a biography for the role, a "past" to motivate the character's present actions. This act of biographical invention serves much the function it does for Stanislavski: it enables the actor to produce the illusion of a single, whole, coherent character whose behavior flows from a concrete past into a determined present. Donald Sinden's approach to playing Malvolio – "What kind of man is Malvolio? What is his background?" (Brockbank, *Players* 43) – is fully reminiscent of Stanislavski's similar question of the role of Roderigo: "What is the *past* which justifies the *present* of this scene: Who is Roderigo?" ("From the Production Plan" 131).[25]

Moreover, in devising this motivating "history" of the role, the actors of *Players of Shakespeare* frequently resort to historical materials in order to specify and concretize the character, to make it respond to the "given circumstances" of Shakespeare's era. In most cases, this research confirms the reality of the character to the actor (and eventually to the audience), by confirming that people *then* were pretty much like people *now*. Ralph Fiennes, playing Henry VI in Adrian Noble's 1988 adaptation of the first tetralogy, *The Plantagenets*, "read a bit about the 'real,' the 'historical' Henry VI" and was pleased to find

some historians' assessments of him to coincide very much with Shakespeare's plays, not so much in terms of dates and accuracy of events, but in essence, as it were. The character they described fitted very much with the character I found myself playing: someone obstinate, certain of their faith, wishing to appease people through granting favours, talking them into loyalty, into peaceful ways of conducting their affairs, but, on finding himself crossed, as Henry is by Suffolk, passionately decisive, however unwise the actual decisions may be. (Jackson and Smallwood, *Players 3* 113)

Shakespeare responds to history by catching the essence of the man; the modern actor responds to Shakespeare by transmitting that recognizable essence to the audience. More often, however, "history" serves an almost purely instrumental role, to render the illusion of a consistent, coherent character. For example, when Tony Church compared his Polonius (in Peter Hall's 1965 *Hamlet*) to Lord Burghley, he was able to cast several parallels between Burghley and Polonius into his performance. Nonetheless, he admits that the historical evidence for such a comparison is inconclusive, and that the figure of Burghley functioned for him "in *character*, and as a fertilizer for the actor's imagination" (Brockbank, *Players* 105).

Of course, the historical dimension of the actors' work is evanescent in performance, traced only in the vision of character, action, and culture that is encoded in their behavior onstage. Though absent in performance, this sense of history provides one of the conditions from which the performance emerges. The actors' "historical sense," like T. S. Eliot's sense of poetic tradition, is a sense "not only of the pastness of the past, but of its presence," a sense of history in which the "temporal" is ineluctably troped by the "timeless" ("Tradition" 49).[26] The actors use history to confirm this "traditional" sense, to confirm a continuity in the "radix traits" of a stable human nature between Shakespeare's era and our own. Working on Portia for Bill Alexander's 1987 *Merchant*, for example, Deborah Findlay remembered

reading a court ambassador from Spain or Italy of the period who wrote home about this passionate, volatile English nation. He spoke of our forebears in terms which we would reserve, suppressed as we now are by Puritanism and Victorianism, for the hot Latin temperament. It was my ambition to catch some of this full-bloodedness and for us all to embrace characters who could hate and love, and feel joy and sorrow, passionately. (Jackson and Smallwood, *Players 3* 53)

The Spanish ambassador's portrait of the volatile English first enables Findlay to distance herself from the modern English character, and to justify her sense of the play's surprisingly passionate energy. At the same time, however, this portrait also seems to confirm Findlay's stereotype of the rambunctious "nature of the Elizabethan man and woman," a full-blooded passion that Findlay implies might still flow through "us all." The ambassador's letter enables Findlay to annihilate the historical difference it appears to summon between fiery Elizabethans and repressed moderns, for in the end Findlay's romantic attraction to this "full-blooded" sensibility is what attracts her to Portia, and helps to forge her identification with "the vibrant, excellent person that she is" (53, 52).

Gregory Doran's brilliant essay on playing Solanio in the same production is more notable in this regard. Solanio is a small and thankless part, but Doran worked to render it with a fine clarity of persuasive detail, work that clearly paid off in Salerio and Solanio's brutal treatment of Antony Sher's Shylock. As a role in the play, Solanio's function in the plot clearly predominates over his individualized character, and Doran worked hard to find ways to make the part concrete, individual, and his own:

In researching the period I discovered that the young Henry III of France had visited Venice on his way back from Cracow, where as a young general he had won the throne of Poland. When he returned from Venice, however, he was a different man. The court was stupefied to see him caked in powder, hung with precious stones, and surrounded by a flock of parrots and little dogs. He began to hold fêtes in the royal parks, decked out in a pink damask dress embroidered with pearls, emerald pendants in his ears, diamonds in his hair, and his beard dyed with violet powder. . . . Adreana Neofitou, the costume designer, drew the line at the violet beard powder, but created a very dashing outfit for Solanio, in russets and umbers, with a splendid orange panache, and for further ornament I added an ostentatious pearl rosary, commas of rouge on the cheeks, kohl on the eyes, and a pickadevant beard and moustache. All this gave plenty of scope for Solanio's "outward show" to fall apart as the first half progressed, and pull himself together by the trial. (Jackson and Smallwood, *Players 3* 71)

Needless to say, Henry III has little to do with Solanio, *The Merchant of Venice*, or Doran's performance, for that matter. What does function here is the image of Venice as the site of elaborate ostentation, reduced to a significant detail – the violet beard – which, though finally absent from the production, specifies the kind of display animating Doran's Solanio. The violet beard epitomizes Solanio, centers the character in Doran's imagination, and enables him to discover a journey through the fragmentary Solanio scenes. Though Doran's wished-for violet beard is perhaps an extreme example, it dramatizes the function of history in the *Players of Shakespeare* volumes: a soup of nuance, image, and detail internalized toward the production of character, usually in ways that claim to reveal the human essence of recalcitrant classical roles and so to enable their intrinsic "properties of being human" to speak again to today's public.[27] Reading for "character," the actors use a kind of historical bricolage to assimilate the centrifugal energies of the role to the modern demand that their performance incarnate a single, undivided, modern subject, a readable self.

This (promiscuous, inspirational, what you will) use of anecdote to situate an unfamiliar discourse (the behavior of Shakespearean roles) in relation to a familiar one (the modern "self") may not seem entirely unexpected. The actors' practice almost parodies the new historicist penchant for "episodic, anecdotal, contingent, exotic, abjected, or simply uncanny aspects of the historical record" (White, "New Historicism" 301).[28] This likeness is more than a glancing one. To seize on an eccentric yet dramatic detail drawn from the character's period, and make it signify in an apparently remote discourse, is somewhat more reminiscent of contemporary new historicism than of traditional "historical" representation in the theatre. Although Victorian actors like Charles Kean and Henry Irving would set *Macbeth* or *King Lear* in the dramatically appropriate historical period, the practice of today's actors resonates with the eclecticism of contemporary staging, which tends to strike a more overt and unstable relationship between the play's historical setting, the period of the play's composition, and other periods signaled by costume and set design.[29] It might be thought that new historicism – with its often shrewd tension between excavating the otherness of history and revising the present by revising the past – has a similarly eclectic feel, claiming likeness between historical eras in terms of their internal symbolic and representational dynamics rather than in the narrative causality of more conventional historiography. Much as new historicism has been criticized for removing "facts," events, or texts from their original context to make them signify in other, surprising (or eccentric) registers, so it might be argued that the *Players of Shakespeare* actors use history in similarly surprising ways, deploying details to register the contingency of terms like "past" and "present." Does Solanio's violet beard work on the contemporary audience like the invisible bullets of Stephen Greenblatt's seminal (and much revised) essay, providing a way both to "other" the past, and to suggest the continuities between some of its ideological categories and operations (character, subversion and containment) and those of the present day? Is it possible that in their strategies of reading Shakespeare, and reading history, the actors are in some unacknowledged way more Greenblatt's contemporaries than Dover Wilson's?

As many commentators have noticed, it is difficult to generalize about new historicism, which (like acting) can seem like a practice – or aggregate of practices – in search of a method. Nonetheless, new historicist inquiry has, by now, come to have a recognizable shape. First, as historical/critical practice, new historicism is urgently differential, engaged in the intense scrutiny of the local specificity of Renaissance literature as a means of distancing it from us, rendering the text as the register of the particular and local, rather than the essential or universal. Arguing, for instance, for a political analysis "which examines how Shakespearean texts have functioned to produce, reproduce, or contest historically specific relations of power (relations among classes, genders, and races, for example) and have been used to produce and naturalize interested representations of the real" (Introduction 3), Jean E. Howard and Marion F. O'Connor position this historical practice in opposition to the Shakespeare of the liberal humanist cultural and intellectual tradition, a tradition in which "Shakespeare has been used to secure assumptions about texts, history, ideology, and criticism" rather than interrogate them, a tradition in which Shakespeare functions "as a kind of cultural Esperanto, a medium through which the differences of material existence – differences of race, gender, class, history, and culture – are supposedly canceled" (4).[30] Yet while it weaves literature deeply into the rhetoric of its originating culture, new historicism also claims its inquiry into the past as an inquiry into the circuits of power in the present as well. This conception of history departs from an inert Eliotic tradition, in which the categories of the "timeless" and universal constitute a "simultaneous order" informing the categories of contemporary experience. Instead, as Louis Montrose has elegantly argued, this sense of history is powerfully dialectical, and

> necessitates efforts to historicize the present as well as the past, and to historicize the dialectic between them – those reciprocal historical pressures by which the past has shaped the present and the present reshapes the past. In brief, to speak today of an historical criticism must be to recognize that not only the poet but also the critic exists in history; that the texts of each are inscriptions of history; and that our comprehension, representation, interpretation of the texts of the past always proceeds by a mixture of estrangement and appropriation, as a reciprocal conditioning of the Renaissance text and our text of the Renaissance. Such critical practice constitutes a continuous dialogue between a *poetics* and a *politics* of culture. ("Professing the Renaissance" 24)

This understanding of the function of texts in history engages those involved in reproducing Shakespearean texts – critics, actors, readers – in a complex enterprise. For as Montrose argues, in "its anti-reflectionism, its shift of emphasis from the formal analysis of verbal *artifacts* to the ideological analysis of discursive *practices*, its refusal to observe strict and fixed boundaries between 'literary' and other texts (sometimes including the critic's own), the emergent social/political/historical orientation in literary studies is pervasively concerned with writing, reading, and teaching as modes of *action*" (26). The new historicism blurs or erases the boundaries between the literary and the nonliterary, undertakes a determinedly anti-authorial understanding of the production of textual meanings, and is concerned not only with the ways in which texts signify in the era of their initial production but with the interested ways they continue to be appropriated and reproduced in subsequent history. As a result, many critics argue as Jean Howard does that "an analysis of Renaissance culture can be made to speak to the concerns of late twentieth-century culture," particularly if we conceive of "our own historical moment as the post-humanist epoch in which essentialist notions of selfhood are no longer viable" ("New Historicism in Literary Studies" 15–16).

Like some new historicists, many actors may appear to "eschew overarching hypothetical constructs in favor of surprising coincidences."[31] Yet while the explanatory power of new historicist argumentation relics on the contested "assumption that any one aspect of a society is related to any other. No organizing principle determines these relationships: any social practice has at least a potential connection to any theatrical practice" (Walter Cohen, "Political Criticism" 34), this sense of the interplay of cultural discourses in Shakespeare's era is sharply different from ways contemporary actors sample history. As Michael Bristol notes, the "notorious new historicist 'anecdote' is much more than colorful décor; it has an indispensable function in making historical descriptions sufficiently thick" – the thick description of the "practical, symbolic, and moral life of diverse and shifting communities, their level of technical knowledge, their politics, and the important social and religious conflicts of the period" being the way new historicism foregrounds its characteristic emphasis on "conflict, difference, and complexity" as well as on "marginal or excluded figures within the social landscape" ("How Good" 34). The actors' commitment to character, on the other hand, suggests a fundamental resistance to the kind of discursive interplay typical of new historicist inquiry, in which the subject is conceived less as an "identity" or "self" than as a shifting site where the claims of competing discourses – of the state, religion, the economy, class, gender, sexuality, and so on – are focused. Despite an analogous commitment to seeing Shakespeare in the past and in the present, actors' engagement with history reveals strikingly different commitments, commitments which really become visible in how they conceive of Shakespeare's commentary on the *present*.[32]

One way to phrase this distinction would be to say that actors are (paradoxically enough) interested in what "Shakespeare" *is* rather than what "Shakespeare" can be made to *do*.[33] The use of historical detail in actors' preparation, geared to the service of character, locates meaning in the text rather than in its *use*. Performance turns out to be a vehicle for representing the naturalized truths of an Eliotic tradition – cultural Esperanto – rather than contesting them, or even showing how such "truths" are our own creation as well as Shakespeare's. This tendency is particularly evident in plays where Renaissance and modern sensibilities are clearly misaligned; *The Merchant of Venice* provides one telling example. Writing about his 1978 Shylock, Patrick Stewart notes that because "of the Nazis' Final Solution and six million deaths, those passages of anti-semitic expression in *The Merchant* will reverberate powerfully for any audience in this second half of the twentieth century." Yet Stewart is concerned that the play's significance will thus be read too narrowly by modern audiences, who will miss its larger – indeed, its justifying – frame of reference.

But however important Jewishness and anti-semitism are in the play they are secondary to the consideration of Shylock, the man: unhappy, unloved, lonely, frightened and angry. And no matter how monstrous his cold-blooded attempt on Antonio's life, it is the brave, insane solitary act of a man who will defer no more, compromise no more. Taking Antonio's life is his line of no retreat and, although justified on commercial grounds, this murder is also, therefore, symbolic. Perhaps this makes of Shylock a revolutionary in modern terms. Certainly, when as Shylock I stood in the court and said "my deeds upon my head", I felt closer to *all* those oppressed and abused who stand up in the face of a hostile and powerful enemy. This was not one Jew, but all victims who turn on their persecutors. (Brockbank, *Players* 19)

Stewart's redemptive reading of Shylock resonates with a theatrical tradition extending at least to Henry Irving's tragic *Merchant* (in which the solitary exit of Irving's Shylock ended the performance), and with familiar modern critical attitudes as well: the sense that Shakespeare's values are essentially humane, and that Shylock's claim to an essential humanity in the play ("Hath not a Jew . . .") points to the play's desire to claim an underlying humanity uniting the variously (class, gender, ethnically, sexually) identified castes of the play. To make Shylock a universal victim, Stewart must self-consciously generalize the explicit function of Shylock's ethnicity in the play, the specific terms in which his identification as a Jew enables the romantic Christians to stage their privileged values as the signs of mercy rather than oppression. As Frank Whigham argues, Shylock demonstrates that Venetian society's "oppression of one . . . reveals its oppression of many"; unlike Stewart, Whigham sees the victimization of Shylock as a function of the abstract and universalizing rhetoric the Christians use to destroy him. Where Stewart makes of Shylock a symbol of oppressed humanity, Whigham sees the generalized category "humanity" as part of the self-interested "ideology of universal harmony" that the play opens to demystification ("Ideology and Class Conduct" 109, 108).

It should be clear that I am not attempting to choose between Stewart's reading – which promoted a rich and moving performance – and Whigham's, but am instead trying to elaborate the continuities and discontinuities between two representative ways of reading the play.[34] Stewart's assumptions about Shakespearean meaning are grooved on the theatre's belief in Shakespearean morality. Although Shakespeare's plays represent profoundly disturbing evils – the blinding of Gloucester, Macbeth's cancerous imaginings, Leontes' engulfing jealousy – "Shakespeare" finally stands for a just vision of human nature and action. If critical reading evokes a hermeneutic of suspicion, the sense that Shakespearean drama negotiates (and is sometimes betrayed by) its densely ideologized theatrical, political, and cultural milieu, reading for the theatre appears to involve a hermeneutic of transcendence, the belief that the values asserted most positively in the play express its core meanings, the meanings that speak equally to Renaissance and modern audiences.

Portia's treatment of Shylock in the Act 4 trial scene throws these divergent perspectives into sharp relief. Like Patrick Stewart, Deborah Findlay, Portia in Bill Alexander's 1987 *Merchant*, takes "racism" as "an element of the play, but not the main one. It is encompassed by the broader debate about mercy and justice, about commitment and loyalty, about the nature of choice and its consequences, and most broadly about how we should treat each other" (Jackson and Smallwood, *Players 3* 56). Contemporary critics, as we have seen, tend to see the "debate about mercy and justice" as an ideological screen that normalizes and naturalizes the play's antisemitism. And yet there is a striking symmetry between Findlay's sense of Portia and critical accounts of the role's ideological functioning in the play. In a provocative reading of Shakespearean set speeches, Thomas Cartelli develops Whigham's sense that the play's characters, Bassanio and Portia in particular, slip "into a stylized rhetorical mode that fore-grounds a set of abstract values," values often taken as identical to the play's – or Shakespeare's – meaning. Yet, Cartelli contin-ues, this rhetoric "simultaneously embodies the speaker's most personal projections" ("Ideology and Subversion" 16), projections that reveal the speaker's complicity in the play's ruling order. Though "innocent of consciously employing the mercy speech as an ideological weapon against Shylock," Portia's speech on mercy registers her immersion in the dominant ideological dis-course of Venice: she is instrumental to Shylock's scapegoating (17). For "the mercy speech is an unanswerable proposition that gilds its speaker in the trappings of all things bright and beauti-ful" (17), offering the bright horizon of a fantasy or utopia clearly detached from the play's actual politics, which repeatedly insist on the rule of a law that lies in the hands of its social elite. So, once Shylock refuses to cooperate, mercy is withdrawn, and the terms of the law are shown to be infinitely fungible.[35] Cartelli concludes, "Portia's initial insistence on mercy resonates with the mercilessness of her ensuing treatment of Shylock in such a way that it renders the very concept indeterminate and her unquali-fied hold on its validity tragic, insofar as it radically distorts her consciousness of things as they are" (20).

Deborah Findlay's response to playing Portia eerily echoes Cartelli's description. Director Bill Alexander and Antony Sher – her Shylock – "wanted an idea of ritual sacrifice in the trial scene," emphasizing the "Christian-Jewish conflict" by having "an image of Antonio strung out on a cross" and by "having Shylock perform an improvised ritual before he kills Antonio. The ritual included spattering blood on a sheet before Antonio's prostrate body and he suggested that this would be a marvellous way for Portia to get the idea of 'no drop of blood'" (Jackson and Smallwood, *Players 3* 63). Findlay found the complexity and power of this conception disorienting, and sensed that Portia must be "in control of the scene from the moment she enters." Bringing Portia into the center of the scene, Findlay also makes Portia the register of the play's dominant ideology, in ways that seem to echo Cartelli's and Whigham's readings.

Far from being vindictive, she follows a simple rule of thumb: mercy, or justice. Having learnt about the nature of choice and its consequences from the caskets, Portia brings this wisdom to the trial and seeks to educate everyone there. It is her only option. She certainly can't compete physically and she is incorruptible. She has only that logic and her wit to see her through. She holds scrupulously to the letter of the law, since that is what Shylock has chosen. [. . .]

Portia gives Shylock as many chances as she can to choose mercy, but once he has made his choice (for me when Tony produced his knife) she follows the consequences through to their final terrible conclusion. Hers is an act of strict impartiality, explaining the law to everyone present. If you reject human mercy then there is only the implacable face of justice to fall back on. If you seek to pervert that, chaos follows. (64)

But of course, chaos doesn't follow, only the seizure of Shylock's property and his brutal conversion to Christianity. What's striking about Findlay's nuanced account of her playing is that it confirms Cartelli's sense of Portia's "innocence," and of the dramatic (and practical) effect of that innocence, an unknowing that enables both Portia and Findlay to act as though the only alternative to Shylock's "mercy" is his "implacable" ruination. Addressing her reading to the lineaments of character alone, Findlay duplicates the character's immersion in the play's ideological given circumstances: Portia could wish for no better defense of her "innocent" implementation of Venetian hegemony. To play the character's journey from the character's perspective, freighted with the weight of Shakespeare's transcendent morality, is to reproduce the ways the play naturalizes the character's behavior to its larger suasive purposes, its attempt to achieve the effect of the real. In succumbing to the "vibrant and excellent *person* that she is," Findlay succumbs to the play's larger designs (52, emphasis mine).[36]

Although Cartelli and Findlay agree about the content of Portia's speech, they differ sharply on its effect, and its relation to the play's larger concerns. This difference marks a larger divergence between how scholarly and theatrical institutions regard the purpose of interpreting Shakespeare. If new historical scholarship tends to regard the play's manifest assertions as the mask of ideological negotiation, actors tend to regard these assertions as the play's essential meaning, what makes the play continue to speak to modern audiences. This attitude comes into view in the ways actors understand the plays to comment on contemporary life. Writing of his fascinating performance as Thersites in Sam Mendes's 1991 *Troilus and Cressida*, Simon Russell Beale recalls acting "*Troilus and Cressida* in Stratford on the night that war was declared in the Gulf, and I was powerfully aware then that Thersites's despair was shared by everyone in the theatre. Shakespeare's discussion of institutionalized machismo seemed more powerful and more relevant than ever, and I was reminded that it was an enormous privilege to have a part in presenting this great play and this extraordinary character" (Jackson and Smallwood, *Players 3* 173). In a similar vein, Brian Cox suggests a variety of historical parallels that have rendered *Titus Andronicus* an important play in the twentieth century:

In our century the context for this play has never been more powerful. When Peter Brook produced it in 1951 the shadow of totalitarianism was very much upon us: Stalinism and the purges of the thirties, Hitler's Germany and the subsequent revelations of the Nuremburg trials. And now we have the rise of Islamic fundamentalism, the breakdown of social units, the mindless violence of soccer hooliganism, the sectarian violence of Northern Ireland, the disaffection of individuals within society resulting in mass murder sprees, not to mention the ever-increasing rise in rape crimes over the last forty years.

This may seem an over-generalized spectrum of events relating to just one play by Shakespeare, but every one of those incidents has its parallel in *Titus Andronicus*. (Jackson and Smallwood, *Players 3* 176)

In these performances, as well as in Roger Allam's account of *Measure for Measure* – where in the city scenes, the "grey cut-away coats and knee-breeches of the court gave way to outrageous cycling shorts and Doc Marten boots. Most of our whores were rent-boys, run by Pompey, working a gents' toilet that rose from the floor" (Jackson and Smallwood, *Players 3* 27) – reference to a contemporary setting, and to contemporary politics, is taken to "de-anaesthetize" the plays, "and thus shock and awaken our audience anew to the meaning of the scene" (27). Remarkably, these accounts cast performance as a parasite on the text: modern settings find "parallels" but don't produce new meanings, new Shakespeare, anti-Shakespeare. In all three cases, the meaning of the Shakespearean original is seen to be constant, despite the many contradictory "parallels" that can be drawn to contemporary life through felicitous and imaginative design and direction. Putting Shakespeare on the modern stage may give us insight into our condition, but it doesn't change Shakespeare – it just dresses him in new clothes.

While critical activity locates the rhetoric of Shakespearean drama in its ideological milieu, in performative accounts – and, surprisingly, in academic "performance criticism" – "Shakespeare" remains a point of repair, a touchstone of value beyond the actions and events the plays criticize. Much as *The Merchant of Venice* is taken to be about antisemitism but not to participate in it or produce it (as it evidently did throughout its first two or three centuries onstage), so *Troilus*, *Titus*, and *Measure for Measure* are shown to criticize from the timeless Shakespearean perspective those temporal elements of social life which parallel meanings already somehow "there" in the play. To engage contemporary culture more critically, Shakespearean production – and Shakespearean acting – will have to engage the rhetoric that reproduces that culture more directly. Such a strategy would demand a more self-evident decentering of the privilege of character, and a more skeptical regard for how "Shakespeare" is produced and implemented.

Indeed, what is finally most striking about actors' accounts of their work is how deeply it converses with an absent authority, with "Shakespeare." Surely actors have a clearer sense of their own creation, and would be unwilling to see themselves haunted by the ghostly presence of the author, a ghost largely exhumed by professors of English? As we have seen, actor training tends to release the actor into the "natural" freedom of the body, only to discover the author already there. Despite the sense, that is, that performance/performers and the text are somehow opposed, when describing their work, actors often summon Shakespeare to justify an interpretation of the play. In *Being an Actor*, for example, Simon Callow lists some of his notes for *Titus Andronicus*:

Revenge. No confidence in ability of law to settle righteous grudges: revenge regarded as legitimate (Cf. vigilantes).
Honour. Cf. Punk boy who killed a man who *smiled* at him. "'E was bringing me down in front of me mates."
Dismemberment. Cf. young Getty's ear from the kidnappers. (157)

Like Beale and Cox, Callow locates his production of character firmly on the horizon of contemporary social life. Believing that until "ideas become translated into sensations, they're of no use whatever to acting" (156), Callow uses vigilantes, punks, and the news to generate the sensations that will substantiate his enactment of Titus, and so define his engagement with the character, and through the character with the audience. It is surprising, then, to find Callow – who emphasizes the actor's creative experience of the role throughout his book – finally suggesting that the actor no longer confronts the author, but communes more directly with the author's designs: "The important thing is to restore the writer – whether dead or alive – and the actor to each other, without the self-elected intervention of the director, claiming a unique position interpreting the one to the other. We don't need an interpreter – we speak the same language: or at least we used to" (221).

Actors deploy a specialized regimen of technique and training to produce the dramatic text in the idiom of behavior. As their use of history implies, actors often have a sharp sense of the aleatory play of performance, and of its constitutive authority over the script of the play. Yet when describing their work, actors also represent their activity onstage as a conversation with authority. It is, again, easiest to raise these questions in terms of characterization, the production of a fictive "subject" as an effect of the signifying behavior of acting. In the process of characterization that the actors describe, "character" emerges both as a product, something latent in the play script, the author's proxy, and (often simultaneously) as a process of production that arises only through the de-authorizing intertextuality of the actor's performance. Brenda Bruce, for example, describes the Nurse in *Romeo and Juliet* in this way: "In my opinion, Nurse is no country bumpkin. She holds a very important position with an important family in Verona. She is the Italian equivalent of a bright Cockney with all the same energetic vulgarity and warmth, and the only interest in her life is Juliet and Juliet's happiness" (Brockbank, *Players* 93). Moving from the Nurse's social situation, Bruce begins immediately to particularize the role, in ways that imply not only an orientation to the character's psychology (compassionate, intimate with Juliet, maternal), but also an approach to playing, a feeling of sensory and physical embodiment ("bright Cockney," "energertic vulgarity and warmth"). Like acting, reading tends to obscure the "otherness" of characters, blurring the threshold between self and role, inside and outside. In this sense, Bruce's retrospective account of her preparation almost necessarily distorts her actual working process; Bruce's trained, affectual responses to the role's activities seem more immediate, and possibly to have produced the "textual" justification of the Nurse's class and social position. Does Bruce play the Nurse, or does the Nurse play Bruce?

This relationship between self and other, actor and role is typical, I think, of the way actors frequently talk about their work, about the necessity of self-exploration as part of the process of characterization. Describing Hamlet, for instance, Michael Pennington responds both to the extraordinary demands of the role, and to "the fact that finally to pull it off will take the actor further down into his psyche, memory and imagination, and further outwards to the limits of his technical knowledge and equipment, than he has probably been before" (Brockbank, *Players* 117). Making "Hamlet" requires the actor to explore his "theatrical self" (122), a "self" that evidently combines features of both writer and text. The "theatrical self" is both inscribed by the role (which forces Pennington "further down into his psyche") and constitutes the role in performance ("Hamlet" is staged through Pennington's mastery of "technical knowledge and equipment"). Pennington describes his work as a complex engagement between identity and artifice, work that finally renders these categories inadequate. The journey to performance seems to require the negotiation of these boundaries, a mutual act of writing in which both "actor" and "character" become each other's author. The text inscribes itself in the person of the actor, textualizing his or her experience and identity; the actor represents the text, rewrites it in the dynamics of the "theatrical self." In this sense, the Death of the Author is, in modern stage practice, accompanied by the Death of the Actor and the Death of the Character: neither actor nor character remains a self-present authority prior to their production in performance; both emerge as effects of representation. In *Being an Actor*, Simon Callow puts a finer point on it: "It's an incomparable feeling. Another person is coursing through your veins, is breathing through your lungs. But of course, it's not. It's only you – another arrangement of you" (166).

Even so, this deconstructive rearrangement of character and actor is finally accompanied by another gesture: "It's not simply a question of seeing the character, knowing who he is. Nor is it a matter of impersonation (though that can help). What it needs is for you to locate him in you. Only then will the energy spring from within, instead of being externally applied; only then will you have renewed the umbilical connection between the character and the author" (166).[37] Actor and character are both rearranged by the text of the other, yet this mutual rewriting is finally referred to an author, who appears *ex nihilo*, mysteriously present in the flesh of the actor/character. The appearance of the author in Callow's remarks is arresting not least for the way in which his or her presence is known: coursing through the veins, breathing through the lungs, something is materialized in the actor's body, transforming the body into an "umbilical connection" where two fictive beings, two sites of ideological activity, are collapsed into one: character and author. We might expect the actor's body – so local, so immediate – to provide a final point of resistance, the zero degree of the author. And yet the author is frequently summoned not only to substantiate a conception of character, but its bodily enactment as well.

Geoffrey Hutchings's account of his Lavatch in Trevor Nunn's 1981 *All's Well That Ends Well* is a case in point. At the outset of the acting process, "the work of an actor on a text is like that of a detective":

You have to look for clues to the character's behaviour in what he says, to a certain extent in what others say about him, in what he does and the way in which others react to him. You then have to interpret those clues and bits of information and create in your mind an "identikit" picture, which is then processed through your senses. Using your own experience, talent and ability, you hope to arrive at a comprehensible and recognizable human being as near as possible to the dramatist's original intentions. (Brockbank, *Players* 80)

Having sleuthed his character back to "the dramatist's original intentions," Hutchings runs into difficulty finding "a modern function for the character that would allow him to behave in the way that he does" (84). First, Hutchings decides to speak the role in his own South Dorset dialect, bringing Lavatch more into line with his own class affinities. Then, deploying the rhetorical instruments of New Criticism, Hutchings notices that Lavatch makes "more than a dozen references to the Bible and the clergy," a texture of imagery that enables him to define a moral and psychological perspective on the character: "There seems to be within him a continual battle between the forces of good and evil" (84). This preparation still fails to animate the body. The life of the role eludes Hutchings until he hits on the idea of using a physical deformity to isolate Lavatch, to motivate his aggressiveness, and to explain why others allow him the license of speaking the way he does. Hutchings's seamless binding of past and present here is striking:

I began, though, to think about other ways of setting him apart, and wondered if he should be in some degree physically abnormal. The history of professional fools is full of references to dwarfs and hunchbacks being used as a butt, a figure of fun and, in time, they developed a reputation and skill in providing their patrons with a constant and ready source of wit and invective. When confronted by some physical deformity it is natural for most people who believe themselves to be normal to extend towards that person an element of generosity and licence that would not be granted to a so-called equal. This would allow Lavatch the freedom to express himself without fear of censure. (85)

Hutchings necessarily thinks the role in the present tense as a way of particularizing it; yet he authorizes his enactment by inserting "Lavatch" into a vision of human nature and "normal" social interaction that identifies Shakespearean society with an idealized version of his own. The body naturalizes a distinctly political vision of social process to a particular conception of character, a conception assigned finally to "the dramatist's original intentions." The "organic growth of the character" that Hutchings describes is, in other words, a powerfully rhetorical process in which the actor's body reciprocates the principle of closure initiated by the author-function; "Shakespeare" informs the cultural work of acting. Characterization represents fictive individuals through a variety of shared codes – movement, language, behavior, dress, acting style, *mise-en-scène*, disposition of the audience – that render performance an act of ideological production, much as Hutchings's conception of Lavatch is traced by a kinder, gentler view of interpersonal and social relations. Shakespeare grounds characterization by effacing its rhetorical agency, its rhetorical complicity in specifically contemporary modes of ideological production. The author inscribes contemporary ideologies in the body of the actor, where contemporary modes of corporeality make them at once powerful and unquestionable.[38]

It is hard to imagine that we can inhabit the body in ways even approximating those of Shakespeare's era. Although sight, pain, cold have probably not changed, our ways both of understanding the body and of mapping it into the signifying web of culture are radically altered, and so the experience of the body has been altered as well. It is also difficult to denaturalize the working of our bodies, in part because our modes of corporeality provide the first, most internalized, and so most fully ideological means of structuring our being in the world. Yet the body's implication in the practices of modern social interaction ought to .make it a vehicle for decentering the author, provided of course we could bring the dialectic between body and author into view. We can, perhaps, get a sense of one way in which such questions might be raised from Antony Sher's account of working on the Fool in Adrian Noble's 1982 *King Lear.*

> The first breakthrough came in a rehearsal of the heath scenes when Adrian asked each of the actors involved to find an animal to play, in order to release the savagery and wildness of the situation. I chose a chimpanzee, chattering and clapping hands, hurling myself around in forward rolls, and found this very liberating for the role. That weekend I hurried to London Zoo to watch the chimps and became even more convinced that they had all the requisite qualities for the Fool – manic comic energy when in action, a disturbing sadness when in repose. (Jackson and Smallwood, *Players 3* 154–55)

Using animals to explore the physical dimension of characterization is a familiar training and rehearsal technique, one that – like "body centers" in some respects – attempts to get the actors away from all that "head work" and into a more "natural" engagement with physicality, with the animal body.[39] In the chimps' behavior, Sher finds a useful model for the Fool's movement and gestures, but what is more arresting is that the strange likeness/otherness of animals seems to concentrate his attention to the role in a new register. Describing the chimps, Sher seems lightly to characterize them, and to internalize their attitudes as well; the chimps become, in a sense, the authors of Sher's Fool. Sher inhabits himself and the Fool differently, not through the umbilical connection to the author, but by acting against the grain – of the self, of the text, of Shakespeare. As Francis Barker has remarked, the body's meanings arise "in a system of liaisons which are material, discursive, psychic, sexual, but without stop or centre" (*The Tremulous Private Body* 12). I don't want to place too much weight on Sher's visit to the zoo, but attempting to discover the character's humanity in the gaze of a near-human other images a distinctly postmodern liaison/rupture between the body and the social world, and between the actor's work and the legitimation of Shakespeare. Moreover, Sher was not alone at the zoo. He discovered his Lear, Michael Gambon, "presumably also in search of his character, leaning against the plate-glass of the gorillas' cage, man and beast locked in solemn contemplation of one another" (155). What's striking about this scene is not only its brilliant approach to the savagery of *King Lear* – in which, after all, man's life is cheap as beast's – but the image of acting it provides. Contemplating himself in the other, and the other in himself, the actor's economy of production finally excludes "Shakespeare" altogether.

Drama, in the theatre, is a means of textualizing the body, making the body and its actions – gesture, movement, speech – readable in specific ways. Anthony Dawson suggests that the "body signifies in the theatre as a crucial part of the performance; it establishes person" ("Performance and Participation" 37), and Michael Bristol takes "the recognition of character as fundamental to any competent interpretation of Shakespeare's plays" (Rev. of Desmet 227). This use of the body does not take place in isolation from other forms of social signification, as though the textual formalities – conceptions of character, action, language, behavior – were somehow already complete and immanent in the text of the play. Instead, textual formalities of the drama collide with the practices of the theatre, forcing a negotiation between the organization of the written text and the material discourse of the *mise-en-scène*. In actors' descriptions of their work, as in the wider scope of performance scholarship, "Shakespeare" works to legitimate meanings that are in fact constructed as the effect of our own ways of reading, thinking, acting, *producing* texts as plays. Perhaps the fiction of the author is just a way of gaining some leverage as spectators, critics, and performers, a way of speaking that enables action. Possibly so; but it seems to me that recourse to "Shakespeare" is also a way of turning away from the question of how representation is implicated in the dynamics of contemporary culture, a way of passing the responsibility for theatrical and critical activity on to a higher authority.

Brian Cox's account of his performance in Deborah Warner's 1987 *Titus Andronicus* points in another direction. Describing the production's brilliant finale, Cox notes how the play deliberately unmoored its audience from a conventional position of tragic judgment, an unmooring to which *Titus* is perhaps particularly well suited. Not parody, not irony, not Brechtian alienation, Warner's *Titus* seems to have released other, alternative ways of responding to the play. Cox recalls how Titus and his attendants entered, whistling "the *Snow White* dwarves" song, "Hi-Ho" as they set the table for Tamora:

> And then, in full starched white chef's garb, I came in, leaping over the table, with the pie. The world had gone crazy; the audience's embarrassment about serving the boys in the pie was released in laughter – but laughter from which you could cut them off. You could allow another laugh in the welcome:
>
> > Welcome, my lord; welcome, dread Queen;
> > Welcome, ye warlike Goths; welcome Lucius;
> > And welcome, *all* . . .
>
> – the last words addressed to the pie. (Jackson and Smallwood, *Players 3* 187)

Cox is right to see the tension between horror and laughter as akin to the way violence is represented in more recent plays. He suggests that Warner's scene, and Shakespeare's play "out-Bonds Bond. It is a cruel play, deliberately cruel" (188). But for all the didactic energy of Edward Bond's prefaces and other writings, Bond's plays tend not to present violence as the human condition, as an inevitable expression of human nature. The overwhelming brutality of Bond's plays stems from the voluntary quality of their violence, the fact that characters (and audiences) choose violence when they are *not* tragically compelled to do so. Warner's playful horror seems directed toward this end, recomposing the play's violence away from the key of high tragedy and toward something else, perhaps that "free-floating and impersonal," affectless euphoria typical of postmodern aesthetics.[40] It might be argued that this pastiche of Seneca, Shakespeare, and Disney represents an effort to decenter the constitutive "subjects" of the play: Shakespeare, Titus, the actor, the ineffably self-present spectator. Perhaps – but the recuperative power of hegemonic ideologies is considerable, and in Cox's view, *Titus* ultimately tells a different story: "The way human life is prized, the value of man and of his destiny – these things have never been as severely under question as they are now. *Titus Andronicus* examines the values by which we live" (188).

Comparing *Titus* to Bond, or as he might have done, to Peter Barnes or Howard Barker, Cox opens another way of conceiving the scene, a more problematic one. The use of Shakespeare to comment on the contemporary horizon almost always assumes that the conditions of Shakespearean production are themselves outside that horizon, that Shakespeare articulates a moral critique of contemporary life through his native language, the timeless language of the stage. The stage is often said to apply the "test" of performance to critical readings of Shakespeare, a "test" that screens out meanings unsuitable to the rhetoric of contemporary performance as innately illegitimate, un-Shakespearean. But there is no way to translate between different modes of producing the text; acting practice and critical practice remain in dialogue precisely because they are incommensurable. Placing actors' reading in dialogue with cultural theory and contemporary scholarship, it becomes possible to denaturalize the practices of the contemporary theatre, to ask how the ways of putting Shakespeare onstage resonate not only with contemporary theatrical conventions, but with the beliefs and attitudes that inform the wider reproduction of culture. Is there a way, for instance, in which the "intensities" of Warner's spiky, untragic *Titus* are reminiscent of the "Singing in the Rain" scene from Stanley Kubrick's *A Clockwork Orange* – more a part of our cultural condition, representing and reinforcing it, than a critique of it? Asking how contemporary performance practice, how actors learn to read Shakespearean drama and rewrite it in the text of stage behavior, might respond in its own idiom to the more alienated perspective of contemporary criticism is to ask how Shakespeare in the theatre can become our contemporary in a very different sense than the one imagined by Jan Kott: not a Shakespeare who mystically anticipates our trials, or merely reflects the deeply ideological contours of human nature, but a Shakespeare whose production is involved in our own deceptive and slippery rhetoric of self-fashioning.

CHAPTER 4

Shakespeare's page, Shakespeare's stage: performance criticism

> [M]y own major interest has always been Shakespeare in
> the theatre; and to that my written work has been, in my
> own mind, subsidiary. But my experience as actor, pro-
> ducer and play-goer leaves me uncompromising in my
> assertion that the literary analysis of great drama in terms
> of theatrical technique accomplishes singularly little. Such
> technicalities should be confined to the theatre from which
> their terms are drawn. The proper thing to do about a
> play's dramatic quality is to produce it, to act in it, to attend
> performances; but the penetration of its deeper meanings is
> a different matter, and such a study, though the commen-
> tator should certainly be dramatically aware, and even
> wary, will not itself speak in theatrical terms.
>
> (G. Wilson Knight, *The Wheel of Fire* vi)

I would like to pause briefly over these remarks, taken from the
preface to G. Wilson Knight's *The Wheel of Fire,* to begin thinking
about the relation between text and performance in Shakespearean performance criticism. An "actor, producer and playgoer," Knight candidly describes the difficulty of assimilating
commentary on the dramatic text to the "dramatic quality" that
can only be seized in performance. Yet while Knight finds this
"dramatic quality" to be producible only in the language of the
stage, "theatrical technique" is, surprisingly, incapable of penetrating to the "deeper meanings" available to "literary analysis."
This is an arresting limitation: critical commentary can disclose
the text's "deeper meanings" precisely because it is not coexten-
sive with the text it represents. Performance, on the other hand,
naturalized to the drama, exhausts the play's "dramatic quality"
at the moment that the text is staged. Conceived not as a

discourse for representing the text, but as a "technique" for realizing the drama onstage, performance can only reiterate the text in its own technical terms. As a result, performance criticism – the "literary analysis of great drama in terms of theatrical technique" – fails to approach the play's "deeper meanings" because the "theatrical technique" it imitates is not itself seen to be critical, invasive, interpretive. Performance criticism becomes an expendable enterprise, offering neither the "meanings" of literary criticism nor insight into the truly "dramatic quality" provided by performance.

Knight brings a basic problem in dramatic criticism into focus, one that has preoccupied one branch of Shakespeare studies for decades: how to relate the signification of the dramatic text to the practices of performance. What is surprising, though, is that the extensive "tradition" of performance criticism – reaching from Granville-Barker's *Prefaces to Shakespeare* through M. C. Bradbrook, to the writing of John Russell Brown, J. L. Styan, Bernard Beckerman, Michael Goldman, Philip McGuire, Gary Taylor, and others – has often been more successful in reifying Knight's polarity between text and performance than in suspending, clarifying, or interrogating it. Despite an impressive body of scholarship, in some respects performance criticism remains stalled at Knight's impasse, bound by an opposition between a "subsidiary" literary criticism nonetheless sustained by a rich, and richly authorized, text, and a conception of performance – and so of performance criticism – enervated by this "detextualized" understanding of the practices of theatre.[1] The text/performance dichotomy, and the interpretive priorities and assumptions it governs, stands at the center of the disciplinary ambiguity that characterizes performance criticism *as* criticism, and has prevented Shakespearean performance criticism from developing an acknowledged complex of aims, methods, and theoretical consequences. More important, it prevents performance criticism from pursuing its justifying critical agenda: to locate the space and practice of criticism in relation to the practices of performance.

In the twentieth century, the critical derogation of performance is engrained in the rise of formal literary studies, associated particularly, and perhaps unfairly, with the widespread influence of the New Criticism. New Criticism treated the drama in terms of its normative literary genre – the lyric – and so presented the dramatic text as a verbal icon. More important, it located the values of New Criticism – verbal irony, ambiguity, and complexity – as definitive of "literature" itself.[2] Applying its powerful interpretive technology to formal, verbal, thematic, and generic features taken to be determined by the text, New Criticism necessarily discredited stage performance, as well as criticism speaking "in theatrical terms," as extrinsic to a play's literary design. Yet while New Critical practice sharply discriminated against stage performance as a means of interpreting drama, performance did have an oddly important function in New Critical thinking. For despite its investment in the text as a closed, organically coherent system, the "heresy of paraphrase" implicit in much New Critical writing and pedagogy points to the reader's engaged performance of the poem as finally exceeding and enriching the formal, verbal, and thematic determinations of critical analysis. Needless to say, New Criticism placed strict limitations on the validity of interpretation generated by reading-as-performance. As performance, reading was guided by the text's internal dynamics, seen as a mode of recovery rather than as a means of producing the text in a different order of signification. While an informed reading can enact the pleasure of the poem, critical analysis can reflect on and identify the poem's means for producing that pleasure. New Criticism, in this sense, takes criticism as a refinement of reading, merely extending the determining order of the text itself. As Hugh Grady argues, despite its technical approach to interpretation, New Criticism emphasized "the experience of literature 'from the inside', as Cleanth Brooks once put it, and this meant an opening to emotion and hence to the values which underlie the emotions – an opening all the more potent because disguised, as was [G. Wilson] Knight's, as simply a submission to the text object which was given primacy and authority" (*Modernist Shakespeare* 124). Stage performance, on the other hand, enlarges on the text, forces it to speak in languages not determined (as the language of critical analysis appears to be) by the words on the page. "In acted drama," Brooks and Heilman remind their readers, "we have costumes, settings, and 'properties'; but drama as

literature has no such appurtenances" (*Understanding Drama* 25).
To the New-Critical temperament, theatrical performance and a
criticism derived from it are merely interpretive free play.[3]

   More recently, of course, literary criticism has tended to disperse "*the* text" of New Criticism, displacing meaning from
within the verbal design that was said to contain it to the contingent relationship between *a* text and the contextualizing, even
constitutive practices that are seen to produce it: the interests and
affiliations of its initial production; the habits of the interpretive
communities that have transmitted it throughout history; the
technologies that have reproduced it materially; the metaphysics
of which it is a part; the pressures of social class, politics, ideology,
gender, global expansion, race. Jean E. Howard and Marion F.
O'Connor introduce their collection *Shakespeare Reproduced* in just
this way, remarking that "Far from distorting the 'true' meaning
of an unchanging text, however, such constructions *are* the text"
(Introduction 4). This relocation of meaning from within the text
to the ways in which a text can be made to perform has fundamentally altered the practice and the consequences of literary
criticism of the drama, especially in Renaissance studies. And yet
the textualizing function of stage performance has remained
largely isolated from this wider effort to place dramatic performance within the discourses of cultural life. The essays in
Shakespeare Reproduced "collectively" place "the Shakespearean text
in relationship to Elizabethan texts other than the text of nature;
and they examine the ideological function of Renaissance theatrical practices and representations in light of a range of other
cultural practices" (Introduction 12). With a few important exceptions, however, actual stage performance is omitted from the
catalogue of "discourses" that inform criticism of "theatrical
practice" and the ideologies it represents. Robert Weimann is
right to point out that ideological criticism of the drama – like
New Criticism in this regard – currently finds in performance a
puzzling indeterminacy. Much as performance cannot be
reduced to the verbal order of the text, so the "pleasure" of the
theatre "cannot exclusively be defined in terms of ideological
structures and categories, any more than other forms of corporeal activity, such as eating, laughing, smiling, and sneezing can

be reduced to ideological gestures of subversion or rehearsal" ("Towards a Literary Theory" 272). Fair enough. Yet while the body is not exclusively ideological, it is not exclusively material, either: to neglect the spectrum of performance merely because its signification exceeds description is finally to reposition "Renaissance theatrical practices" – and modern theatre as well – back within the text of nature. Whether by design or by default, literary criticism of the drama tends to assign the textualities of performance to the subjective caprice of the actor's freedom.

Performance criticism seeks to replace purely textual interpretation with a critical practice that uses stage performance to represent the truly "dramatic quality" of Shakespeare's plays. And yet the persistence of the "text against performance" question points precisely to the ongoing dependence of performance criticism on the categories of literature and literary interpretation, particularly on the legislative power of the authorial work. Performance criticism often takes performance as a way of preserving the authentic literary work, as though stage performance merely replays the formal structures of Shakespearean character, language, and meanings, in the corporeal idiom of theatre.[4] I am thinking here of most treatments of "subtext" in Shakespearean characterization, metadramatic and metatheatrical criticism, iconographical readings of stage imagery, and what might be called "directorial criticism" – the idealized description of how Shakespeare's plays "control and shape what an audience hears, sees, and experiences moment by moment in the theater" (Jean E. Howard, *Shakespeare's Art* 2). Such moment-by-moment studies of Shakespeare's plays have been crucial in opening a space for stage-centered readings on the wider horizon of Shakespeare scholarship and criticism, and for alerting critics to some of the perspectives that thinking about the plays in the theatre can make available.[5] These versions of Shakespearean performance criticism undertake a scrupulous engagement with the texts of Shakespeare's plays in the potential space – rather than the material, historical space – of theatre, and outline a range of productive ways to think about the performative designs of drama. Yet James H. Kavanagh rightly implies that this "ostensibly alternative 'stagecraft' commentary" tends "to produce a kind of para-literary ideological discourse," one that casts the stage in a lapsed relation to the authority of the "literary" text ("Shakespeare in Ideology" 147). To the extent that "performance criticism" frames performance as a way to recover meanings intrinsic to the text, it can hardly be said to oppose merely "literary" methods. Performance criticism emulates "literary" methods by locating the text as the source of performative work, which exists as a secondary elaboration of meanings – of a "work" – that have already been produced elsewhere: in "literary" criticism.

"What means," Jay L. Halio asks, "are available to help us analyze performances so that we can properly understand and then judge the significance of the production? How can we know whether we are seeing Shakespeare performed or something that passes under the name of Shakespeare but is really something else, not Shakespeare at all?" (*Understanding Shakespeare's Plays* 3). This anxious regard for the role of Shakespearean authority in performance can be traced – like so much else in performative reading of Shakespeare – to J. L. Styan's landmark study, *The Shakespeare Revolution*. Styan charts the ways that the modern theatre and modern scholarship have worked in tandem to discover the original performance environment of Shakespeare's plays; restoring that environment provides, Styan argues, a way of recovering an authentic "Shakespeare experience" (5). The phrase is a revealing one, correlating three moments where an author-effect is accomplished: in the author's original intention, in a mode of theatre understood to reproduce that authority, and in the response of the audience, whose "experience" of performance recapitulates the author's imagined designs. The effort to synchronize these three moments sustains the argument of Styan's history.

Readers and performers can approximate Shakespearean intentions by recovering the circumstances of the Elizabethan public theatre and asking how the plays of that period exploited them. Of course, Styan is not calling for more tights and rapiers in today's productions. Rather than reproducing Shakespeare's medium, ersatz Elizabethan stagings impose a basically pictorial (Victorian, naturalistic) aesthetic between Shakespeare and his audience. Instead, the modern ability to restore "what he intended" arises from a fortuitous constellation of otherwise disparate experiments in the modern theatre. Pioneers like William Poel worked to reproduce the circumstances of Shakespeare's stage, but Styan suggests that such antiquarian impulses only served as inspiration to the "new Shakespeare," who "did not, however, make his appearance on any make-shift Elizabethan stage." Instead, the widespread repudiation of stage realism throughout early twentieth-century Europe forged a complicity between Shakespearean and modern performance practice. The modernist stage, as a result, could recharge "the play's first meaning," and so restore "the Shakespeare experience." By the second decade of the twentieth century, Styan suggests, "the notion that theatre had to reproduce life by verisimilitude was already succumbing to the non-illusory assaults of the theatre men [Appia, Meyerhold, Craig, Fuchs, Reinhardt and others]. Had they known, the students of Elizabethan dramatic convention might eventually have found themselves marching in step with such scandalous avant-gardists as Pirandello, Cocteau, Brecht, Genêt [*sic*] and others who have returned its former elasticity to the stage" (4–5).

In this history of modern theatre practice, Shakespeare serves a strangely neutralizing purpose: the historical particularity of the modern stage and of the various avant-gardes noted here is reduced to a single Shakespearean essence – non-illusionistic representation. Yet the elasticities devised by the modern theatre are neither recuperative of Shakespeare's actual practice nor particularly similar to one another. Craig's largely unrealized impressions, Meyerhold's use of carnival and biomechanics, and Reinhardt's secular rituals all oppose stage realism in different ways, and so necessarily construct Styan's key notions – *author, audience, experience, intention,* and *realism* – in different ways as well, and in ways different from how they might have been constructed in sixteenth-century London. Moreover, when modernist theatre practices are trained on Shakespeare, directors as diverse as Nigel Playfair, Barry Jackson, and Tyrone Guthrie turn out to be involved in a single effort: "to give their audiences what they took to be the stuff of the Shakespeare experience. As far as it could be reclaimed three centuries later, they tried to capture and translate the temper of the original. Each man's search was for an authentic balance between the freedom a Shakespeare script grants the actor and the responsibility of recharging the play's first meaning" (5). By essentializing the "elasticity" of non-realistic staging, Styan asserts a continuity between sixteenth-century and twentieth-century theatricality, and a continuity between the audience's experience and Shakespeare's artistic intentions. The flexible stage is the opening to authentic Shakespeare: "The secret of what he intended lies in how he worked" (4).

Styan rightly takes modernist theatre to provide new ways to think through the process of Shakespearean drama onstage. But the claim that the modern stage restores an essentially Shakespearean meaning implies that this revolution is really a covert operation, a restoration in disguise. Seeing stage modernism as an accident of history that providentially makes Shakespeare once again legible, Styan brings a third term to bear: the work of modern scholars to recover the original performance circumstances of the Renaissance public theatre.

A surprising post-Second World War spurt in scholarship on the Elizabethan playhouse is associated with a much longer list of distinguished names: G. F. Reynolds, G. R. Kernodle, G. E. Bentley, Cranford Adams, Walter Hodges, Leslie Hotson, Glynne Wickham, Richard Southern, Bernard Beckerman and Richard Hosley. Although most of these would not claim to be dramatic critics, it is clear that each shares the idea of non-illusory Elizabethan performance, controlled by the medium of the playhouse. The flexible Elizabethan mode of performance, playing to the house, stepping in and out of character, generating a stage action allegorical and symbolic, making no pretence at the trappings of realism, encouraged a verbally acute, sensory and participatory, multi-levelled and fully aware mode of experience for an audience. (5)

The practices of the Elizabethan playhouse, and so the practices of the modern theatre are, by and large, not significantly inflected by history, social conditions, the composition of the audience, language, nationality, and so on: "flexibility" constructs a distinct mode of experience for any audience. This notion of a transcendent "flexibility" lends *The Shakespeare Revolution* its palpable teleology, in which "the new direction and focus of scholarly thinking about Shakespeare" and "the new freedom from the constrictions of realism and the proscenium arch" – and, presumably, the re-installation of an authentic Shakespeare experience – "should culminate in Peter Brook's landmark production of *A Midsummer Night's Dream* at Stratford in England in 1970" (6).[6]

By laminating a monovocal Shakespearean theatrical practice to a similarly homogenized modern stage tradition, *The Shakespeare Revolution* provides the modern theatre with a unique relation to Shakespearean authority, for the author-function that Styan finds in this revolution is in most ways eccentric to the history of the theatre. Modern notions of authorship have little relation to the production of dramatic texts in Shakespeare's theatre, in which plays were often written by several hands and revised by the company of performers who owned them. When stage practice has sought to recuperate the authority of "Shakespeare," it has more often than not had to resort to recomposing the play: rewriting the text in the case of Dryden, Tate, Cibber, Garrick, and Barton; reorganizing it in the case of Irving and Olivier; or editing and cutting it, the nearly universal practice today. Styan's sense that Shakespeare emerges authentically on the stage only in the twen-tieth century necessarily defines the modern stage as a belated, subordinate institution, working – as earlier theatres clearly did not – only to reproduce the constitutive meanings ascribed to Shakespeare. The modern stage becomes a site of interpretation, rather than a place of production, a place where meanings are found, not made. Described in this way, Styan's history of Shakespeare production is self-evidently at odds with the stated goals of the modern theatre's most influential practitioners – Meyerhold, Brecht, Artaud – and works both to contain and to delegitimate the centrifugal and disruptive power of the stage. *The Shakespeare Revolution* in this sense seems no revolution at all: a revolution that invokes the past to erase it, and that finally denies the historical and material specificity of the present. Although the "students of Elizabethan dramatic convention" might be flattered to feel themselves "marching in step" with the avant-garde, it's hard to believe that the feeling would have been mutual. *Brecht?* Marching *in step?*

The Shakespeare Revolution is a deservedly celebrated and influential book, and in quarreling with Styan's situation of Shakespeare in the action of history I have largely sidestepped his real achievement: making stage production central to a critical history of Shakespeare in the twentieth century. And yet, the role performed by Shakespeare in this history finally represents modern performance almost exclusively as a mode of interpretation, committed to replaying meanings already inscribed in the text or, much the same thing, in the text's potential signification when performed in its original theatrical environment. This work has been widely influential, and this sense that stage meanings are authorized by the text alone pervades most critical writing – both academic and journalistic – about Shakespearean performance today. Much as Styan's history forges an identity between the modern stage and the "flexible" practices of the Globe (Styan, like others, tends to regard the circumstances of the Globe as normative, taking little account of the different performance environment at other public theatres, at the private theatres, and at various court performances), so Shakespeare performance criticism tends to regard performance – or *some* performance – as a way of realizing the text's authentic commands.

A more polemical version of performance criticism grounds itself in the drama's theatrical origin as a means of displacing merely "literary" interpretation. In practice, this kind of criticism either limits interpretation to the presumed capacities of Elizabethan performance practice, or frames the play within a universal definition of the purposes, forms, and meaning of "the theatre." Merely inverting the New-Critical valuation of text-against-performance, this brand of performance criticism urges the priority of the lively and spontaneous performance over the "impractical" insights reached by criticism altogether. As Richard David has it, "It is for this reason that half (I sometimes think all) the subtleties exposed by commentators are not, as actors would say, 'practical'"; if "meaning" can't be played, it "cannot be integral to the drama as drama" (*Shakespeare in the Theatre* 16, 17).[7] Performance is marked out as a special zone of individual expression, set apart from the institutional practices of criticism, and the signifying formalities of modern culture.

Despite its salutary rethinking of Shakespearean drama in the practices of theatre, though, has this theatrical approach to Shakespeare really changed anything? Granted, John Russell Brown's complaint (of 1962) that critics "trained in literary disciplines, are apt to think that theatrical experience is coarse and vulgar" ("Theatre Research" 224) has been fully replaced by Richard David's "commonplace of criticism" that "Shakespeare's plays were written for the theatre, and only in the theatre develop their full impact" (1).[8] Has this "shift from page to stage, from analysis of the plays as literature to a new interest in the plays as performance" (Hawkins, "Teaching the Theatre of Imagination" 519), really changed the mapping of performance onto the literary design of texts? Writing in the 1984 *Shakespeare Quarterly* special issue devoted to teaching Shakespeare, Homer Swander takes a typical position: "To read a script well is to discover what at each moment it tells the actor or actors to do"; "Shakespeare's words, deliberately designed by a theatrical genius for a thrust stage with live actors and an immediately responding audience, cannot be satisfactorily explored or experienced in any medium but his own" ("In Our Time" 529, 540). To understand what the text "tells the actor or actors to do," however, is to regard acting as both an interpretive and a signifying practice, articulating a dialogic relationship between a text and the *mise-en-scène*, and between the *mise-en-scène* and the audience. How does acting reproduce a text? How does their training enable the actors to conceive the text as *telling* them to *do* anything in particular? How does a range of perceived acting opportunities constitute a strategy for reading the play *as* actable, as representable to an audience in the theatre? And to what extent does acting, or criticism modeled on it, avoid a fundamentally "literary" valuation of the text?

A similar line of questioning might, of course, be trained on directors, designers, and so on, but that's not the point. As the history of theatre demonstrates, stage performance requires a highly formalized body of activities: techniques for training and preparation; conventions of acting and staging style; habits of audience disposition, behavior, and interpretation. Richly diverse and historically local, these practices articulate the text as "acting" within the wider range of signifying behavior familiar to a given theatre and culture. Swander's view of "dramatic quality" appears to oppose the New-Critical priority of text-to-perform-ance, but in fact duplicates it: while the text produced by criti-cism is irrelevant to the stage, the performance-text speaks directly to the actors through a privileged "technique" that retains the authority of the text precisely by emptying perform-ance of its textualizing, ideological function. John Russell Brown is more blunt about it: "Readers and critics have become increas-ingly aware that the plays were written for performance and reveal their true natures only in performance" (*Discovering Shakespeare* 1). Garrick, Irving, and Olivier each applied a different histrionic technology to their roles, performances that not only required different acts of attention from their audiences, but that incarnated action, character, and meaning in distinctly different ways. To preserve the unchanging "true natures" of Shakespeare's texts in performance requires a delicate negotiation of the chang-ing history of stage practice. In a more recent revision of his chapter on stage Shylocks, Brown argues that the history of act-ing shows how actors of a given role "were all, in their partial interpretations, responding to the opportunities of the text" ("Creating a Role" 79), searching for the strong "subtext" that will bring them "closer. . . to Shakespeare's intention" (77). In a sense, though, while the style of performance has changed, the essential relationship between the governing design of Shakespeare's text and the practice of acting is largely unaltered. Since "Shakespeare has ensured" that Shylock "is the dominating character of the play," "various interpretations that have become famous" are merely "responses to an unmistakable (and unavoid-able) invitation to make a strong, adventurous and individual impression in the role" (85). Actors have not made different Shakespeares, they have merely seized Shakespeare's governing design – the role – with different instruments.

"His theatre was different from any we know today, but the essential act of performance was the same" (*Discovering Shakespeare* 8). Although it questions the adequacy of "literary" interpreta-tion in order to advance stage-oriented reading, this sense of per-formance casts the *mise-en-scène* as a vehicle for reproducing the authority of the text, a text whose "dramatic quality" is both determined and recovered through an authorized stage technique. Striving to legitimate performance as a mode of inquiry independent of literary criticism, performance criticism uses the sign of "Shakespeare" to repress the rhetorical character of performance; rather than understanding the *mise-en-scène* as a strategy for producing Shakespeare's plays in the differential medium of theatre, performance criticism takes the *mise-en-scène* as a recovery device, finding authentic Shakespeare in the designs of the stage.[9] As Robert Hapgood implies, performance criticism attempts to answer the question, "What reliable guidance *does* Shakespeare give his interpreters?" (*Shakespeare the Theatre-Poet* vii).

Indeed, Hapgood provides a useful example of how performance criticism uses "Shakespeare" to regulate potential signification, and to cast the stage as an interpretive institution for the recuperation of Shakespearean authority. Hapgood locates Shakespeare's "voice" or "presence" not in any of the characters or lines of the play, but as an effect of the "performance ensemble" itself, arising in the collaborative relationship between playwright, players, and playgoers in a theatre event (1). Hapgood argues that meaning arises in the theatre through the interactive relationship of the ensemble of performers. This is a particularly rewarding perspective when the ensemble's players – author/text, actors, audience – are understood to be constituted in and by the performance itself. Such a "performance ensemble" implies a creative collectivity among the theatre's participants, and locates a specifically *theatrical* meaning in their mutual performance. But the authority of Hapgood's performance is hedged in striking ways. Styan recognizes Shakespeare in the historical synchronicity of the modern and Renaissance theatres, and Brown takes theatre practice as the privileged register of authentically Shakespearean intention. Hapgood finds Shakespeare's "presence" in the perdurable economy of theatrical relations, the unchanging ensemble of interactions that shapes characters, actors, and audiences in performance. Passing over the fundamental discontinuities between what such terms – *actor, character, spectator* – might have meant in Shakespeare's era and what they might mean in our own, Hapgood defines the equilibrium of

authority that animates the ensemble of Shakespearean performance: "In these realms Shakespeare's presence is to be felt, and
the players' function defined, by surveying the widest range of valid
possibilities that the text leaves open to interpreting performers,
by marking the outer limits of these possibilities, and by considering the pros and cons of the principal options within them" (130).
The range of "possibilities" that the performance ensemble can
engage is finally grounded in the already-authorized meanings
left open by the text. The ensemble's freedom is the freedom to
interpret and enact only what one of the players – Shakespeare –
has already invented.

By mapping the author into the design of performance, performance criticism hesitates to move "from work to text," to consider the play in terms that conform (or *should* conform) more
closely to the working of the script in the theatre: "as play, activity, production, practice" (Barthes, "From Work to Text" 162).
Although this sense of textuality seems imperative for a truly performance-oriented criticism, Hapgood and others assign the
Shakespearean text a more overtly theological function: the text
determines a range of potential meanings which the performance
works to discover. This interpretive sense of performance legitimates "readings" which mask the historical, social, and institutional particularity of the theatre at any given time, in order to
privilege the "essential" operations of *the* stage, Shakespeare's
stage.

Hapgood's reading of the performance ensemble at the opening
of *Henry V* is a case in point:

Shakespeare challenges his spectators to a large-mindedness that can
rise to his occasion. In the rest of the Prologue, the Chorus is very direct
about the appeal he would make to our imaginary forces. First he con-
fers upon us some of the nobility he had wished for in his ideal behold-
ers: he dubs us "gentles all". Although in other places Shakespeare regularly refers to his spectators as "gentles", the Chorus's earlier wish for
"monarchs to behold" the performance puts special emphasis on our
implied ennoblement. He then proceeds to specify how (*noblesse oblige*)
we can live up to our given title and grant his concluding appeal "gently
to hear . . . our play". (20)

The Chorus can, and in many productions probably does, accomplish something of this kind, flattering the audience into a sympathetic engagement with the action to be seen, a gesture that perhaps still retains its original class inflections: the spectators become "gentles all" if they see the scene in the way that the Chorus invites them to see it. And yet to say that this must happen in any legitimate performance today overlooks the extraordinary richness of this scene in Shakespeare's theatre, where terms like "gentle" exerted a complex and *differentiating* function, as well as (perhaps instead of) a blandly homogenizing one. In performance, of course, this speech would have been delivered by an actor who was anything but "gentle."[10] How might this have affected the meanings constructed by the performance ensemble, an ensemble much more evidently heterogeneous in demeanor, dress, behavior, and social privilege than the RSC-National-Stratford-Ashland-regional theatre audiences of today? Would the Chorus's invitation to the stinking crowd have been an affront to those who *were* "gentle" in the audience? Would it have been taken, as Meredith Anne Skura suggests, as part of the "tendentious formality" of the prologue convention, in which the player's "flattery was taken to be a cover for self-serving greed, if not arrogance" (*Shakespeare the Actor* 60, 61)? Might the invitation have been directed specifically toward some of the "gentles" in the house, reifying the class divisions already self-evident in the theatre audience, and between the audience and the performers as well? Although the "Chorus spells out precisely the faculties required for this particular play" (Hapgood 20), in 1600 those faculties emerged in a densely particular milieu, one that is imaginable but not any longer recoverable in performance. While contemporary stagings might aim for analogous effects – and so analogous ensembles – these are new vehicles for different kinds of meaning, and presumably require and produce different "faculties" in the performance ensemble. The performance ensemble of Shakespeare's era was differently related, differently constituted, and so differently *present* in the production than a performance ensemble today. Presumably a different "voice" and "presence" of Shakespeare – and so a different Shakespeare – emerged as well.[11]

To conceive the performance ensemble as interpreting the author means that the ensemble is interpreting an author it creates: "Shakespeare" is a necessary fiction that organizes and stabilizes this interpretive community, working not to provide access to privileged meaning, but to legitimate the relationship between actor and text, between spectator and stage, between critic and performance. Regarding the absent author as the privileged origin of meaning in the ensemble's closed circle of interpretation, Hapgood elides the historically diverse materiality of performance with the intrinsic, permanent designs of the text; repressing the differential character of performance, Hapgood blinds us to the uses of Shakespeare in the past and to the uses of Shakespeare in the present as well.

Some consequences of this conception of performance – that actors "realize" the text, and so realize Shakespeare – are dramatized by John Barton's highly-regarded television series *Playing Shakespeare*, and the useful book that accompanies it. *Playing Shakespeare* has more to do with pedagogy, with staging performance criticism so to speak, than with producing live theatre. For just that reason, though, the series brings performance and criticism into an unusually revealing counterpoise. Playing the part of avuncular critic/director, John Barton repeatedly urges his actors to discover the "infinite" interpretive freedom at their disposal through a scrupulous reading of "the text" and its "ambiguities." As Douglas Lanier remarks, "Barton's strategy of recasting the text as a theatrical 'score' paradoxically invests the text with even more authority, with the consequence that its every jot and tittle articulate a theatrical intent that any given enactment can only aspire to" ("Drowning the Book" 190). Viewers of the series may well feel that the performances and Barton's direction are far from infinite in their variety, and Barton's illustration of the divergence between criticism and theatre provides an arresting instance of the ideological complicity between his directorial practice and the "literary" notions he repudiates. In the "Set Speeches and Soliloquies" episode, Barton invites David Suchet to read a convoluted passage of criticism "from one of the world's leading theatrical magazines." The passage begins, "This ambiguity is one of the significant aesthetic counterparts of the broad philosophic drift defining the modern age... In theatre, *Hamlet* predicts this epistemologic tradition. ... The execution of the deed steadily loses way to a search for the personal modality of the deed..." and continues on for a few more heavily edited sentences (Barton, *Playing Shakespeare* 101, Barton's ellipsis).[12] The passage is hardly amusing; what makes it funny is how it is performed. In part, the text's emphatically "academic" quality seems inflated, pretentious in contrast to Barton's ingratiatingly low-key style. But the passage becomes funnier in Suchet's delivery, for he not only hectors the camera, he speaks in what – to me at least – sounds like an oddly aggressive, distinctly American accent, one perhaps touched by a trace of Brooklynese – "*duh* leading *uh*sthetic problem." The use of dialect here is not motivated by any visible feature of the text; it points instead to the textualizing function of performance style. The dialect suggests that this voice speaks in the wrong accents, accents that mark its critical perspective – its origin in America, and in "literary" study – as unspeakable in the powerful, legitimating sonorities of the RSC style. Spoken in the wrong accent, it must be saying the wrong thing.

Barton then turns to Michael Pennington, about to deliver Hamlet's "To be, or not to be" soliloquy, and says, "Michael, come and follow that." Pennington first gives an underplayed, obviously "intellectualized" reading, one that seems to illustrate the unsatisfying results of following the dictates of an overabstract and literary conception of the part. Then Pennington gives the soliloquy a second try. Following Barton's direction to "share it with us," to "open himself to his audience," Pennington gives a lively reading, broadening his range of movement, and making explicit contact with the audience offstage. In other words, Pennington produces the speech through contemporary conventions of Shakespearean stage characterization: a concentration on psychological motivation complicated by a degree of openness to the theatre audience, the post-Brechtian compromise between "realistic" and "theatrical" characterization typical of the RSC since the mid-1960s.[13]

The results here are confusing, despite Barton's enthusiasm and the elegance of Pennington's enactment. For Pennington's

performance seems oddly to conform to the thematics of character described by the vulgar American. Pennington and his
"Hamlet" seem engaged in a "search for the personal modality of
the deed" in the public confines of the stage, a search typical of
"the leading aesthetic problem of the actor in the modern theatre
– the interpretation of action through characterologic nuance."
The camera narrates this thematic as well, showing Pennington
full-length in front of an approving audience, then closing to a
head shot which stresses the interiority of Pennington's performance. The point here isn't that the critic is really in the right, or
that Pennington's performance "illustrates" such critical conclusions about *Hamlet*. It's that theatrical practice – the production of "character" as an effect of "acting," in this case – is not an
unconstrained means of realizing the text, but a practice related
to other modes of cultural transmission, signification, and
interpretation. The acting that Barton praises as a matter of "com-
mon-sense rather than of interpretation" clearly owes its "com-
mon-sense" precisely to its ideological redundancy; Barton
represses the powerfully theoretical capabilities of the stage, taking
acting merely as the reflection of more widespread and familiar
habits for identifying characters and selves, acting and behavior.[14]

Much as Styan's *Shakespeare Revolution* claimed a unique access
to Shakespeare for the modern stage, so performance criticism of
this kind claims for performance an exclusive (yet indeterminable) access to the "dramatic quality" of the text, and so to
Shakespeare. Yet, the "test question" of such criticism – "Can
this be played?" – dramatizes the limitations of regarding playing
as the realization of an immanent authorial intention
(Samuelson, Preface, *Theatrical Dimension* xv). For determining
how such a "test" would work – or what it would test for – turns
out to be anything but straightforward. The idea of the "test" is
that any meaning claimed for a play in critical discourse is only
authentically Shakespearean if it can be directly represented (?),
translated (?), or enacted (?) in Shakespeare's medium – modern
stage practice. Since performance can't restate meanings that
emerge from a different mode of articulation (criticism), it can't
test them; *no* performance can directly articulate meanings
framed in another discourse. Nor, of course, can criticism directly

represent – or "test" – the kinds of meanings that emerge in the discourse of performance. If such a "test of performance" were possible, it could only confirm those critical meanings already assimilable to the privileged presentation of the performer, and the reigning understanding of the purpose and limits of theatre; the "test" tests only the symmetry between conventional ways of reading and the conventions of stage performance, their mutual ways of evoking Shakespeare.[15]

Let me try to suggest what is at stake here. Regarding performance as realization represses the institutional practices already inscribed in the theatre, in gesture and intonation, in the body and its behaviors, the textualizing formalities that render theatre significant. To do so is to disqualify the processes that produce meaning in the theatre as legitimate objects of attention and scrutiny. A variety of such practices intervene between the text and its stage production, much as they do between the text and its production as reading experience or as critical activity. Terry Eagleton remarks that "text and production are distinct formations – different material modes of production, between which no homologous or 'reproductive' relationship can hold. They are not two aspects of the same discourse – the text, as it were, thought or silent speech and the production thought-in-action, articulate language; they constitute distinct kinds of discourse, between which no simple 'translation' is possible" (*Criticism and Ideology* 66). Merely to say that text and performance are incommensurable is, I think, again to miss the point that the text is "against performance" of all kinds. It differs from *any* discourse that represents it, from the practices of reading and of criticism as well as acting; and as Peter Shillingsburg, Jerome McGann and others have argued, the text itself has an unstable, differential relation to the immaterial work (see ch. 1). Text and performance are dialectically related through the labor of enactment. The instruments of representation – literary and theatrical, critical and performative – transform the text that they constitute into something else, an act of reading, a rehearsal, an essay, a performance that could not be anticipated merely from an "inspection of the text" (65). The production of the text's meanings in the theatre requires the application of a complex machinery of interpretation and of signification, whose adequacy cannot be derived from the text because it is engaged in making the text, producing it as theatre. Criticism cannot recapture or reproduce stage performance; stage performance – where meaning is always at some level irreducibly nonverbal – cannot speak the meanings of reading or criticism. Where homology may be possible, then, is not between text and performance, nor between the results of literary interpretation and stage production. Instead, performance criticism might attend to one interface between these modes of production, how the organized systems of the stage "textualize" – however metaphorically – performance. To regard performance in this way without inscribing it as a text, *the* text of "Shakespeare," poses a variety of problems, a few of which have been sketched out here: a performance's claim to transmit an authentic realization of either the "text" or the immaterial "work" is largely rhetorical, imbricated in the theatre's conventional means for framing the authority of its productions, their proximity "to something we value" (Taylor, "End of Editing" 129). This phantom – and nonetheless pragmatic – authority informs the ways that Shakespearean performance criticism uses the "textualization" of performance – "the extension of the notion of text beyond things written on paper or carved into stone" (Geertz, "Blurred Genres" 31) – as a way to characterize Shakespeare's work on the stage.

Identifying Shakespeare's legitimate medium as the theatre, performance criticism attempts to displace the merely literary insights of critical discourse. At the same time, however, performance criticism has been sustained by a sense that its critical activity can recover authentically Shakespearean insights and meanings, meanings which reside in the essential stabilities of Shakespeare's text, and the privileged access that the stage has to them. As any visit to a library catalogue, *Shakespeare Quarterly*, or *Shakespeare Survey* will confirm, Shakespearean performance criticism remains a diverse and somewhat eccentric corner of Shakespeare studies and of theatre and performance studies more generally, and all the traditional – and valuable – modes of performance criticism (metadramatic, "directorial," phenomenological, figural) are still very much on the scene. In recent years, however, several critics have attempted to negotiate a clearer articulation of the textuality of performance with the perform-ance of criticism. Clifford Geertz noted in 1973 that the "idea" of conceiving cultural forms as texts "remains theoretically undevel-oped; and the more profound corollary, so far as anthropology is concerned, that cultural forms can be treated as texts, as imagin-ative works built out of social materials, has yet to be systemati-cally explored" (*Interpretation of Cultures* 449). In the past two decades, the practice of treating cultural forms as texts, or of treating performance as a kind of textuality has been widely invoked, refined, and contested throughout the humanities. In Shakespeare studies, Geertz is most often associated with the rise of new-historicist discourse, but the "textualization" of perfor-mance has come to have important consequences in performance criticism as well. Although it would be surprising – and dis-appointing – if a single critical practice were to emerge as a consequence of treating performances "textually," much of this writing has swirled around the relationship between reading plays, seeing them in performance, and representing the work of performance in the discourse of criticism.

To see a play in the theatre is to engage it in a rich and various performance, as a spectator; to read a play is to engage it in a rich and various performance, as a reader. Only reading pro-duces "texts," and to "read" performance as a mode of textuality models performance on the paradigm of texts, often on an unduly stable understanding of what "texts" are. Given the authenticating discourse informing Shakespearean stage produc-tion, it's not surprising to find this tendency in one vein of performance criticism, which derives its critical practice directly from the viewing of plays in the theatre: it "reads" actual per-formances as a way of "reading" the plays, taking "the record of performance" as an index of "what the plays *are*" (Ralph Berry, *Shakespeare's Plays in Performance* vii). Roger Warren's *Staging Shakespeare's Late Plays*, for example, focuses on Peter Hall's pro-ductions of *Cymbeline*, *The Winter's Tale*, and *The Tempest* at London's Royal National Theatre (which began rehearsing in December 1987 and opened the following May), in order to

record the "discoveries" (3) they made about the plays. The performances provide the authentic theatrical "text" of Shakespeare's
"work," which Warren then "reads" as a spectator. Warren's discussion of *Cymbeline* 4.2, in which Imogen awakens to the headless
body of (apparently) Posthumus, provides a telling example of this
strategy, how reading performances in this way strikes a particular relation between the critical textualization of performance
and the apparent prescriptions of the text. Warren points out that
the scene "can be the grim confirmation of something that
Innogen [*sic*] has feared, glimpsed in her half-asleep state; but
nothing in the speech indicates unequivocally that she realizes
before this moment [the line 'a headless man'] that the corpse is
in fact headless (as opposed to merely bloodsoaked)" (66). In
Hall's production, Geraldine James did not immediately see a
"headless man"; flowers seemed to conceal the head when they
in fact replaced it. Concealing the body's headlessness enabled
James to discover – rather than to recognize immediately – "the
awful truth":

This interpretation made excellent sense: on recognizing "the garments
of Posthumus", she turned away, only half-looking at the body as she
identified it. This helped to explain the very specific identification more
convincingly than the usual method of exploring the parts of Cloten's
body and identifying them as Posthumus', a method carried to an
extreme by Helen Mirren in the BBC Television version, where she
even nodded with an increasing, terrifying certainty as she proceeded
with the identification. I do not intend this as an adverse criticism: it
takes great courage to play the scene in Mirren's way, and it makes the
valuable point that what is factually untrue is nevertheless horribly real
for Innogen. But I think James's version both more convincing and
more in line with Innogen's habit of analysing her emotions; and her
jumping to the wrong conclusions here links her with Posthumus
earlier. (67)

What impresses Warren is that James's performance activates a
psychologically consistent character and integrates it with other
thematic elements, in a way that registers the truth of the play.
Given Hall's sense of Shakespearean acting as a "journey," it's
hardly surprising that "one thing that has emerged above all others

from recent stagings of Shakespeare's late plays" is "the sense of
the central characters going on spiritual journeys, voyages of discovery and self-discovery" (239). Reading these productions,
Warren discovers the values he already associates with theatre
and with Shakespeare. Textualizing the performance is finally a
way merely to reread the text.

Anthony Dawson's fine book *Watching Shakespeare* takes a related
perspective, reading "each play from the point of view of key
decisions about it that actors and director must make in order to
put it on the stage" (xi). Granting that "the possibilities for performance are almost limitless," Dawson nonetheless argues that
"each play poses particular questions and challenges which performers have to face," and writes to alert spectators to this range
of choice. As Dawson's reading of eighteen plays implies, while
the actual decisions are probably "limitless" in their local variety,
they appear to stem less from the plays *per se* than from the relationship between the plays and theatre practice: the "choices"
that a theatre must make as it presents a play in a different –
physical, visible, enacted – mode of production. Like Warren,
however, Dawson frames these "choices" as features of the play
rather than as formalities latent in modern performance practice,
formalities of behavior that re-textualize the play within the conventions of contemporary theatre. For example, in his reading of
The Merchant of Venice, Dawson suggests that "There are at least
three possible approaches" to the part of Portia.

First, and this works well in a nineteenth-century setting, is the bored,
rather self-pitying little rich girl. This leads to a petulant reading of the
expository lines about her father's will, and to a smug, perhaps even
nasty, and self-consciously clever presentation of the caricatures of her
various suitors that make up the rest of the scene. . . .

A second, median position on Portia would be one that handles the
first line with graceful self-irony, stressing playfulness rather than bore-
dom or cynicism. This is perhaps the most common strategy. The
caricatures might then follow naturally from a sense of her witty irre-
pressibility (that Elizabeth Bennett spark). . . . This Portia is in general
a younger, more innocent one than the first, not intensely bothered by
the terms of the will and quite ready to fall in love with a handsome,
dashing young man like Bassanio. . . .

A third approach, based on a serious reading of the opening line and the later speech about the harshness of her father's will, would emphasize the restrictions she feels, her inability to act freely in the world and control her own life. A possible problem with this is that the passage about her various suitors does not suggest a Portia that is too weighed down or distressed. (31)

The broad outlines of these three Portias depend on a variety of assumptions about the character's journey, her integration into the physical environment onstage, the need to register a single dominant tone or tenor to the part and to establish a clear pattern of visual "focus" onstage.[16] Again and again in *Watching Shakespeare*, Dawson outlines dominant conceptions of characterization – the mechanicals in *A Midsummer Night's Dream* are either played with "all the old gags" or "more seriously" (21); Sir Andrew Aguecheek is "a goofy, foolish knight" but is "much richer" in productions expressing his "dignified and slightly pathetic side" (52); Lear is susceptible to characterization as "ill-used father," "titanic, godlike Lear," "tough, arrogant, authoritarian King, who commits folly and invites retribution," or "the mad, or senile, old man, mad that is from the beginning, who moves upward to sanity, not downward to madness" (182).

Where do these paradigms come from? Although Dawson's focus on character implies that these options arise solely from the text, they are more clearly involved in how the modern theatre stages Shakespeare, how it recomposes the "text" as acting, formalized behavior designed to *represent* behavior *as* significant in identifiable ways. As the theatre changes, however, new "choices" heave into view. *Henry V,* for example, was once routinely taken as a celebration of English military power and national identity, but now seems to register a brooding doubt about the ethics of imperial expansion, the difficulty of integrating a "nation" through force, about the relationship between nation and gender: "What used to be simple is now perceived as complex, what was clear is now ambiguous" (115). The play-text now presents "choices" that did not seem to be there, say, fifty years ago. Changing ideas about nationalism, about gender, about heroism, about "character," have brought these choices into view, choices which (like the

three Portias or four Lears) are now part of a contemporary horizon of theatrical expectation, part of the "text" that actors and
directors read when they imagine the play's possibilities and
explore them in the idiom of stage behavior. Dawson attempts to
locate performative meanings in Shakespearean potentialities,
but makes a different, more important, recognition possible: that
theatrical choices arise at the intersection between the text and
the formal strategies of its meaningful production as theatre.
These strategies are not "texts" or "textual" in a literal sense, nor
do they arise in the text itself. Yet in posing a system of choices
for reading the text and producing it as stage performance – and,
just as important, in suppressing some kinds of reproduction
altogether, as beyond the range of "choice" – theatre systematically reproduces the play in another mode of representation, the
textualized conventions of contemporary stage Shakespeare.

Watching Shakespeare illustrates the problems that arise from
regarding theatre as a mode of reading, and of regarding stage
practice as merely interpreting or reflecting the designs of the
text. Harry Berger's *Imaginary Audition*, on the other hand, attempts
to deploy a version of reading as a direct analogue of theatrical
viewing, spectating. Developing from Berger's series of articles
on the intersection between theatricality and textuality, *Imaginary
Audition* sketches out a related model of stage-oriented reading.
Rather than reading the plays through individual performances,
Berger tries to see reading as a mode of spectating, incorporating
the illocutionary aspects of speech – definitive of performance in
this book – as an aspect of critical activity. Berger skeptically
reviews the anticritical cant of much performance criticism, the
disabling sense that "the empirical experience and psychology of
playgoing" should provide "the exemplar whose privileges and
constraints are to be reproduced in armchair interpretation" (xii).
Berger, that is, attempts to clarify the relationship between critical
and spectatorial reading as a means to develop a legitimate performance *criticism*.

Berger takes plays to be intrinsically theatrical in their framing
of an interlocutionary situation essential to performance, a situation that can be analytically deployed by the "armchair" critic to
frame theatrically sensitive "readings." This interlocutionary

situation enables Berger to move beyond the disabling impasse of stage-oriented criticism, "only mildly caricatured by reconceiving it as a contrast between the Slit-eyed Analyst and the Wide-eyed Playgoer: the former subtle, suspicious, cynical, ironical, elitist, deviant, neurasthenic, forever skulking about in his or her armchair; the latter simple, vigorous, normal, trusting, true, attuned to the larger-than-life effects of Shakespeare's Human Opera, and, above all, *there* – in the presence of the real thing, face to face with the veritable play-in-itself" (xiv). While the ironic, self-reflexive mode of literary criticism reciprocates the complex and overdetermined evasiveness of writing for Shakespeare's theatre, it can seem to deploy critical practices remote from or irrelevant to the representational conditions of that or any theatre; while stage-centered criticism leads "to a vivid apprehension of some of the ways performance can interpret the complexities of the text" (28), it often rests on three untenable assumptions: "first, that the criterial status of actual performance conditions is self-evident; second, that any interpretation that does not conform to those conditions must be non- or antitheatrical and violate the Shakespeare text (by treating it as a text rather than a script); third, that a valid interpretation must match or reproduce the experience of actual playgoers" (32).[17]

Focused on the question of *reading* drama, *Imaginary Audition* turns away from broader theories of performance, responding to the condition of theatre by imagining dramatic speech solely within the shifting relations of interlocution, the text's representation of a speaker and a deeply embedded congeries of auditors. Imaginary audition is what we do when "in a dialogue between A and B, we imagine the effect of A's speech on B; listening to A with B's ears, we inscribe the results of this audit in the accounts we render of B's language" (45). Berger argues that Shakespeare's language encourages a more complicated activity: by listening to "B's language with B's ears," we realize B as his own audience, an audience akin to the audience in the theatre. Berger develops an interpretive practice based on this "imaginary audition" that claims not only to mediate between reader and spectator, and so between the contradictory agendas of the Slit-eyed Analyst and the Wide-eyed Playgoer, but to provide a critical, *reading* practice that responds to the essential dynamics of stage meaning.

> Centered on the practice of imaginary audition, attentive to the structure and conditions of theater, maintaining the fiction of performance as a control on reading yet firmly committed to the practice of decelerated microanalysis, the literary model of stage-centered reading perforce shuttles back and forth between two incompatible modes of interpretation, reading and playgoing. Whether one chooses to privilege the page or the stage, neither can do without the other. Any performance of a play actualizes what is (always) already an imagined performance, an imaginary performance, and this prior virtual status is inseparable from the interpretive reading that led to it. (140)

Berger's sense that dramatic performance is already virtually complete in the interlocutionary relations posed by the text should give us pause. First, Berger implies that reading, audition, and acting – imaginary or otherwise – stand in a constant relation to one another, that decoding a text's signs of audition (what "reading" is in this model) is to decode in some way signals that are unequivocally and uniformly seized by the practice of acting (which consists mainly of speaking and listening). Yet when contemporary actors and directors read Shakespearean texts, their activity is in many ways tangential to "imaginary audition," and indeed to a sense of theatrical performance defined by "audition" – the construction of character principally through speaking and listening. As we have seen, contemporary acting is informed by a range of attitudes toward Shakespeare, the text, the body, the audience, and the purpose and meaning of theatrical performance, that in some sense shape how "speaking" and "listening" emerge in performance, what they mean as activities, and what they *do* in dramatic action onstage. While "imaginary audition" approaches some of the conditions of performance, Berger's focus on the text as a structure of speech acts renders other kinds of activity impalpable to the "armchair" reader. His brilliant reading of *Richard II* conceives Richard's speech acts as taking place on an unlocalized, even "imaginary" stage, in which the specific contours of theatrical practice – the textualized conventions of acting, movement, gesture in a given era that frame the meanings of "audition" – are absent. Like many literary scholars (Andrew Parker's and Eve Kosofsky Sedgwick's introduction to *Performativity and Performance* comes to mind) who base their understanding of performance on speech-act theory, Berger's sense of the "structure and conditions of theater" tends to assume the conditions of modern theatre as normative: silent audience, darkened auditorium, clear boundaries between stage and audience, acting and behavior, onstage and offstage. Nonetheless, the particularity of stage behavior specifies the interlocutionary force of speech acts in the theatre, and without the outline of these behaviors, "audition" may seem too isolated from the way theatre – a specific theatre – signifies, too plainly "imaginary," as unconstrained as the imaginary "stage" that other Shakespeare critics use to discover Shakespeare's "theatrical" sensibility. The armchair reading of speech as interlocution oddly removes speaking from the theatrical practices that contextualize it as activity, as production.[18]

Such efforts to locate a reciprocity between reader and spectator frame performance to the Procrustean bed of Shakespeare's text; performance becomes merely another way of reading. Indeed, it is precisely this impasse between readers and spectators as the implied agents of performance criticism that Anthony Dawson addresses in a more recent series of articles. Asking whether performance criticism can "offer a workable theory of performance as something separate from text, or does it simply read performances as though they were texts?" ("Impasse over the Stage" 309–10), Dawson has come to oppose the "inescapably concrete" practice of the theatre to "theory," an urge for system and order "uncomfortable with the ungoverned and the heterogeneous" qualities of performance ("Performance and Participation" 30). Dawson's theatre "is inescapably practical, concrete, anti-theoretical" ("Impasse over the Stage" 310), meaning that the practice of theatre – individual bodies, specific working conditions, the restrictions of time, budget, location – is finally contingent and undetermined, too: "the very contingency of performance in whatever venue generates uncontrolled interpretations. The materiality of the theater thus contributes to its heterogeneity," a heterogeneity that cannot be adequately represented within any theoretical perspective (315). Much as performance transcends representation in writing, so too the application of "reading" as a way of understanding the impact of performance denatures the experience of actual spectators, actual performers.

Dawson reinstates a familiar distinction between practice and theory, actual and virtual, theatrical and literary, one that has afflicted Shakespearean performance criticism, theatre studies, and even performance theory for some time. The impasse between criticism and performance, in this view, has less to do with the literary-or-theatrical ontology of Shakespeare's plays – whether the reader or the spectator is the more authentic consumer of authentically Shakespearean meanings – than with the inability of critical discourse, of *any* verbal discourse, fully to capture the embodied particularity of the stage, and the spectator's rich experience of it. To the extent that performance critics model their practice as an implied act of "spectating," they represent the spectator's engagement with the process of a play as a readerly "selection, focus, and emphasis" of attention, transforming performance into "yet another text," a rich field for critical interpretation, but a nonetheless "theoretical" construct that evades the immediate vivacity that performance holds for all its actual participants, performers and spectators alike.[19] Interpreting performances as "texts" to be "read" by spectators, retextualizing them in this "theoretical" way, crudely distorts the material working of theatre, artificially systematizing the casual process of performance, its inexpressible immediacy.

Dawson, that is, takes the principal "theoretical" moment of performance criticism to arise in reception. The work of the stage is pure *doing*; "theory" arises in the effort to represent performance by other means. Much as critical "readings" cannot be directly reframed or translated into performance, so meanings that arise through the process of performance are denatured when represented in criticism. Ethnographers have long recognized that representing a performance is not the same thing as performing in it, and the analytical leverage gained by transforming oneself from "observer" (or "theorist") into "participant" (or "spectator") necessarily dialecticizes these roles. Textualizing performance creates an insurmountable impasse, though, only to the extent that we accept Dawson's understanding of performance as unconstrained and indeterminable, and also accept his implication that performance criticism works to represent the experience of performance, rather than analyzing the (rhetorical, ideological, aesthetic) work it accomplishes. Instead of seeing performance as the undetermined activity of which criticism is the theoretical reduction, we might consider performance as a kind of "'immanent theory'" (Lanier, "Drowning the Book" 204): in its concise ways of transforming the text into something else, performance can be seen as doing material and theoretical work, something concrete that is not captive to the designs of the text nor an entirely unconstrained and contingent practice, but a way of working that shares some of its determinants, values, and activities with other kinds of signifying labor. To the extent that it can represent this work, criticism may be able to appropriate some of the insights and responses of spectators; at the same time, like reading or acting, criticism transforms what it represents – Shakespeare's text, the performance onstage, the performance of a spectator – into something else, a new production neither "homologous" with nor immanent in these events, these "texts." I don't meant to suggest merely that "all signifying activity is to be seen as 'performance,'" which, as Dawson rightly argues, is "to flatten the debate instead of energizing it" ("Impasse over the Stage" 318 n.18). As we have seen, though, a given dramatic performance operates within a fluid but palpable range of institutional, formal, practical, historical, cultural, and geographical pressures, that both recall and distinguish it from other dramatic performances, and that are like and unlike the pressures that frame other kinds of performance. Performance is an individual and indeterminable way of producing meaning, that is nonetheless not entirely undetermined, not merely individual. Acting, spectating, reading, and writing are strikingly different means for producing plays. What they share is that they are modes of production, operating in a given social and historical horizon.[20]

One way to broach this impasse is to see performance and reading as modes of textuality, ways of making "textualized" versions of the plays they produce. This is, as Dawson might complain, already to transform performance into something else, but while it fails to grasp some dimensions of performance, it also enables other dimensions to be recognized for the representational work they perform, work which emerges *as work* precisely because dramatic performance *is* systematic, part of a concerted representational apparatus, a texturing of the world. This possibility even lurks in the shadows of Dawson's demonstration of the failure of "theory." Toward the end of the essay, Dawson describes a scene from the Stratford, Ontario, Young Company production of *As You Like It* of 1987. The scene (4.1) was played on a bare stage, with lighting (and Jaques' fishing) used to establish a "stream" area downstage. Orlando arrives and "throws himself in the 'water' fully dressed" and shortly Rosalind does, too.

The tone is light and mocking, but it begins to turn to "a more coming-on disposition" as she speaks, moving magnetically toward him as he "floats" on his back (lying on the stage, turning slowly in the shifting light): "Ask me what you will, I will grant it." "Then love me, Rosalind." As Orlando turns, still on his back, she's on her knees between his spread legs, evoking a wondrous and slightly humorous sexiness, a passionate attraction that they both feel, but that Orlando can't quite comprehend. "And wilt thou have me?" "Ay," she replies, "and twenty such." The lines are spoken with full erotic power and only a touch of comic detachment, evoking bewilderment on Orlando's part. The combination of sex and game-playing sends them into the play-marriage (Orlando regaining a little of his composure), which takes place with the two of them kneeling in the "water" facing Celia on the "bank." All this is absolutely convincing on a bare stage. (324–25)

It's a luminous scene, one that Dawson plainly fails to recapture in prose: "That I have failed to do it justice in writing about it is both absolutely true and part of my point. Here was something that no amount of reading could produce, something totally unconceptual, a demonstration once again that theater is a physical art. Certainly the shifts in tone, the psychological play, the oscillation of passion and detachment can be traced in a literary way. But what the bodies of the actors did to the bodies of each other and the audience, cannot, could not" (325). No reading of the tone, characters, or action of *As You Like It* could have anticipated the precise inflections of this production, and no description of it – or attempt to account for its intricacy – can capture the bodily grace, the grain of the voice, the elegance of the actors' (and director's, and designers') labor.

In a later essay, Dawson argues that the "body does carry messages, no question. But those messages are so heterogeneous and dispersed that they are difficult to trace" ("Performance and Participation" 31). One place to trace those meanings is in the marking of a performance, its ways of assigning meanings to bodies, its ways of seeing the body as susceptible to meaning anything. Dawson's description of *As You Like It* seems fully to evoke the apparatus of the modern theatre, some of its typical ways of constituting Shakespearean meanings (lighting, bare stage), and particularly its tendency to display the body as the emotive, physiological, "natural" ground of spoken words. The scene visibly encodes verbal discourse in the register of heterosexual eroticism, using the (literally) transparent fiction of the "stream" to stage an elegant visual image of sexual contact. Merely understanding the familiar conventions of modern Shakespeare production is, of course, not sufficient to account for the compression and beauty of this scene, and no description of it fully conveys its work as performance. Nonetheless, this scene is recognizably "modern"; its economy of means – doing so much more than can be readily described – points precisely to its mastery of them, and to a confidence that it will strike its audience as powerful, surprising, appropriate. These meanings could not be foretold from a reading of the text; nor does reading Dawson's description of them approach Dawson's experience of seeing the production; nor does Dawson's effort to chart and register his experience entirely grasp his own experience of the scene. Words fail. Yet to say that the performance was "totally unconceptual," that "theater and theory have very little to say to each other," is to discount the kind of thinking and the kind of theory enacted in modern performance, and to reserve "conceptualization" for other kinds of representation. Textualizing the performance – as Dawson does merely in describing it, and as I have done in describing its modernist rhetoric – loses it, while at the same time dramatizing its transformation of brute materiality into meaning or, more accurately, showing how theatrical practice has already thematized its materials as susceptible to a range of activity and meaning. A theatrical performance is not a text, but considering performance as though it participated in textuality helps us to see some of the work, the theoretical work, it performs.

Dawson's writing moves from reading performances as though they were texts to a sense that any effort to represent performance *as* a "readable" field of textuality, deforms it past recognition. In a celebrated series of articles and in her book on Shakespeare's history plays, *The End Crowns All*, Barbara Hodgdon explores the textuality of performance as a way of intervening in this permutation of the text-against-performance controversy. Hodgdon considers the "Shakespearean play" to exist "in multiple states – as the words constituting the playtexts, as the readings based on those texts, and as their concrete, historically particular theatrical representations, or performance texts" – and her readings of Shakespearean drama work to encompass "all these forms of textuality, or, to put it another way, several different 'Shakespeares,' each an altered, provisional state of what First Folio's title page calls 'the True Originall copies'" (*End Crowns All* 3). Hodgdon avoids collapsing reading and stage production into the designs of the text, distinguishing between "playtext" – used to "refer specifically to the words that are traditionally construed as 'Shakespeare's play,'" and "to convey some sense of their indeterminacy and to differentiate them from other, more determinate textual categories" – and "performance texts," a term meant to destabilize "the notion that the written word represents the only form in which a play can possess or participate in textuality," an "apparent oxymoron that freely acknowledges the perceived incompatibility between the (infinitely) flexible substate(s) of a Shakespearean play and the (relative) fixity of the term 'text'" (18–19). Hodgdon charts a fluid boundary between malleable material texts and the materialized textuality of performance, not so much to grasp the experience of the spectator in the discourse of criticism, but to frame the dialectical relationship between these incommensurable modes of Shakespearean production.

In practice, Hodgdon's "performance text" is a compact oxymoron, conveying the sense that stage production produces meanings as well as interpreting them, meanings which have to do with the precise specificity of location, history, and audience. Citing Pierre Bourdieu's observation that "The 'eye' is a product of history reproduced by education" (quoted in "He Do Cressida" 270), Hodgdon's ways of reading performance move away from the determinations of the text most clearly at those moments when she constructs a dialogic history of Shakespearean representation. In "Katherina Bound," the dynamics of gender representation evoked in the text of *The Taming of the Shrew* sustain a kind of conversation between Douglas Fairbanks and Mary Pickford, Elizabeth Taylor and Richard Burton, Cybill Shepherd and Bruce Willis – not to mention Charles Marowitz, Stephen Orgel, Carol Neely, and Lynda Boose. Hodgdon uses a series of "performance texts" to interrogate the possibility that the play "can be reconfigured progressively" (538), dramatizing the ways the text of *Shrew* is transformed by the locality and medium of its production (mainstream and experimental theatre, film, television) and yet continues to substantiate the production of masculinist fantasies of gender/power. In a reading of the reception of Robert Lepage's 1992 *Midsummer Night's Dream* – a production notable for its infusion of both British and Canadian styles of ethnic and racial identity performance – Hodgdon acknowledges the impact of "knowledges drawn from literary as well as theatrical cultures, knowledges which are necessarily implicated in particular economies of truth, value, and power" in the constitution and reception of performance, arguing that the work of performance criticism should take place not at the imaginary level of the text, nor "at the locus of examining director-auteurs and the ideotexts of their mise en scènes or the theatrical apparatus itself, but at the point of historical reception, where 'theatre' collides with spectators who may transform it into a 'strange, eventful history'" ("Looking for Mr. Shakespeare" 86). Hodgdon negotiates several reading strategies here: the work of the stage can't be reduced to a good/bad echo of the "text," nor can it – or should it – attempt merely to reconstitute the (real or imaginary) experience of spectators. A play in performance resonates with other ways in which the play is produced, other ways it is authenticated, other ways it is made to represent "something we value."

Hodgdon's citing of the textuality of performance is necessarily delicate. To read performance as mere text risks collapsing its work into the history of literary production; to avoid the textualizing dimension of production marks performance as a kind of unmediated meaningfulness, unconstrained by the ideological pressure it reshapes and is shaped by. Conceiving performance in the mode of textuality enables Hodgdon both to assess its figural labor, and its engagement with other acts of representation, not only with the critical reception of performance, but with the critical "production" of Shakespearean texts. This relationship animates Hodgdon's distinction between play-texts and performance texts:

> Once purchased, a playtext is literally "free" for repeated rereadings, whereas seeing a particular performance more than once – a practice that allows a spectator to reexamine, if not to stop, the text – may, at present-day ticket prices, cost the spectator quite a bit of money. But a more basic distinction exists: on the one hand, there is a self-individuated private project, resulting in a text (the critical reading) that replaces the play with another text; on the other hand, a collectively understood and collectively mediated performance, a public project that re-*places* the play within a theatrical and cultural space. Although the final *products* (the critical reading, the performance) do indeed differ, the *processes* that generate each text, each "performance," so to speak, share more similarities than differences. Indeed, alteration, interruption, and intervention are features endemic to imagining and creating both sorts of texts. To focus on one example, alteration, critical practice regularly makes cuts, additions, and digressions that may be not only more considerable, but, often, more drastic than those found in the theater; furthermore, in the process, whole sections of the "play as text" go by even more rapidly in the theater – if indeed they are cited at all. (*End Crowns All* 16–17)

To attend to performance is to engage in a public and collective kind of activity, different in most respects from the privacy associated with modern reading (though this collective dimension usually seems largely virtual given the privacy assigned to most spectators in modern theatre, sitting silent and uncommunicating in the dark). Hodgdon implies that both the private and public acts of producing Shakespeare are nonetheless acts of replacement, the

making of a new thing – a reading, a performance, a viewing –
that materializes a new work, a new play, in dialogue with the
text but not immanent in it. Made as they are through different
means, of different materials, for different audiences who con-
sume them differently, these "plays" must differ, diverging from
one another as much as they diverge from the written text.
Performance scholarship – historical, theoretical, critical – can
work to suggest both the force of these divergences and their
points of reciprocity. But to do so requires a certain skepticism,
not only of the authority of the text and the implications of textuality, but of the ways it invades thinking about performance, most
insidiously at the moment, perhaps, when performance seems
most free.

Textual and performance criticism share – or might come to
share – an interest in determining how Shakespeare's plays have
been produced as cultural artifacts, and how the process of production inscribes itself into – and perhaps constitutes – the
"works" it represents. Susan Bennett's *Performing Nostalgia: Shifting
Shakespeare and the Contemporary Past* attempts to grasp this final
concern, the reproduction of Shakespearean authority. Bennett
considers a fascinating collection of Shakespearean occasions, to
ask how Shakespeare becomes both the sign and the agent of a
regulatory use of the "past," a factitious and fungible nostalgia.
Bennett's Shakespeare is largely a figure of coercion, the instrument of enforced hegemony, grounding a panoply of ersatz,
manipulative "traditions" (the new Globe on the South Bank);
buoyed by the educational system, popular and academic publishing, state-subsidized theatres (and their own publishing and
educational arms), and the movie and television industries,
Shakespeare could hardly be anything else. Nonetheless, contemporary Shakespeare often appears to have an oppositional edge,
in the "left/ish impetus" of some recent Shakespeare scholarship
(31), in the "Jacobean" alienation of "not-Shakespeare" films like
Derek Jarman's *Edward II,* in dramatic rewritings and performative adaptations of Shakespearean narratives, and – very rarely
– in performances of Shakespeare's plays. Since the work of nostalgia is to naturalize a monolithic and monumental past as a
means of governing the representation of the present, it's not sur-

prising that such oppositionality is often *only* apparent, sustained at some deeper level by "the psychic experience of nostalgia," a desire to revive "an authentic, naturally better, and material past" (7) imaged in the production of "Shakespeare."

Performing Nostalgia is much less about the ideological work of particular performances of Shakespeare's plays than the wider frame of Shakespearean cultural production. For example, Bennett considers a gaggle of *Lears* produced in the 1980s, not only stage, film, and video productions of Shakespeare's play(s), but a variety of responses, confrontations, and transgressions as well. She takes a dim view of *Lear* in the 1980s, not least because the ample over-production of the play "performs a nostalgic identification with greatness – of the text, of Shakespeare" (77), a nostalgia visible in the ways productions of the 1980s obsessively reiterate a surprisingly narrow range of design, acting, and conceptual "choices": the "red nose" becomes a striking metonymy for the constricted range of *Lear* in stage practice. The consistencies informing stage *Lears* in the 1980s disarmingly mark the limitations of "mainstream" theatre production, of theatre training and practice more generally, and of *Lear* in contemporary production: both "authenticity and/or originality are impossible with the recognized theatrical script" (47).

Bennett then considers how a "multiplicity of competing Lears" might foreground "precisely that understanding which a hegemonic authenticity works to negate" (47). Edward Bond's *Lear* (1971, 1982, 1983), a "modern classic," is too "carefully and easily contained within the frame of a mainstream cultural concept identified as theatre" (49); Howard Barker's *Seven Lears* (1989) adopts a "Shakespearean antecedent as an intriguing and absolutely marketable device" for Barker's habitual misogyny and violence (51). But other works mark the potential for *Lear* to perform another kind of work, to evade mere nostalgic reiteration. The Women's Theatre Group's *Lear's Daughters* (1987) uses multiracial casting and a dispersed narrative structure to stage a "herstory" that both "produces the gaps and absences of Shakespeare's (and Bond's and Barker's) texts" (51) and challenges the conservative collocation of Shakespeare with the civil regulation of "family values" (53). Similarly, Barrie Keeffe's *King of England*, performed at the Theatre Royal (Stratford East) in 1988, concerns a "Lear" who is a contemporary black London Underground driver dividing his wealth among his daughters before emigrating to Trinidad. Like The Women's Theatre Group, Keeffe uses *Lear* to interrogate contemporary race and class dynamics; *King of England* is finally not "concerned with the question 'what have we done to Shakespeare's play?'" but with another more pertinent question: "'how can this material be useful to us?'" (56). Welfare State's *The Tragedy of King Real* (filmed as *King Real and the Hoodlums*), involved townspeople of Barrow-in-Furness – whose principal employer, Vickers Shipbuilding and Engineering, manufactured nuclear submarines – in an anti-nuclear performance that dramatized the social, moral, and political dynamics of the local economy. The chapter concludes with a survey of several *Lear* reinventions, including the *Kathakali King Lear* project of David McRuvie and Annette Leday (1990); Amal Allana's 1989 environmental production of *King Lear* in a "constructed village complex on the site of the New Delhi Trade Fair," a production that precisely addressed the "irreconcilable presence of the indigene and the tourist" (74); and the Mabou Mines cross-gender and Americanized *King Lear* (1990). Bennett evokes the wide horizon in which any Shakespeare production takes place, a horizon not limited to Shakespeare's plays, to their performances, nor even to the theatre.

Performing Nostalgia treats Shakespearean and non-Shakespearean productions in a variety of media. In this sense, Bennett participates in a wider body of work considering the conceptual economies of contemporary performance, including dramatic performance, the performance of plays. While performance studies and performance art have generally regarded this kind of ideological critique as taking place only within avant-garde performance – or, sometimes, in studies of avant-garde performance – Bennett resists the trivial notion that some modes of cultural production (say, performance art) are essentially oppositional, while others (say, dramatic theatre) are essentially hegemonic. As Raymond Williams argued, the distinction between residual, dominant, and emergent forms of cultural production is not intrinsic to such forms (as though new forms were always contestatory), but arises through their *use*, through the kind of work they are made to do (*Marxism and Literature*, ch. 8). Generalizing "performance" to embrace the production of Shakespeare in/as nostalgia, *Performing Nostalgia* is able to figure the work of Shakespeare in cultural formations that extend well beyond the Shakespearean stage – in criticism and scholarship, in films, in a host of contemporary plays. Moreover, Bennett's sense of Shakespeare in performance is not limited to the textualities of the stage. Like Geertz, Bennett circles "within a single, more or less bounded form" (*Interpretation of Cultures* 453) – "Shakespeare" – to evoke the ways in which Shakespearean authority is produced and used to textualize – represent, make significant, euphemize, regulate, conceal, *interpret* – the meanings of contemporary culture.

Performance criticism of Shakespeare has moved through several phases. An initial phase worked to legitimate "performance" as a means of critical access to Shakespeare's plays. This theatrically oriented paradigm was in some sense related to a more readerly approach that attempted to find an inscription of performance in the writing of the text, placing the interpretive dynamics of performance in a more direct dialogue with other critical, philosophical, or aesthetic traditions. At the present time, to judge by the essays in James C. Bulman's *Shakespeare, Theory, and Performance*, by Susan Bennett's work, by recent studies of Shakespeare as cultural icon (Michael Bristol, *Shakespeare's America*; Lawrence Levine, *Highbrow/Lowbrow*), performance scholarship is engaged in an effort to discover how to read what Isobel Armstrong calls "some symbiosis . . . between theory and performance" ("Thatcher's Shakespeare" 12) in the effort to find a contestable Shakespeare.

Discovering a critical paradigm for performance criticism and theory requires a sufficiently dialectical notion of paradigm and discipline to frame our activities. New paradigms are often ghosted by their history in ways that are difficult to recognize, acknowledge, and transform; to understand performance criticism through a simple opposition between text and performance is to remain captive to the spectral disciplines of the past, the disciplines of the text. Both texts and performances are materially unstable registers of signification, producing meaning intertextually in ways that deconstruct notions of intention, fidelity, authority, presence. At the same time, texts and performances retain the gesture of such semiosis, and discussions of both text and performance remain haunted by a desire for authorization. If I have fairly captured even part of the complexity of this situation, it should be clear that no simple opposition between text and performance – or, I would argue, between the paradigms we constitute to frame them – will be sufficient to capture the rich, contradictory, incommensurable ways that they engage (or fail to engage) one another. Theatrical production writes the drama into stage practice. Performance criticism should exhume the affiliations between this writing and the very different acts of inscription that make the theatre readable.

To describe how the theatre subjects texts and performers to its process is a daunting challenge, one that performance critics have pursued with energy and success. But to make such insight valuable, we need to locate its claims as criticism. The first move in such a venture would be to displace the enervating polarization of "text *against* performance," (or, more accurately, of "criticism against performance"). Access to a work is always through its performance, a performance continually taking place offstage – as editing, reading, education, advertising, criticism, and so on – before any stage performance is conceived. The hermeneutics of text and performance in Shakespearean performance criticism and in other areas of literary and performance theory remains troubling because the repudiation of "the text" often masks an underlying investment in it, a desire to retain its peculiar, familiar forms of authority. Perhaps performance scholarship should more tenaciously expose what Kenneth Burke might have called the "lie" at the heart of theatre (*Rhetoric of Motives* 23).[21] This would mean conceiving the rhetoric implicit in conceptions of performance and in performance practice, particularly the way performance as a "body of identifications" works (or refuses) to write "Shakespeare" into the designs of the stage (Burke 26).

The complex invocation and subversion of the author confirms, I think, the volatile place where Shakespeare lives in the institutions (university classrooms, books, theatres) of cultural production today. This Shakespeare points not so much to an Eliotic tradition, but to the function that such traditions fulfill: effacing the dynamic of cultural change behind the mask of permanence. Performance, as Clifford Geertz recognizes, is a way of interpreting ourselves to ourselves; performance of the "classics" necessarily threatens to become an act of transgression, in which the cultural tradition embodied by the work is forced to tell a new story. Of course, this act is transgressive only if we believe that there are other alternatives, if we think that both the work and the tradition it metonymically represents can be known apart from their performance, if we think that the past is not constantly being remade by – and remaking – the present. Legitimating the author *is* a way of authorizing ourselves, which perhaps explains the anxious acts of filiation that, surprisingly, continue to animate accounts of stage performance. Allowing Shakespeare such authority, we reify Shakespearean drama – and the past, the tradition it represents – as sacred text, as silent hieroglyphics we can only scan, interpret, struggle to decode. We impoverish, in other words, the work of our own performances, and the work of the plays in our making of the world.

Notes

1 AUTHORITY AND PERFORMANCE

1 On the notion that the theatre of cruelty is a non-interpretive theatre, see Derrida, "Theater of Cruelty," esp. 245.

2 Michael Vanden Heuvel presents a more subtle version of this distinction: "dramas are written within an aesthetic and semiotic framework that includes theatricality or spectacle" ("Textual Harassment" 160–61). On the Wells and Taylor *Oxford Shakespeare*, see Bevington, "Determining," and Ann Thompson, et al., *Which Shakespeare?* 16–20.

3 On "ministerial" transmission, see Bristol, *Shakespeare's America* 105.

4 In his own work, and in various commentaries he has written as editor of *The Drama Review – The Journal of Performance Studies*, Richard Schechner has envisioned the "shift" to performance studies with considerable passion and intelligence. See "Once More, With Feeling," "Performance Studies: The Broad Spectrum Approach," "The Canon," "Toward the 21st Century," and "New Paradigm."

5 One area in which the intersection between textuality and performance has proven particularly rich is in the field of dance studies; see Susan Foster, *Reading Dancing*, and Susan Foster, ed., *Choreographing History*. For a representative example of the generative power of this discursive revision of performance, see Sue-Ellen Case, Philip Brett, and Susan Foster, eds., *Cruising the Performative*.

6 In "The Materiality of the Shakespearean Text," Margreta de Grazia and Peter Stallybrass argue that the materiality of Renaissance texts – the "old typefaces and spellings, irregular line and scene divisions, title pages and other paratextual matter" – insist "upon being looked *at*, not seen *through*. Their refusal to yield to modern norms bears witness to the specific history of the texts they make up, a history so specific that it cannot comply with modern notions of correctness and intelligibility" (256–57). In an era in which a play might appear under several different titles, and in which even Shakespeare's signature can be conceived as "a collaborative field, not the private property of a single individual" (278), it is difficult to maintain print as the transparent vehicle for the immanent authorial work. For a counter-reading of this issue, the sense that a work's various forms are all "good enough approximations of

the playwright's *ipsa verba* in a determinate order to dispell doubts about their identity. . . . There is no deep tension between stable self-identity and an intractably complex textual history," see Mueller, "Redrawing the Boundaries?" 615 and *passim*. In "How Good Does Evidence Have to Be?" Michael Bristol undertakes a more shrewd critique of how de Grazia and Stallybrass configure the materiality of Renaissance texts as evidence for shifting notions of authority; he suggests that this "essay represents an odd kind of wishful thinking that flows from a sincere aversion to certain pernicious effects of an exacerbated individualism and from a sincere belief that these effects would be greatly diminished if only the demons of authorship could be exorcised" (41).

I am not able here to develop a comprehensive overview of the state of contemporary textual studies of Shakespeare; in addition to works discussed here, readers unfamiliar with this body of work might turn to Urkowitz, *Shakespeare's Revision of "King Lear"*; Taylor and Warren, *The Division of the Kingdoms*; Wells, *Re-Editing Shakespeare*; and Braunmuller, "Editing the Staging."

7 Peter Shillingsburg's definitions of *authorial* and *authority* may be useful here; he defines "authorial" as "originating with the author," and "authority" as "the person, persons, or conceptual or institutional framework that has the right to generate or alter the *text* for the *work of art*" (*Scholarly Editing* 169).

8 In "Contemporary Textual and Literary Theory," Michael Groden provides a canny overview of contemporary editorial theory, to which I am much indebted. Groden suggests that for Tanselle the author "reappears in the conception of the work; any attempt to manifest the work in print, in speech, or even presumably in a word-for-word formulation in the author's mind, is already an imperfect text." Tanselle's author "is an isolated, stable entity," who is the source of the work imperfectly realized in the text, and who in effect collaborates with the editor ("Contemporary" 270). For a complementary reading, see Cohen and Jackson, "Notes on Emerging Paradigms." In addition to works discussed here, see also McGann, *Critique*; Tanselle, "Editorial Problem" and *Textual Criticism*; and Zeller, "New Approach." It should be clear that Tanselle, Shillingsburg, and McGann take very different views of the role of the author, the work, and of the editing of texts.

9 This understanding of reading as a mode of performance is one point of conflict between what is conventionally understood as a "literary" and "theatrical" understanding of performance: conventional (and in my view, sentimental) articulations of the relation between text and performance maintain "reading" as non-perfor-

mative, as a work of production already immanent in the design of the text, while stage performance undertakes a distinctly different mode of representing the text. In "Text as Matter, Concept, and Action," Peter Shillingsburg makes a careful distinction between three ways in which *performance* might be said to model relations of textual authority: "Creative Performance," which "is primarily inventive but usually involves some sort of mechanical work to inscribe through writing, typing or dictating," and consists of what we more generally take to be the act of authorial creation (57); "Production Performance," which determines "what material form the Linguistic Text shall have" in the forms of "public distribution" (57), and "Reception Performance," which "refers to acts of decoding Linguistic Texts," or "what we do when reading and analyzing" (58). These three terms bear obvious affinities with notions of the theatrical production process, though in stage production these kinds of performance may be closely linked: an actor reading a play is engaged in some sense in both reception performance (as a reader/analyzer), production performance (reproducing aspects of the text as acting), and creative performance (taking the text as raw material and making it something different – acting). Although it may be possible to ascribe these three terms to different phases of the actor's process, at many points they are overlapping.

10 In a fascinating reading of the editing of early music, Philip Brett takes a similar, though perhaps more temperate, position; see "Text, Context" 111–14. I am grateful to Professor Brett for providing me with a copy of this article.

11 In Foucault's terms, the work is always absent from performance, an ideal construction assigned to an equally absent "principle of rarefaction," the "author" ("Discourse on Language" 221). Much as the "author's name manifests the appearance of a certain discursive set and indicates the status of this discourse within a society and a culture" ("What Is an Author?" 147), so the work is a site of regulation, containment, a way to fix and stabilize meanings by predetermining the range of appropriate interpretation, of licensed reading.

12 See Gaskell, *Writer to Reader* ch. 12, and Donohue, "Character."

13 As McGann rightly remarks, "To read, for example, a translation of Homer's *Iliad* in the Signet paperback, in the edition published by the University of Chicago Press, in the Norton Critical Edition, or in the limited edition put out by the Folio Society (with illustrations), is to read Homer's *Iliad* in four very different ways. Each of these texts is visually and materially coded for different audiences and different purposes" (*Textual Condition* 115).

14 For instance, Weimann's concern with mimesis ("Mimesis in *Hamlet*")

might be seen to be an anxiety openly registered in Marowitz's collage, but repressed in the Gibson film version, with its emphasis on character consistency and narrative integrity.

15 As far as stage production is concerned, Grigely's iterative model might look something more like this:

$$W \rightarrow T_x \text{ (script)} \rightarrow T_{x1}(T_x \text{ modified by director}) \rightarrow \text{rehearsal} \rightarrow \text{prompt copy} \rightarrow P$$
$$\uparrow$$

(incorporation of T_1, T_2, T_3 . . ., other performances, new decisions, cuts, etc.)

16 As Gerald Rabkin remarks, performers and directors accept "the text's privilege" in a variety of ways, not least when – ignoring stage directions, for instance, or modernizing archaic words – they seem to oppose the authority of the text: "Unlike critics, most actors and directors rarely talk about the text; they talk of the script which they hold in their hands as they rehearse. The script is inscribed, it may indeed be published, but it carries a provisional authority. The script is something to be used and discarded as its textuality is corporealized in performance" ("Is There a Text" 150). Since the script is taken as a vehicle of authority, discarding it does not do away with that privilege; it has merely been rewritten into the performance through the conventionalized practices (lines are more sacrosanct than stage directions, characters have "subtext") of corporealization found in the modern theatre.

17 Remarking that Hamlet's advice to the players privileges "neither the written text, which Hamlet has changed and reinterpreted to suit his own personal and political designs, nor the reader, but *playing*," Barbara Hodgdon goes on to argue that "Even once a play reached printed form, many early quarto title pages carefully assured potential consumers that what they were buying was the play 'as it was sundry times acted,' often by a particular company, on one or another of London's public stages" (*End Crowns All* 18). Merely printing the texts of plays is not enough, in this view, to change their ontology in a given culture. Harry Berger, Jr. argues that "the rules of the game change when the Age of Reading makes plays available in the same medium as the sonnets and when, owing to the spread of literacy and the institution of literary studies, the plays are read and studied more than they are seen" (*Imaginary Audition* 23); but it is only with the spread of literacy and the institution of literary studies that the sense of the "medium" of plays becomes that of "literature." The status of screenplays and teleplays today perhaps more closely resembles the status of dramatic texts in the seventeenth century. Similarly, when Philip McGuire suggests that "Printing encouraged and ultimately compelled us to accept a definition that equates a

play with its words rather than its performances. In Shakespeare's plays, the density and richness of the words made that definition all the more irresistible" (*Speechless Dialect* 124), he collapses a long process – not only the rise and spread of printing, but the development of institutionalized modes of textuality (literature, journalism, historiography) – into the moment of play-printing itself.

18 Michael Dobson's excellent account of the "'authorizing' of Shakespeare" between 1660 and 1769 amply documents the "coexistence of full-scale canonization with wholesale adaptation, of the urge to enshrine Shakespeare's texts as national treasures with the desire to alter their content" in the period. Moreover, in showing that "adaptation and canonization, so far from being contradictory processes, were often mutually reinforcing ones," Dobson documents a fluidity in the *use* of Shakespeare that was not possible in the same way once Shakespeare had become fully an "author" of "literature" in the modern sense (*National Poet* 4–5). As Dobson suggests in his reading of Charles Gildon's comments on Restoration adaptations, for example, Gildon believes adaptation "benefits Shakespeare's texts when its exponents supply thoughts 'which we could justly attribute to Shakespear' – presumably to replace those of Shakespeare's original thoughts which we would rather not attribute to Shakespeare. Shakespeare is thus positioned as the ultimate figure of authority behind original and adaptation alike" (118). On Edmund Malone's role in devising an authentic Shakespeare, see de Grazia, *Shakespeare Verbatim*.

19 Osborne, rightly I believe, suggests that the "Folio editors had no need to convince their readers that their text was close to performance: that relationship was self-evident, as they acknowledge from the outset" ("Rethinking" 173). In this sense, Heminge's and Condell's claim to offer versions of the plays "cur'd, and perfect of their limbes" is not a claim to offer a pre-theatrical text, one purified of theatrical practice, but a text that has passed the "Decree" of the theatrical court and not one of the "diuerse stolne, and surreptitious copies, maimed, and deformed by the frauds and stealthes of iniurious impostors" (*Riverside Shakespeare* 63). Osborne's fascinating article develops McGann's sense of the work as the "global set" of its manifestations, to argue that this lineage of editions tends more directly than "literary" editions to reveal the ideological work of "Shakespeare" at a given moment in history.

20 Osborne develops a fine reading, for example, of the edition of *Much Ado About Nothing, By William Shakespeare: Screenplay, Introduction, and Notes on the Making of the Movie by Kenneth Branagh*, that accompanied the film ("Rethinking" 182–83).

21 On copyright struggles, see Stephens, *Profession of the Playwright* 84–115 and *passim*. My summary of nineteenth-century dramatic authorship and publishing, and of the transformation of dramatic property, is indebted to Stephens's detailed study.

22 On Habermasian "differentiation" and the "development of professionalism and bureaucratisation, and the organisation of science and technology into the systems of economic expansion" typical of nineteenth-century culture, see Grady, "Disintegration" 115; see also Grady, *Modernist Shakespeare* ch. 1. On the rise of the director and the resituation of dramatic texts, see Rabkin, "Play of Misreading" 56. Gary Taylor discusses the development of "expertise" in the production of academic Shakespeare in *Reinventing Shakespeare* 184–91.

23 Describing the fortunes of *Henry V* in the nineteenth-century theatre, for example, Anthony B. Dawson reminds us that the play was routinely mounted precisely for its spectacular possibilities, "in an attempt, it would seem, to belie the Chorus's apology for the inadequacies of stage representation. Audiences were treated to the delights of huge dioramas with richly painted scenes, such as the departure of the English fleet from Southampton, minutely reconstructed castles, interpolated tableaux and ballets, and, in Charles Kean's production, the insertion of 'An Historical Episode: Old London Bridge, from the Surrey Side of the River', which was set up to illustrate and accompany the Chorus's fifth-act speech depicting Harry's triumphant homecoming" (*Watching Shakespeare* 115).

24 Gary Taylor briefly charts the similarity between attempts to restore authentic texts and to insert a notion of authenticity into theatrical production in *Reinventing Shakespeare* 267–85.

25 For a discussion of the impact of the verbal medium on the "visual representation" of Shakespeare's plays, see Kennedy, *Looking at Shakespeare* 109 and *passim*. Kennedy also traces "how Shakespeare has operated on the stage and in the mind outside English-speaking environments" (133) in "Shakespeare Without His Language."

26 The quotation is from Salter, "Acting Shakespeare" 123. As Salter rightly asks, "The totalizing assumption seems to be that since we all speak English, we can all communicate with each other. Can't we – and, if not, why not?" ("Acting Shakespeare" 115). Salter's fine reading of Shakespeare in English- and French-speaking Canada might be paired, for example, with an inquiry into the differential functioning of Shakespeare in both the Republic of Ireland and in Northern Ireland, or Shakespeare's long performance history by African American theatres as well as in the Caribbean. In *Performing*

Nostalgia, Bennett notes the desirability of extending "the field of cultural negotiation to consider the power of texts 'read' and 'performed' outside specifically academic contexts," and outside institutionalized theatrical contexts as well (see 13 and *passim*). On theatrical nationalism in Canada, see also Filewod, "National Theatre/National Obsession"; Knowles, "Shakespeare, 1993"; Lieblein, "Theatre Archives"; Salter, "Declarations of (In)Dependence"; and Wilson, "Staging Shakespeare." On Shakespeare's function within the "canonical counter-discourse" of plays and performances, see Gilbert and Tompkins, *Post-Colonial Drama* 20–21 and ch. 1 *passim.*

27 As Leanore Lieblein remarks, "The resistance to extraperformance communication with an audience by some theatre artists is related to the still asserted (in some places) notion that the creative act results from 'inspiration' and that its authenticity is guaranteed by spontaneity, is contaminated by reflection, and is unchanged by the nature of its audience or the context of its production" ("Theatre Archives" 167).

2 SHAKESPEARE'S AUTEURS: DIRECTING AUTHORITY

1 On the rhetoric of naturalism in theatre practice, see Worthen, *Modern Drama* chs. 1 and 2.

2 See Dennis Kennedy, *Looking at Shakespeare* ch. 2, for an excellent reading of the reciprocal goals of Victorian pictorialism and the Elizabethan revival. Cary M. Mazer, in an indispensable study of Edwardian Shakespeare, remarks, "The traditional pictorial stage recreated the context of the historical event, allowing the spectators to pretend that they were present when the event was occurring for the first time. The Elizabethanist stage took the event out of its historical context and enacted on the open platform in the midst of the spectators, creating instead the illusion that the 'first time' of the event was in fact the moment of its theatrical presentation" (*Shakespeare Refashioned* 56). As Mazer goes on to demonstrate, the "Elizabethan" stages of Poel and others often used a curtain between the downstage pillars, as well as across the upstage "discovery space," in an unacknowledged transposition of nineteenth-century theatrical idioms to Shakespeare's theatre. Moreover, many of the "Elizabethan" stages they constructed were built within the framing architecture of proscenium theatres, often within the proscenium itself; rather than surrounding the thrust stage, the audiences faced it, looking into the "Elizabethan" stage much as they looked into the "historical" dramatic settings of Irving or Tree.

Finally, Mazer notes that many observers – including William Archer and Bernard Shaw – found Poel's experiments impoverished and amateurish, and thought that Shakespeare would have preferred – as they did – the superior illusion created by modern stage technology. See *Shakespeare Refashioned*, ch. 2 *passim*, and fig. 19.

3 Brook is here speaking of Merce Cunningham's exercises for dancers. For a fine account of Brook's approach to rehearsal, see *The Empty Space* ch. 4, "The Immediate Theatre"; see also Mitter, *Systems of Rehearsal*, and Jones, *Great Directors at Work* ch. 4.

4 For one notable exception, see Bogdanov and Pennington, *The English Shakespeare Company*.

5 I don't mean to suggest that Brook's "open" rehearsal methods are without his active, and often controlling agency; for an excellent account of Brook's rehearsal process, see Selbourne, *The Making of A Midsummer Night's Dream*.

6 In addition to Benedetti's *Director at Work*, some of the principal directing textbooks used in the United States are Alexander Dean and Lawrence Carra, *Fundamentals of Play Directing*; Francis Hodge, *Play Directing: Analysis, Communication, and Style*; David Welker, *Theatrical Direction: The Basic Techniques*; George Black, *Contemporary Stage Directing*; and J. Robert Wills, *Directing in the Theatre*. These guides are representative of American theatre in assuming fundamentally realistic attitudes toward acting and dramatic action. British textbooks, such as John Miles-Brown's *Directing Drama* or Hugh Morrison's *Directing in the Theatre* tend to be less formal in their approach, outlining in a more general way the series of tasks the director will confront. In *Directing Postmodern Theatre*, Jon Whitmore takes a semiotic approach to directing and director training.

7 In "Frankie Goes to Hollywood (North)," Richard Paul Knowles characterizes the "two basic traditions, sets of expectations" about how directors in Canada should be trained and should work in the theatre: "The first is the one most commonly inscribed in textbooks, and often also the one most trusted by actors, in which the director is constructed as 'guiding genius', 'missionary', 'ship's captain', or 'benevolent dictator', whose job it is to provide unifying principles, through-lines, intellectual concepts, and other phallogocentric shaping devices. . . . The second is what I think of as the 'empty space' approach to directing, modelled on the trans-cultural process of Peter Brook and other 'experimental' directors who construct the rehearsal process as 'free' exploration of 'deep' and 'fundamental' and 'primitive', and therefore 'universal', human instincts and impulses" (4). Noting the seductive "mimicry of democratic freedom of choice" inscribed in the "open" model, Knowles argues that

"Oppositional directors working within these models are either discredited by their deployment of authoritarian power structures that are willy-nilly inscribed in an industrial model, in which directors produce meaning through the theatrical workers under them for audiences constructed as consumers; or their political intentions are themselves contained or subverted by 'neutral' processes that 'allow' the 'common senses' of a naturalized dominant ideology to 'speak through' the exploratory process as culturally transcendent truth" (5). For a shrewd reading of how the space of the Festival Theatre in Stratford, Ontario constrains directors and designers, see Knowles, "Shakespeare at Stratford."

8 On "translation" as a paradigm for understanding the work of directing, see Knowles, "Focus."

9 One version of the "universalist" Shakespeare is the claim that Shakespeare's command of the theatre – conceived as an unchanging institution designed to deliver "entertainment" – was so complete that he continues to provide much the same entertainment in today's theatre. As Gerald Freedman suggests in comparing the demands of Shakespearean drama with those of American musical theatre, "If you have worked in the commercial theatre, many of Shakespeare's difficult or even inexplicable demands become clear, because they are familiar from your musical script. . . . The content is genius, but the form is a matter of craft" ("From Hitch-kick to Highgate" 32–33).

10 It is sometimes thought that this aporia would be closed if only Shakespeare's original publishers had included more extensive stage directions. Yet as Alan C. Dessen shows in his survey of stage directions in a Jacobean printed quarto annotated with playhouse commentary, the addition of even such extra-textual "information" hardly determines the scope of the events taking place onstage. See "Recovering Elizabethan Staging," esp. 46–47.

11 In his excellent directing textbook, for example, Francis Hodge notes that understanding the dramatic action is in part a function of identifying its genre: "If a character does not finally accept what he dislikes at the beginning of a play, he will probably die or exile himself in the process of resisting the forced change that others bring upon him and become what we call a *tragic hero*. If a character strongly resists being pried loose from what he already likes intensely at the beginning, he will survive, but he will be ridiculed and thus he will become what we call a *comic fool*" (*Play Directing* 26).

12 Yet as Barbara Hodgdon asks, "if this particular play can be reconfigured progressively, why should its seemingly coercive no-choice politics matter?" ("Katherina Bound" 538). As Hodgdon suggests in

an exemplary reading of modern productions and their staging of gender/power relations, it is by no means clear that the fantasized pleasures offered by *Shrew* in its original productions have not been translated into modern forms and guises. In her reading of the performative and editorial problems posed by *The Taming of the Shrew* and the supposedly non-Shakespearean *The Taming of a Shrew*, Leah Marcus suggests "that we start thinking of the different versions of *The Taming of the Shrew* intertextually – as a cluster of related texts which can be fruitfully read together and against each other as 'Shakespeare.' To do that, of course, is to give up the idea that either Shakespeare or the canon of his works is a single determinate thing. It is to carry Shakespearean textual studies out of the filiative search for a single 'authentic' point of origin and into the purview of poststructuralist criticism, where the authority of the author loses its élan and the text becomes a multiple, shifting process rather than an artifact set permanently in print. In the case of *A Shrew* and *The Shrew*, it is also to interrogate the canonical version of a play we may no longer want to live with" ("Shakespearean Editor" 198).

13 Proponents of directing from the 1623 First Folio generally read the composition of the Folio's printed page to contain authorial directions for performers, and sometimes advocate the use of both early and modern editions in directing and acting in Shakespeare. On this practice, see Neil Freeman, *Shakespeare's First Texts*, and my discussion in chapter 3 below.

14 Berry regards this extension of the audience with some condescension. Modern-dress production "immediately breaks through the mental barrier existing for many between (say) kings, queens and consuls and the present day, and appears to establish the authenticity of the production's credentials. Those knowing the text well, for whom the mental barrier is no problem, will nonetheless be engaged and gripped by each piece of modern translation that the director introduces" (*On Directing Shakespeare* 15). I am not certain that it has ever been decisively shown that familiarity with Shakespeare is a necessary condition of historical imagination. Gary Taylor gives a thumbnail sketch of modern-dress Shakespeare in the 1920s and 1930s, and suggests its relation to other critical and artistic trends, in *Reinventing Shakespeare* 269–72.

15 Peter Hall remarks that "in an old play, where the signals are different and are not being made to a society which has the same receivers, the problems are more complex. You have to know what Shakespeare's signals are, and then think of a way of getting them through to a modern audience. That's why I think that doing

Shakespeare in modern dress is on the whole crazy (because though it illuminates much, it always cuts off much). It is a direct and crude way of making *some* signals operate" (quoted in Cook, *Directors' Theatre* 71–72).

16 Amy S. Green, for example, notes a series of period-setting productions at The American Shakespeare Festival Theatre, Stratford, Connecticut, in the 1950s and 1960s: a nineteenth-century Texas setting for *Much Ado* in 1957; a "medieval soap opera" *All's Well* in the 1958–59 season; a 1961 Edwardian *Twelfth Night*; an American Civil War setting for *Troilus and Cressida* in 1961. See *The Revisionist Stage* 36–37. These periods have now become relatively conventional settings for these and other Shakespeare plays.

17 Hall was somewhat less complimentary about Miller's *Measure for Measure*; Hall does not "approve in my puritan soul of moving Shakespeare into a modern period in order to illuminate him. You merely illuminate some things and obscure others." In this case, he thought Miller's production discounted the "Dionysian" side of Vienna – "There is no joy in this city." Hall's most interesting comment, though, is to suggest, "Shouldn't we now, if we want to do Shakespeare out of period, rewrite it? It would be absurd, but at least it's logical. There is something pathetically stupid about Renaissance language in 1920s Vienna. Why didn't Jonathan modernise the text as well?" (*Diaries* 64).

18 It is also notable that the controversies surrounding intercultural performances of Shakespearean drama – Ariane Mnouchkine's series of Shakespeare productions in performance modes derived from various Asian traditions at Le Théâtre du Soleil in the 1980s, for example – throw the cultural work of period staging into higher relief. For while it may be seductive to see Shakespeare providing an anticipatory analysis of, say, the American Civil War, it is less inviting to see Shakespeare providing an immanent, imperial reading of the dynamics of other cultures.

19 Marowitz's view of the trivial character of scholarship is epitomized by the kinds of fictitious projects he suggests are exemplary of scholarly activity: " 'The Erotic Influence of Semi-Colons in The First Folio,' 'Did Prince Hamlet Cut Classes While Enrolled at Wittenberg University' " and so on. He has even "read treatises which have studiously explored the number of times a particular noun has recurred in a Shakespearian play, investing that recurrence with profound significance; how the use of capital letters was a guide to Elizabethan understanding; how printing and punctuation contained telltale hints about the author's secret meaning; how the existence of a particular historical character at a particular time in history was 'the

key' to understanding the veiled significance of a particular play"
(*Recycling Shakespeare* 71). Not claiming such myopia for himself, it's perhaps unfair to hold Marowitz to "scholarly" standards of accuracy:
the source for the claim that "according to a certain school of scholarship, the Elizabethan director was closer to a prompter or stage-man-
ager" is unidentified; one "Harbage" is identified as the author of B.
L. Joseph's book *Elizabethan Acting* (37) – though Alfred Harbage did
publish a fine article entitled "Elizabethan Acting" in 1939; "*The
Shakespearian Quarterly* [*sic*], published by the Folger Shakespeare
Library," epitomizes "the kind of dust they fling up" (70).

20 Marowitz's chapter titles, his remarks on "wanking," and his
general description of directorial authority are, it might also be
noted, openly and offensively masculinist throughout *Recycling
Shakespeare*. Susan Bennett remarks of Marowitz's language that
"Rape, as every woman knows, is all about differentials of power
and not in the least about the kind of interpretive freedom
Marowitz wants to inspire. Frankly, the gendered, sexualized and
violent metaphors of his rally cry are terrifying" (*Performing Nostalgia*
166 n.41). In this regard, though, Marowitz typifies the general conventions of writing about theatrical practice; this emphasis passes
without comment in most books by directors or about directing, as
well as in actor training and voice training books. While this might
be explained – though not excused – by the dominance of men in
the modern theatre, it hardly explains why both acting and directing training manuals and textbooks – which obviously have men *and*
women as their imagined audience – persist in this "convention."

21 These texts have been conveniently collected in *The Marowitz
Shakespeare*.

22 On Miller's career and ideas about theatre, see Romain, *A Profile of
Jonathan Miller*.

23 *Strange Days* is set on New Year's Eve, 1999, in Los Angeles. The
parallels between the setting and the Los Angeles riots of 1992 are
everywhere in evidence: the police force is armed with military
weapons, and the city is in a state of high security, anticipating the
riot/celebration that will break out at midnight, especially from the
young, ethnic underclass shown on the streets. Ralph Fiennes plays
an ex-cop who deals in the black-market drug of the millennium's
end: virtual experience. A device has been perfected that allows
someone to record his/her experience – of sex, murder, etc. – on a
small compact disc. The "user" wears a second device that "plays
back" the CD directly into his/her cerebral cortex: the "user," in
effect, *lives* the experience of the recording subject from the subject's
point-of-view. Because the technology that created the recording

and playback devices is classified, Fiennes's trade is strictly black-market. It is perhaps unnecessary to point out that the highest demand is for discs that record dangerous or illicit experiences. The most insidious of these are "snuff" discs, in which the recording subject died while recording the disc; the plot of *Strange Days* turns in part on such a disc. But it also turns on another disc, which records an eye-witness observing two police officers dragging a famous rap-music star from his car and executing him, in an explicit replay-ing of the Rodney King beating: making this disc public would con-nect police racism and an urban explosion directly, without the intervening "trial" phase.

In the film, then, Fiennes wants to turn the incriminating disc over to the authorities, so that the offending policemen – who are presented as rogue cops, not part of a system of institutionalized racism – will face justice; he is concerned that if the disc falls into the wrong hands, the cops will escape justice, or the disc will be made public and incite the 1992-like riot that is clearly waiting to erupt. Since part of the ethic of the film is to show this mediatized "experience" as a *drug*, the film's comic dimension hinges on Fiennes's ability to see that he is an addict, has wasted his life in sim-ulated experience, and to rekindle a desire to return to authentic experience, i.e. true love. This aspect of the plot is focused in Fiennes's romantic entanglements: his (bad) love for a drug-addicted groupie, and his eventual recognition that his sidekick, an African American woman (Angela Bassett), represents his way back into a useful life in society. Throughout the film, Bassett's character refuses to watch the CDs and can be persuaded to do so only once – to watch the CD of the rapper's execution – so that Fiennes can moti-vate her to help him out. In the film's closing moments, Fiennes finally understands that she in fact loves him, and that his attraction to her is not "virtual" but "real": rather than the simulated sex scenes with his girlfriend that Fiennes plays throughout the film, *Strange Days* ends with a romantic embrace between Fiennes and Bassett, a "real" kiss.

24 In a fine reading of this production, Shannon Steen argues that Sellars's staging of an Anglo judge marked one of the production's clearest engagements with the politics of the Los Angeles uprising; playing videotape of the uprising, and of comments both by the police officers and police chief Daryl Gates during the trial scene, the production seemed to parallel Shylock's trial with a miscarriage of justice in the Simi Valley trial by staging the court as a "white" institution. The power of the Anglo-American gaze might also be considered more broadly: this production enacted racial and ethnic

strife under the watchful gaze of a largely white, Anglo audience. Steen also suggests that by casting African American women to play Portia's servants *as* African American, Sellars seems to subvert the casting paradigm of the production; see "Authority." I am grateful to Shannon Steen for providing me with a copy of her work, and for permitting me to cite it here.

25 Arguing that what "is so brilliant in Shakespeare is he makes everybody as human as everybody really is" ("Peter Sellars Interview" 12), Sellars took the most important consequences of racism in the play to arise in the private sphere: "What's impressive is that Shakespeare is taking on colonialism and the capitalist system at the moment of their creation and is saying: 'If you set this up wrong, nobody will have happiness. You're poisoning your own lives as well as the lives of distant people in foreign lands who you will never meet, whom you will simply exploit.' The play is about exploitative relationships" (13). In an article reviewing Shylock's fortunes as a Jewish stereotype on the eve of the Sellars production, Emily D. Soloff cites historian June Sochen's reservations about Sellars's approach: "Historians also try to universalize experience, to show commonalities between periods and cultures . . . But there is danger in oversimplifying and making all experience the same. Not only do you simplify, you trivialize. It encourages indifference." On the other hand, Chicago actor Byrne Piven remarks "'I think Peter's casting of a black actor is a marvelous idea, especially in this time of black/Jewish tension, because it universalizes the oppressed class. It's not the Jewishness (*per se*) but the oppressedness, to coin a word, of this character, the minority aspect of this character' that makes him so universal" (Soloff, "Merchant of Venom" 20). As Albert Williams suggests, "Even the wrong choices – like drawing a simple parallel between blacks and Jews, who have suffered distinctly different kinds of prejudice and persecution – raises issues most theaters would shy away from" (34). The leading Black newspaper in Chicago voiced its dismay over "such an awful production of Shakespeare's dramatic masterpiece" by concluding that "It is better to feature the Bard's works in their own period and with settings that historically enhance them" (Calloway).

26 Kathleen McLuskie has remarked on a similar kind of analogy between Renaissance and modern "market" economies, and on the incompatibility of such comparisons: "However, the very obviousness of these connections gets in the way of precise historical and critical analysis. It reifies 'the market' into a metahistorical image as applicable to the 1980s and the 1580s, a procedure which may be theatrically creative but is analytically confused. It allows a rhetori-

cal elision between the emergent early modern market and the highly developed, all pervasive, and infinitely adaptable market of late-twentieth-century capitalism" ("Shopping Complex." 89).

27 Joel Henning, for example, remarks that "Despite a stage engorged with audio and video technology, most of these actors struggle through their lines as if their tongues were injected with Novocain while they simultaneously perpetrate amateurish wringing of hands, hunching of shoulders and long, sterile pauses that contain nothing but dead air and empty silence." Perhaps the most cogent reservations were expressed by Albert Williams: "I'm still debating whether the guy knows just how accurately he's invoked TV-influenced contemporary culture in all its shallowness and arbitrary violence. Many of this *Merchant*'s line readings are contrived and sophomoric; that might be because Sellars is under television's spell, or because he's knowingly exposing the medium's influence on the play's characters" (33–34). James Loehlin, in a brilliant and devastating reading of the production, remarks "A curious fact about Sellars' production was that he took what I suspect were, on the whole, a pretty decent set of actors, and made them appear to be absolutely abysmal. In a sense, Sellars is hoist by his own brilliance: his relentless imagination and wilfully perverse directorial tricks sink what is a powerfully-conceived production" (Letter); see also Loehlin's review of the production.

28 Alan Sinfield usefully outlines the complex relationship between Shakespearean characterization and modern notions of identity that Sellars's production helps to bring into view: "None of the opponents of character criticism I have been invoking disputes altogether that dramatis personae in Shakespearean plays are written, at least some of the time, in ways that suggest that they have subjectivities. The objection is to jumping from that point to a Bradleyan or essentialist-humanist conception of character. My contention is that some Shakespearean dramatis personae are written so as to suggest, not just an intermittent, gestural, and problematic subjectity [*sic*], but a continuous or developing interiority or consciousness; and that we should seek a way of talking about this that does not slide back into character criticism or essentialist humanism. This way of talking would not suppose that performances attempted an unbroken illusionistic frame; or that this continuous interiority is self-constituted and independent of the discursive practices of the culture; or that it manifests an essential unity. The key features in this redefined conception of character are two: an impression of subjectivity, interiority, or consciousness, and a sense that these maintain a sufficient continuity or development through the scenes of the play" (*Faultlines* 62).

29 Moreover, the issue of *Onstage: Newsletter of the Goodman Theatre Series* devoted to the production contains photographs not only of Sellars and the cast in rehearsal, and of the Los Angeles "rioting," but also of "N. Y. Crown Heights" – an image not directly relevant to this production (and mentioned nowhere in the text), but recalling Smith's previous work, *Fires in the Mirror: Crown Heights, Brooklyn, and Other Identities.* It should be noted that the visual images behind Smith in performances of *Twilight* were different in different productions, and are not noted in the published text of the play. I am basing my reading on two quite different productions: the Public Theatre production in New York, directed by George C. Wolfe, which I saw in April 1994, and the Berkeley Repertory Theatre production, directed by Sharon Ott, which I saw in March 1996. In subsequent performances, Smith's production of *Twilight* has continued to evolve.

30 *Twilight* was conceived in the aftermath of the April 1992 rioting in Los Angeles, an uprising sparked by a jury's decision not to convict four policemen of brutality in the 1991 beating of Rodney King. It not only built on the techniques Smith had developed for earlier works in her *On the Road* series, but seemed to develop the issues framed in her previous performance work, *Fires in the Mirror: Crown Heights, Brooklyn, and Other Identities* (1991). Smith's working process consists of assembling an archive of tape recordings of conversations she has with individual informants; she occasionally uses telephone recordings as well. She then selects passages from these conversations, and arranges them in a larger sequence (though this sequence is frequently changed as the production develops; published versions of *Fires in the Mirror* and *Twilight* are in this sense not necessarily representative of the "text" of any actual performance). Meanwhile, she uses her conversations with the informants and the tape records to fashion a precise mimesis of each informant's speech and gestural habits. In making *Twilight*, Smith interviewed over 175 people, and used four dramaturgs in composing the Mark Taper production.

Nonetheless, the Los Angeles project posed a variety of unusual problems. Not only was Smith an "outsider" in LA, but the LA rioting was different in character than the Crown Heights, Brooklyn conflict that had been the subject of *Fires in the Mirror*. It was not confined to a single area or neighborhood, embraced a wider variety of ethnicities, and catalyzed a wider network of conflict – not just black/Jewish antagonism, but variously motivated struggles among a variety of differently positioned (and differently oppressed) groups. Smith described the city as "sprawling. It's difficult to feel community. And it's a city that presents to us this new racial frontier. . . . This story is about multiple conflicts. Latinos. Blacks. Asians. Police" (Weinraub, "Condensing" C15), and this quality was evident in the formal irresolution of *Twilight*, as Edit Villareal remarked in her review: "like Los Angeles, which has no urban center to draw its populace together, neither Smith, nor her characters, arrive at a moment of unifying revelation about these events" (111). One of the most persistent criticisms of *Twilight's* Los Angeles production was Smith's deafness to various racial or ethnic discourses surrounding the events. Villareal also suggests that "the large Latino underclass is, relative to other communities, nearly absent from *Twilight*. The media has characterized the civil unrest as a largely African-American and Korean American vendetta, yet a great majority of the poorest Latinos in the city fell prey to lawless behavior. *Twilight*, like the mainstream media, never explores the economic plight of these poor Latinos whose idea of looting was to steal milk, toilet paper, and Pampers" (111). On Smith's working methods, see Sandra L. Richards, "Caught in the Act."

31 "Palimpsest" is Carol Martin's term ("Anna Deavere Smith" 51). Smith's working methods constitute her characteristic mode of identification with/distinction from the characters she plays in a somewhat contradictory manner. As Charles R. Lyons and James C. Lyons suggest in a fine reading of Smith's work, Smith "deliberately attempts to resist the temptation to internalize the other, as subject in the world external to her, and reconfigure that image as an aspect of her own interiority. That resistance to internalization marks the difference between her mode of acting and the dominant subjective processes of most acting in the U.S." ("Anna Deavere Smith" 49–50). Yet Amy Wegener suggests that "Charles Lyons and James Lyons' assertion that 'Smith deliberately attempts to resist the temptation to internalize the other,' then, is only partly true; Smith does characterize her own process as one of becoming, identification, and inevitably, internalization" ("Playing" 5). I am grateful to Amy Wegener for providing me with a copy of this essay and permitting me to quote from it here.

32 Reviewers noted that Smith performs the characters "in the same level and tone," for example (Guy 116); "She makes virtually no judgments and treats everyone with stern objectivity" (Weinraub, "Condensing" C15).

33 In a shrewd comment on the reception of Smith's work, Sue-Ellen Case remarks that "people are most seduced by Anna Deavere Smith, a single woman who sums up the voices of contentious communities in Los Angeles around the Rodney King uprising – that what people find as a viable, historical, theatrical form at this point

is that the individual can tame the Korean community, the African-American community, the Chicano community – the communities that were at unease with one another as much as with the dominant white culture. I think that might be [seen as part of] a kind of neo-individualism" (Edmondson and Odendahl, "Interview with Sue-Ellen Case" 24). As Judith Hamera remarks in her review of *Twilight*, audiences "want, and wanted, an authorial owning up, if for no other reason than to assess the author/editor's investment in, her capacity to be moved and changed by, the voices she offers to move and change us" (117).

34 For a reading of Smith's work that emphasizes the similarity between her invocation of social reality and the theory of metaphor, see Rayner, "Improper Conjunctions."

35 This desire is perhaps most visible in Richard Schechner's sense that Smith's work resembles shamanistic possession. Describing the relationship between Smith and her subjects (in *Fires in the Mirror*), Schechner marks the healing virtue of Smith's performance: "she does not destroy the others or parody them. Nor does she lose herself. A shaman who loses herself cannot help others to attain understanding. As spectators we are not fooled into thinking we are really seeing Al Sharpton, Angela Davis, Norman Rosenbaum, or any of the others. Smith's shamanistic invocation is her ability to bring into existence the wondrous 'doubling' that marks great performances. This doubling is the simultaneous presence of the performer and performed. Because of this doubling Smith's audiences – consciously perhaps, unconsciously certainly – learn to 'let the other in,' to accomplish in their own way what Smith so masterfully achieves" ("Anna Deavere Smith" 64).

36 In a more recent article, Knowles invites a rethinking of the work of directing as "one that foregrounds, rather than mystifies, the ideologies of choice and the productive tension and discursive *stakes* involved in the confrontation of the historicized dramatic source text, the (also historicized) theatrical target text, and the interpretive production of meaning by a heterogeneous audience" ("Focus" 9–10). Though Sellars is in some ways illustrative of Knowles's "'Shakespeare-really-did-know-just-about-everything' school of Shakespearean production" (11), his production seems to have worked in other directions as well, multiplying focus onstage, and so phrasing contestatory – as well as parallel – relations between Shakespeare and the modern audience.

37 Knowles's savvy reading of the 1993 Stratford, Ontario Shakespeare Festival provides an exemplary reading both of the "performances" and of the material, financial, national, and commercial contexts which animated them.

3 SHAKESPEARE'S BODY:
ACTING AND THE DESIGNS OF AUTHORITY

1   One of the most popular acting guides published in the United
     States, Robert L. Benedetti's *The Actor at Work* has been through five
     editions since it was first published in 1970. Benedetti takes these re-
     visions seriously, dropping and adding chapters, exercises, and em-
     phasis in each edition (the back cover of the 1990 fifth edition, for
     example, describes its "clear, less abstract writing style – less jar-
     gon"). In this chapter, unless noted otherwise, I cite from the 1976
     edition. While the 1990 edition may be more jargon-free, in the ear-
     lier edition Benedetti sometimes foregrounds his guiding attitudes
     and assumptions more clearly, principles which continue to inform
     later editions of this fine book.

2   On the relationship between acting and ideology, see Roach, *Player's
     Passion*; Worthen, *Idea of the Actor*; and Worthen, *Modern Drama* ch. 2.

3   Despite his careful and appropriate warning about the reliability of
     texts as indices to the ideology of performance, Phillip Zarrilli is also
     interested in the ideological inscription of modern acting training;
     see Introduction 10–16. As Richard Paul Knowles suggests, while it
     may "seem unfair to interrogate printed texts written by voice
     coaches and teachers rather than the methods they employ in their
     studios and rehearsal halls . . . these books encode and reinforce ide-
     ological structures and assumptions that are both deeply embedded
     in theatrical discourse and too easily overlooked or mystified when
     their methods are applied in practice" ("Shakespeare, Voice, and
     Ideology" 93).

4   On "theatre poet," see Hapgood, *Shakespeare the Theatre-Poet*. The
     impact of "performance-oriented approaches" to Shakespeare has
     been particularly profound in the area of pedagogy; I am thinking,
     for instance, of *The BBC-TV Shakespeare Plays*, John Barton's *Playing
     Shakespeare*, various issues of *Shakespeare Quarterly*, the "Shakespeare in
     Performance" series of volumes devoted to individual plays,
     ACTER residencies in the United States, the generous availability
     of RSC and Royal National Theatre actors and directors to student
     groups visiting the London theatres.

5   On ideology here and its function in the qualification and subjection
     of individuals as subjects, I have been especially influenced by
     Göran Therborn. He argues that the "reproduction of any social
     organization, be it an exploitative society or a revolutionary party,
     entails a basic correspondence between subjection and qualification.
     Those who have been subjected to a particular patterning of their
     capacities, to a particular discipline, qualify for the given roles and
     are capable of carrying them out" (*Ideology of Power* 17). Therborn
     then discusses "*three fundamental modes of ideological interpellation.*

Ideologies subject and qualify subjects by telling them, relating them to, and making them recognize": "*what exists,* and its corollary, what does not exist," "*what is good,* right, just, beautiful, attractive, enjoyable, and its opposites," "*what is possible* and impossible" (18). Though Therborn is discussing modes of ideological interpellation generally, these modes also characterize specific structures of ideological production, such as theatre training and performance. This general view of subjectification is given a somewhat more available reading by Louis A. Montrose: "Thus, my invocation of the term 'Subject' is meant to suggest an equivocal process of *subjectification*: on the one hand, shaping individuals as loci of consciousness and initiators of action – endowing them with *subjectivity* and with the capacity for agency; and, on the other hand, positioning, motivating, and constraining them within – *subjecting them to* – social networks and cultural codes that ultimately exceed their comprehension or control" ("Professing the Renaissance" 21).

6   Despite the critical influence of Artaud, Grotowski, and Brecht on Anglo-American experimental theatre in the 1960s and 1970s, their efforts to redirect theatre and theatre training have been influential mainly at the level of performance style. Where their influence is most significant is in the realm of autoperformance and performance art, a kind of acting that most theatre training explicitly ignores. The difficulty that playwrights like Edward Bond and Howard Barker have faced when trying to implement their own ideas about acting are illustrative in this regard. On the influence of Asian acting and martial-arts training, see Zarrilli, "'On the edge'"; Suzuki, "Culture is the Body"; Watson, "Eastern and Western Influences."

7   Despite decades of impugning Stanislavski and the techniques he developed or inspired, several Stanislavskian principles – continuous characterization, an organic connection between scenes, the need to develop an inner life for the role, a consistent through-line of action – suffuse thinking about acting today, and particularly suffuse actors' descriptions of their work. This is hardly surprising. As the theorist of modern realistic enactment, as much so as Ibsen, Chekhov, or O'Neill, Stanislavski is involved in the production of the bourgeois subject at the heart of modern realism: an individual, delimited, organic, non-commodified, spontaneous psyche. And, Stanislavski or no, it would be difficult to expect actors any more than the rest of us to stand outside this dominant mode of ideological transmission, producing the world by producing us as its subjects invested in particular notions of what such subjectivity entails. For an unsympathetic critique of the role of Stanislavski in contemporary actor training, see Hornby, *The End of Acting.*

In "The Bard Goes to Univers(al)ity," a paper discussed at the 1992 Shakespeare Association of America meetings in Kansas City, Anthony Dawson undertakes a brilliant reading of the relationship between materialist criticism of Shakespearean drama and the "universalist assumptions" implicit in theatre training and production today, assumptions fully formed in the "utterly pervasive force" of notions of "character" in actors' accounts of their work: "It stands as an unquestioned truth that what the actor does is create character."

8 It is notable that Gronbeck-Tedesco's assimilation of contemporary schools of acting makes no reference of Augusto Boal, and cites Brecht only once, citing the Brechtian social *gestus* in relation to Gronbeck-Tedesco's notion of the "geste": "*a pattern of movement that the actor uses to create a fundamental form for the character*" (*Acting Through Exercises* 244). This transformation of Brecht's essentially political device into a purely formal instrument is characteristic of how actor training tends to position modes of acting not designed to reproduce the bourgeois subject as marginal to the essential purpose of theatre.

9 Bert O. States discusses this aspect of theatre with typical subtlety in his reading of Beckett's *Catastrophe*: "So we attend this new play by Samuel Beckett, in whose work we are naturally interested, and we watch a man being complacently, as a matter of business, stripped of his humanity, made into a *thing* before our eyes for our pleasure and instruction, whatever that may mean. But then Beckett overturns his catastrophe – overturns the overturning – and poses the real question: *are we to applaud his play?* What are we applauding if we do?" (*Pleasure of the Play* 207).

10 For a fuller treatment of the ideological and practical consequences of Stanislavski-inspired actor-training in Canada, see Salter, "Body Politics," and the response by Kurt Reis, "Defending NTS." In a treatment of four college acting programs in the Toronto area, Laurin M. Mann remarks that while training programs have worked away from the exclusively psychological dimension of the American Method of the 1950s, now "giving equal emphasis to body, voice and internal work," Stanislavski nonetheless remains as the "basis" of actor training ("Teaching Acting" 34).

11 One of the implications of Peter Stallybrass's reading of the boy actor's body in Renaissance performance is that the body in performance is known through its prostheses, which finally enforce "contradictory attitudes about both sexuality and gender: on the one hand, gender as a set of prosthetic devices (in which case, the *object* of sexual attention is absorbed into the play of those devices); on the other, gender as the 'given' marks of the body (the breast, the vagina, the penis) which (however analogous in Galenic medicine)

are read as the signs of an absolute difference (in which case, sexuality, whether between man and woman, woman and woman, or man and man, tends to be organized through a fixation upon the supposedly 'essential' features of gender)" ("Transvestism and the 'Body Beneath'" 73).

12 In "Shakespeare, Voice, and Ideology," Richard Paul Knowles deftly characterizes the relationship between voice training and the ideology of Shakespeare production at the RSC. In a close analysis of books by Cicely Berry, Kristin Linklater, and Patsy Rodenburg, Knowles traces the construction of four related terms – freedom, nature, identity or character, and Shakespeare or text – in the representation of voice training and performance, and argues that the inscription of bourgeois ideology works much more fundamentally here than the more overt "politics" of famous directors (Peter Brook, Peter Hall) associated with RSC work in the post-war period. This is pioneering work, and I'm indebted to Knowles for his fine reading of the development of Berry's, Linklater's, and Rodenburg's work, which he treats in much more detail than I do here; and my thanks to him and to James Bulman for providing me with a copy of the essay in advance of publication.

13 As Joseph R. Roach remarks, "We tend, therefore, to see our bodies as damaged by the kinds of lives we have lived. In response to this powerful idea, acting theorists have come to believe that before an actor can learn to act, to use his bodily instrument expressively in vital characterization, he must himself learn to move and feel and live anew because in growing up he has disordered his musculature, misshapen his bones, and dulled his sensitivities" (*Player's Passion* 218).

14 Harrop recognizes that contemporary drama often strikes a different relationship between actor and character, predicated on changing notions both of the identity of the subject and of the nature of representation. Yet as his concluding remarks suggest, Harrop finally sees the demands of postmodern performance as merely a shift in the register of style rather than as a fundamental reorientation of either identity or representation; see *Acting* 124.

15 Robert L. Benedetti treats these types in the 1990 edition, 164–65. See also Gronbeck-Tedesco, *Acting Through Exercises* ch. 16. Bud Beyer translates the notion of bodily center into a "period spine," the "way in which the central axis of the body is carried, its degree of fluidity, its degree of expressiveness, its degree of rigidity" characteristic of different historical periods – "Shakespeare, the Greeks, Chekhov, or Ibsen" – and of different contemporary nationalities (quoted in Mekler, *New Generation* 320).

16 This idea appeared in the 1976 edition of *The Actor at Work* in a different though related exercise, the "polarization" exercise. In this exercise, the actors beat out the rhythms of a speech without using the words of the text: "In this and the other polarization exercises that follow, you are creating an extended *visceral* experience that renders the rhythm, tone, imagery or configuration of your character's language into *real* bodily experiences. The body will 'remember' much of these experiences far better than could the mind. In Stanislavski's terms, you are creating *sense memories* based upon the qualities and associations embodied in the text. Later, as you rehearse and perform the text in a 'normal' way, these bodily memories will automatically enrich your performance *without conscious effort* – for your mind, in performance, must be totally free to concentrate on *what* you are doing, not *how*" (153).

17 While the circle exercise helps performers feel the weight of words, the whole-body sensation is the goal of a related exercise: "Each member of the group lies full-length on the floor. . . . Feeling the weight of your body on the floor, simply speak the text through, rolling over at the changes of thought" (*Actor and His Text* 187). Patsy Rodenburg offers a similar series of exercises (*Need for Words* 145–48), such as: "speak whilst pushing something relatively substantial. As you push you can feel a powerful connection to the breath and body. Push against a wall and speak. Feel how the words enter the wall along with your strength" (146).

18 For instance, Antony Sher recalls working on the opening speech in *Richard III* with Cicely Berry. She complains that he is "singing the same tune" throughout the speech, and first has him bang on a wastebasket with each reference to nature, and then has him recite, bang the wastebasket, and sketch a portrait of Richard at the same time (*Year of the King* 192). "This is the most useful exercise of all. The diversionary tactic liberates the words and thoughts. Phrases that I've been shoving around like dead weights suddenly come to life. The pen bites into the hump and the bent legs. Interesting that by using something in which I'm confident (sketching) I liberate something in which I'm not (verse-speaking)" (193).

19 In some respects, the groundwork for a rhetorical approach to acting that derives from Elizabethan practice was developed in Bertram Joseph's *Acting Shakespeare*; while Joseph explores the function of classical rhetoric in the training of Renaissance actors, "It is the author's belief, indeed, that the actor's task is simply nothing more than the truthful creation of character" (xvii).

20 Peter Shillingsburg's excellent discussion of the printing of Thackeray's novels takes up the subject of rhetorical as opposed to

syntactic punctuation. Shillingsburg notes that "The basic concept
of rhetorical punctuation is that different points indicate different
lengths of pauses. Thus, a comma is a short pause, a semicolon indicates a pause twice as long as that for a comma, a colon represents a
pause three times as long as that for a comma, and a period four
times as long as that for a comma"; he suggests that in Thackeray's
case, the manuscripts reveal "the writing of a man who punctuated
rhetorically but who was accustomed to compositors who imposed
syntactical punctuation on his texts" (*Scholarly Editing* 60). Where
Freeman expands the sense of rhetorical punctuation is by attributing motive to the use of various points. In his view, commas, semi-
colons, and periods are not merely the record of duration, but of
duration that can be "filled" with a character's intentions.

21 See, for example, Buzacott, *The Death of the Actor*.

22 See Brockbank, *Players* 131, 153, 155; Jackson and Smallwood, *Players
2* 15, 138, 181, 192; Jackson and Smallwood, *Players 3* 22. Kristin
Linklater recommends John Barton's *Playing Shakespeare*, Cicely
Berry, Bertram Joseph's *Acting Shakespeare*, Caroline Spurgeon's
Shakespeare's Imagery, and E. M. W. Tillyard's *Elizabethan World
Picture*, among others (*Freeing Shakespeare's Voice* 1); in ch. 4, she pro-
vides an overview of Tillyard as "a description of the medieval
philosophy that implicitly governed the way in which the
Elizabethans lived in their world" (62). In *The Actor and His Text*,
Cicely Berry provides an overview of "Elizabethan thinking" (116)
drawn mainly from Tillyard; see 116–19.

23 This sense of character consistency, of a "character" unfolding its
history on its "journey" through the play is common to actors – like
Ian McDiarmid – who dispense with an "over-generalised understanding of Stanislavsky" as a "by-product of the naturalistic
theatre" (Jackson and Smallwood, *Players 2* 47). Like his colleagues,
McDiarmid nonetheless develops a fully Stanislavskian preparation,
using the "Ghetto Nuovo" of Venice to provide a kind of sensory
image/memory guiding his characterization: "I was fascinated to
see that all the windows looked inward towards the square. None
looked outward to the city and the sea beyond. So, I extrapolated,
the Jew was not permitted to look outwards. He had no alternative
but to look inwards. Light was shut out. He was left obsessively to
contemplate the dark" (48). For actors' use of the "journey," see
Brockbank, *Players 2*, 142, 159; Jackson and Smallwood, *Players 2* 55
("voyage of discovery"), 56; Jackson and Smallwood, *Players 3* 41, 52,
113. Carol Rutter also notes, describing her plans to inteview five
Shakespearean actresses for *Clamorous Voices*, that she "wanted them
to follow the journey their character makes through the play" (xv).

In this sense, it's hardly surprising that Roger Warren singled out "one thing that has emerged above all others" from Peter Hall's 1988 staging of the late plays: "the sense of the central characters going on spiritual journeys, voyages of discovery and self discovery" (*Staging Shakespeare's Late Plays* 238).

24 I am thinking here, of course, of Fredric Jameson's use of *pastiche* as one of the identifying markers of postmodern representation; see *Postmodernism* 16–25.

25 "What kind of man is Malvolio? What is his background? I see him as a military man; unpopular at school, he joins the army and, while he displays no quality of leadership, he is so damned efficient that he now finds himself, at forty-five, a Colonel in the Pay corps, embittered, with no prospect of further promotion. He has bored every woman he has met and he stays unmarried. A certain widowed Count I suppose needed a major-domo to manage his Mediterranean estate, and who better than this totally efficient and honest tee-totaller?" (Brockbank, *Players* 43). Compare Stanislavski: "What is the *past* which justifies the *present* of this scene: Who is Roderigo? I imagine that he is the son of very wealthy parents, landowners who took the produce of their village to Venice and exchanged it for velvet and other luxuries. These goods were in turn shipped to other countries, including Russia, and sold at great profit. But now Roderigo's parents are dead. How can he manage such a tremendous business? All he is capable of is squandering his father's wealth. It is this wealth which made his father, and consequently himself, acceptable in aristocratic circles. Roderigo, a simple soul and a lover of gay times, constantly supplies the young blades of Venice with money which, obviously, is never returned. Where does this money come from? Well, thus far the well-established business, managed by old and faithful workers, is still running through force of inertia; but certainly it cannot continue like this much longer" ("From the Production Plan of *Othello*" 131). These are Stanislavski's notes for Roderigo's first entrance in the play.

26 Eliot's well-known passage reads, "The historical sense, which is a sense of the timeless as well as of the temporal and of the timeless and of the temporal together, is what makes a writer traditional. And it is at the same time what makes a writer most acutely conscious of his place in time, of his contemporaneity" ("Tradition and the Individual Talent" 49).

27 Roger Allam, the Duke in Nicholas Hynter's 1987 *Measure for Measure*, describes reading Richard Sennett's *The Fall of Public Man* and Quentin Skinner's *The Foundations of Modern Political Thought* "in a quite dilettantish way to stimulate my imagination" while playing

Brutus in *Julius Caesar.* This reading, a visit to Pentonville prison,
Michael Ignatieff's *A Just Measure of Pain,* and Ignatieff's television
series *Voices* blended together in a "varied soup of thoughts and
experiences I brought in at the start of rehearsals to begin the more
practical task of finding some sort of character for the Duke"
(Jackson and Smallwood, *Players 3* 23, 24–25). "Historical" research,
in Allam's practice, ameliorates the difference between a character
whose mode of being seems remote and strange and the assumed
sensibility of a contemporary audience. See also Tony Church's
comments on his "oppressive Victorian-style paterfamilias" Polonius
in 1980 (Brockbank, *Players* 107); and Geoffrey Hutchings's reading
of "the metaphysical poets" and "poems about war" for his 1981
Lavatch (Brockbank, *Players* 83).

28 On the function of such anecdote, see the openings of each chapter
of Stephen Greenblatt's *Shakespearean Negotiations,* including ch. 2,
"Invisible Bullets." Yet as Jean Howard has asked, "with Greenblatt's
use of the illustrative example, one wants to know more about the
process by which disparate phenomena are chosen for juxtaposition
and discussion; the juxtaposition can seem arbitrary to those reared
on the notion of 'coverage,' that is, on the idea that all the texts and
all the documents need to be surveyed before one can say with
confidence that any two stand in a pivotal cultural position.
Greenblatt's practice implicitly challenges this mode of thinking, but
one wishes for an overt articulation of his oppositional point of
view" ("New Historicism in Literary Studies" 41).

29 For example, the American Repertory Theatre's 1994 production of
Henry IV, Parts 1 and 2 created the court "with images from the
American Civil War, while Falstaff's tavern world is very much of
the 1990s, with a punk Prince Hal (Bill Camp) and his biker bud-
dies. Some critics found such anachronisms distracting but [director
Ron] Daniels maintains that his interpretation is by no means cynical. 'This is an interpretation of integration – of how this young
man is very cleverly synthesizing within himself the feminine and
masculine principles. The interesting thing about the play is the way
it brings the warring aspects of a nation together through the person
of the new king, who is himself a synthesis of these opposing forces'"
(Tropea, "Ron Daniels" 41).

30 It should be noted that Howard and O'Connor, with their emphasis
on material history, sit somewhat uneasily within the general rubric
of "new historicism" – as do nearly all of its practitioners; see also
Howard, "New Historicism in Literary Studies" for a critique of the
practice of new historicism.

31 H. Aram Veeser's remark in its entirety reads, "Suspicious of any
criticism predetermined by a Marxist or liberal grid, New Historicists

eschew overarching hypothetical constructs in favor of surprising coincidences" (Introduction xi–xii).

32 In a letter to H. R. Coursen, Cary Mazer rightly notes that for a contemporary audience – and for contemporary actors – the only discourse through which Shakespearean character can be registered is our own, a situation that raises challenging problems for him as a director: "After all, I think my [new historicist] colleagues are essentially *right* about the interiority stuff; I just don't think you can play it. So, instead, I work with the actors on a) the action of each scene, in the most Stanislavskian sense of the word: what does the character want, what is *happening* in the scene in terms of conflict, energies, etc. *without* discussing *why* the characters are the way they are yet; and b) I identify, thematically and theatrically, the relevant systems of meaning that reflect the characters' dilemmas, i.e. Ferdinand's [in *The Duchess of Malfi*] voyeurism; images of twinning, mirrors, purity of blood, etc. We discover (in the case of Ferdinand) that he has almost no sense of boundaries between himself and his sister, that he's afraid, not of wanting to sleep with her, but that her desires (for someone outside of their twin-ness) and her sexual activity somehow violates the integrity of his own ill-defined and misplaced sense of his 'self.' The result of this is that we tap the energies of the play (ambiguities about the status of the 'self') unlocked by historical conceptualizing, and we make *that* the issue that a modern actor can play, and that a modern audience can perceive: i.e., that this is a character who has a tenuous grip on his sense of self, and his terror about this drives him to sororicide and madness" (quoted in Coursen, *Reading Shakespeare* 264). What it is important to recognize here, however, is that to the extent that one accepts the "new-historicist" critique of subjectivity in Shakespeare's era, Mazer's fascinating efforts are able to provide only new, analogical meanings; presumably, performances in Shakespeare's theatre were capable of registering subjectivity in terms not available to modern actors and audiences.

33 Yet as Edward Pechter notes, "From inside a practice that raises potentially unsettling suspicions about fixed identity, the hermeneutics of suspicion may seem *de trop*. For professionals whose work is sporadic and transient, dependent on corporate and government funding and on an appeal to a general audience, a stable Shakespeare embodying universal human values may accommodate a powerful need" ("Textual and Theatrical Shakespeare" 17). My thanks to Edward Pechter for providing me with a copy of this essay in advance of its publication, and for this shrewd, materialist critique.

34 As Barbara Hodgdon has argued, new historicist discourse often treats actual performance only tangentially: "Conceptualizing and

reading such spatial models requires thinking of performance texts not as the realization of an ideal text that is being 'brought to life,' but as constituted by critical as well as production processes that stretch and, at times, even break through that textual envelope to generate a specific series of radical interventions. And writing the cultural history of such reinterpretations and interventions is crucial if the profession's newly dominant discourse, new historicism, is to separate itself from 'essentialist old historicism.' The new historicism, which by and large equates plays with their texts, and thus focuses on that which gives the illusion that it 'abides,' reproduces the assumption that only reading can yield insights about those texts" (*End Crowns All* 20).

35 As Whigham argues, when Portia "finds no mention of a jot of blood, she reveals the language of the law as infinitely interpretable, as the ongoing creation of its native speakers, who maintain their power precisely by 'ad libbing' with it. Portia discovers the necessary escape clause in the white spaces between the lines, where no strict construction is possible" ("Ideology and Class Conduct" 110). For a position that questions this use of ideology, see Ferber, "Ideology of *The Merchant*" 462.

36 In a lucidly detailed and informative reading of this production, James C. Bulman outlines how "Alexander dramatises how alienation born of ideological difference leads inexorably to violence" (*Shakespeare in Performance: The Merchant of Venice* 131; see ch. 6 *passim*).

37 The difficulties of this dialogue where living writers are concerned, though, points to the extent to which the author is (perhaps) a necessary fiction of the actor's work. Callow provides an arresting account of working with Edward Bond on *Restoration*, in which Bond's inability to communicate a more lively sense of Lord Are's character to Callow forces him into an anxious inspection of Bond's intentions (*Being an Actor* 134–35).

38 On "modes of corporeality," see Barker, *The Tremulous Private Body*.

39 Michael Howard, like many of the acting teachers in Eva Mekler's collection, finds animals useful: "It's useful for the actor to go to the zoo, choose an animal suited to his character, and study it in every detail, muscularly. The actor then can make choices as to what elements of the behavior of the animal will be useful" (quoted in Mekler, *New Generation* 10). Sher later used animals when thinking about his brilliant Richard III, in Bill Alexander's production, which he played on crutches: "Back at home, a video treat – two episodes of David Attenborough's *The Living Planet*. You can find any character by watching animals. Insects rubbing their front legs together – could do that with the crutches. Spiders move in a nimble

dance, their legs going like fingers on a keyboard, they rotate on the spot. Too lightweight for Richard, I think" (*Year of the King* 122).

40 I am thinking here of Fredric Jameson's discussion of the relation-ship between postmodern art, the death of the subject, and what he calls "the waning of affect": "The end of the bourgeois ego, or monad, no doubt brings with it the end of the psychopathologies of that ego – what I have been calling the waning of affect. But it means the end of much more – the end, for example, of style, in the sense of the unique and the personal, the end of the distinctive indi-vidual brush stroke (as symbolized by the emergent primacy of mechanical reproduction). As for expression and feelings or emo-tions, the liberation, in contemporary society, from the older *anomie* of the centered subject may also mean not merely a liberation from anxiety but a liberation from every other kind of feeling as well, since there is no longer a self present to do the feeling. This is not to say that the cultural products of the postmodern era are utterly devoid of feeling, but rather that such feelings – which it may be better and more accurate, following J.-F. Lyotard, to call 'intensities' – are now free-floating and impersonal and tend to be dominated by a peculiar kind of euphoria" (*Postmodernism* 15–16).

4 SHAKESPEARE'S PAGE, SHAKESPEARE'S STAGE: PERFORMANCE CRITICISM

1 On the "detextualization" of the body, "the transfer of meanings from language to nonhuman forces in 'nature,'" see Berger, "Bodies and Texts" 144–66.

2 On the practice of New Criticism in Shakespeare studies, and the relationship between New Criticism, the professionalization of literary studies in general, and Shakespeare, see Grady, *Modernist Shakespeare* ch. 3. Sam Crowl notes the rise of performance criticism as a displacement of New Criticism, and in passing suggests the influence of F. R. Leavis on Peter Hall (*Shakespeare Observed* 7, 5).

3 That the lyric is the normative mode of *Understanding Drama* is per-haps suggested by the subordination of visual to verbal in the drama: "That is, if drama seems on the one hand to give up so many means of expression that it must become blunt and fumbling, it at the same time makes compensating adjustments. For it gains the precision and exactness essential in literature, first, by the very act of eliminating everything but a bare central theme and, second, by dealing with that theme in the most expressive but at the same time the most controlled kind of language. So, ironically, in consid-ering the special symbols of drama we have inevitably come around

to an earlier point, its sharing of the symbols of poetry. One cannot strictly compartmentalize drama, for at its height it combines two modes of concentration" (26). That Brooks and Heilman do not take performance as intrinsic to dramatic analysis is confirmed in Grady's fine reading of *Understanding Drama*, in which performance is not mentioned (*Modernist Shakespeare* 128–48). For a brief history of the development of New Criticism's treatment of Shakespearean drama, see Charles Frey, "Teaching Shakespeare" 130–33.

In Britain, F. R. Leavis and *Scrutiny*, though often opposed to what Leavis saw as the sterile professionalism and purely academic orientation of the New Critics, also expressed an emphasis on formal literary analysis combined with disregard for (sometimes antipathy to) performance. While Grady is right to suggest that the British critics most influential among American New Critics – I. A. Richards and William Empson – had a sometimes tangential relation to Leavis (see *Modernist Shakespeare* 148–53); Leavis's sense of the literary text as record of authorial intention has had a profound effect on British theatre, largely through his teaching of a generation (or two) of Cambridge undergraduates. As Christopher McCullough notes, "Peter Hall [a Leavis student] exemplifies the ideological conflict between literary criticism and theatre, by his own seemingly contradictory position: 'radical' modern theatre practitioner; and advocate of the process of privileging the literary text as an absolute value, the latter belief implied by his view that there is one Shakespeare for all time, transcending, as culture, the historical-material forces of its own original production" ("Cambridge Connection" 114).

4 See Marvin and Ruth Thompson, "Performance Criticism From Granville-Barker to Bernard Beckerman and Beyond," Thompson and Thompson, *Shakespeare and the Sense of Performance* 15. For a fuller account of this collection, see my review.

5 For a convenient gathering of recent examples, see the essays in *Shakespeare and the Sense of Performance* by Marvin Rosenberg, Inga-Stina Ewbank, and J. L. Styan, as well as books considered here. In other words, some of the standard approaches to performance criticism seem to operate in ways that subordinate performance to designs said to be located in the text: most metadramatic and metatheatrical readings; generally phenomenological accounts of the plays' histrionic designs (Michael Goldman, *Shakespeare and the Energies of Drama* and *Acting and Action in Shakespearean Tragedy*); contextual accounts of performance ideology (W. B. Worthen, *The Idea of the Actor: Drama and the Ethics of Performance*); studies of the symbolic function of stage position and gesture (Robert Weimann, *Shakespeare*

and the Popular Tradition in the Theater, David Bevington, *Action is Eloquence*); and perhaps even deconstructive readings of text/performance, such as Harry Berger, Jr., "Text Against Performance: The Example of *Macbeth*." See also Richard Levin, "The New Refutation of Shakespeare." While Marvin Rosenberg's crucial series of books on *Othello*, *King Lear*, *Macbeth*, and *Hamlet* considers the different ways actors have approached their roles in these plays, these books, too, are informed by a sense that the performances are revealing potentialities latent in the plays rather than producing new meanings through the plays; this sense is shared to some extent by Anthony B. Dawson's fine reading of the questions and challenges of various Shakespearean roles in *Watching Shakespeare*. In *Imaginary Audition* Harry Berger, Jr. engages a critique of "page and stage" readings that I consider below.

In the "directorial" mode of dramatic criticism, I would include Bernard Beckerman, *Dynamics of Drama*; Ralph Berry, *Shakespeare and the Awareness of the Audience*; Harley Granville-Barker, *Prefaces to Shakespeare*; Jean Howard, *Shakespeare's Art of Orchestration*; Emrys Jones, *Scenic Form in Shakespeare*; Ann Pasternak Slater, *Shakespeare the Director*; J. L. Styan, *Shakespeare's Stagecraft*. Although such work has been extremely, and rightly, influential in opening the stage (in the abstract) as a site of signification, it tends to ask how staging can be made to contribute to or to articulate textual "meanings" without raising the intervening practices of acting or directing as a mediating discourse. As Sidney Homan remarks, "my subsequent commentary 'recreates' an ideal performance, ultimately *my* ideal performance, and thereby treats what *might* happen, not during a single performance but potentially during *any* performance of the play in question" (*Shakespeare's Theater of Presence* 9).

6 Styan's narrative of modern stage production and how it approximates the flexibility of the Elizabethan stage has been unusually influential. In his Introduction to *Players of Shakespeare*, Philip Brockbank also argues that "It may well be that our present experience of Shakespeare's plays is closer to that of the audiences of his time than it has been for many generations," a proximity enabled by a "keener respect for Shakespeare's text than was usual on the stages of the eighteenth and nineteenth centuries" (2). And like Styan, Brockbank tends to essentialize the functioning of the empty stage, arguing that "Bertolt Brecht did much to return European traditions of theatre to public and social modes of thought and feeling, but in England the communal styles have not, from present evidence, displaced those techniques of empathy and illusion practised, for example, by the player of Priam in the court of Elsinore"

(9). Much as Brecht's massive effort to reconceptualize the ideological functioning of the theatre is assimilated to (pre-capitalist) modes of popular theatre, so the notions of empathy and illusion represented within *Hamlet* are continuous with, even identical with, those common in the theatre today (this despite the fact that the Player's Priam speech, and "The Mousetrap" already seem dated in the context of the play, part of a residual dramatic and theatrical style).

7   See also J. L. Styan, rev. of *Shakespeare the Director* 71. A version of this attitude sustains much current thinking about Shakespeare teaching practice; see Halio, "'This Wide and Universal Stage'"; and see *Shakespeare Quarterly* 35 (1984): 515–656, and *Shakespeare Quarterly* 41 (1990): 139–267, special issues devoted to "Teaching Shakespeare." As Richard Levin has remarked, the claim that "these plays can be really understood only in performance, or even that they really exist only in performance" leads to a subversion of textual authority not desired by even the most "extreme performance critics." To take performance criticism at its word, Levin argues, is to disseminate the play's authority over any and all performances of it, an assumption that reverses the New Critical tendency to conserve authority within the bounds of the text itself: "If a play really exists only in performance, then, since there would be no way to determine *which* performance (since that would bring us back to the author's text, and so confer 'reality' upon it as well), it would have to mean *any* performance. This would mean that any alterations made in the text during any performance, even including actors' errors, would become parts of the 'real' play. Then there would be no 'real' play, but only the aggregate of all the different performances, which would all be equally legitimate, since the author's text, and hence his meaning, could no longer be relevant, and the sole criterion for judging them would be whether each one 'worked' in its own terms. But then it would make no sense to say that a play can be really understood only in performance, because there would be no independent 'reality' apart from the performance that could be understood. Thus the assertion that a play can be understood only in performance would seem either tautological (if the play and the performance are identical) or self-contradictory (if they are not)" ("Performance-Critics vs Close Readers" 547–48).

8   Brown's essay was originally published in *Shakespeare Quarterly* 13 (1962): 451–61.

9   A sense of how markedly performance-based teaching has shifted in the past twenty years may be gained from Jackson G. Barry's remark in the 1974 *Shakespeare Quarterly* teaching issue: "This essay attempts to show that the dramatic medium does not in itself distort

a play" ("Shakespeare with Words" 161). A longer view of the insti-
tutionalization of Shakespeare is taken by Charles Frey in
"Teaching Shakespeare," and by Alan Sinfield, "Give an Account."
On the ideological significance of various Shakespearean perfor-
mance institutions, see Sinfield, "Royal Shakespeare," and
Holderness, "Radical Potentiality."

10 At best, an actor like Shakespeare, Burbage, or Alleyn – that is, a
successful sharer in the company – might be seen today in economic
and class terms as a member of the bourgeoisie, but in the early
modern period, the volatility of acting/theatre as a profession, the
still-incipient nature of modern economic classes, and the theatre's
identification with the court would certainly have interfered with
this perception (perhaps not least for the sharers themselves). In
most cases, actors were identified economically as artisans, but socially
and legally as servants or vagrant "rogues and vagabonds." In the popular imagination, of course, actors were routinely associated with pros-
titution, gambling, vice, "effeminacy," and social corruption in general.

11 On the different ways that stage and film versions of the Kenneth
Branagh *Henry V* constructed the performance ensemble, see Collier,
"Post-Falklands, Post-Colonial."

12 Barton elides three passages which in the original occur in three separate paragraphs covering two pages of text. Barton's target, Donald
M. Kaplan, is much more directly interested in the relationship
between text and performance than Barton's heavily edited quotation would suggest to a listener or to a reader: "As for staging, the
theatre of modern realism thrusts the actor into the very center of
the theatrical event. Like Paganini, Shakespeare, in the writing of
Hamlet, casts the performer as virtuoso, a role elusively part of, yet
apart from, the play's central personage. *This* treachery plagues
every staging of *Hamlet* and *exemplifies the leading aesthetic problem of the
actor in modern theatre – the interpretation of action through characterologic
nuance and rarefaction*" – italicized portions quoted by Barton and read
by Suchet (Kaplan, "Character and Theatre" 103). At least, however, Barton cites his scholarly straw-man. Other stage-centered
critics vaguely allude to "Some commentators" or the "currently
influential view" as a means of situating their own perspective, without identifying who these influential commentators might be (see
Roger Warren, *Staging Shakespeare's Late Plays* 6).

13 On the problems of a "radical" style in the RSC, see Walter Cohen,
"Political Criticism" 31.

14 On Barton's part in the politicization of RSC productions, see
Sinfield, "Royal Shakespeare."

15 In a letter to H. R. Coursen (discussed above, chapter 3), Cary

Mazer outlines the difficulties of tapping "energies of the play . . . unlocked by historical conceptualizing" and making them into concerns "that a modern actor can play, and that a modern audience can perceive" (quoted in Coursen, *Reading Shakespeare* 264).

16 On the rhetoric of "choice" in directing practice, see Knowles, "Focus."

17 For a fuller reading of Berger, see my review; also see Dawson, "Impasse over the Stage" 315–18, and Hodgdon, *End Crowns All* 16–18, which treats some of Berger's earlier articles.

18 J. L. Austin's oft-cited remark – a "performative utterance will, for example, be *in a peculiar way* hollow or void if said by an actor on the stage" – assumes, of course, a fixed, spectatorial relation to that utterance characteristic of modernist – especially realist – theatre: it is hardly hollow or void to the other actors, though the action it performs is perhaps not the same as it would perform were it to be said outside the theatre (quoted in Parker and Sedgwick, Introduction 3). Like many literary scholars now interested in "performativity and performance," Andrew Parker and Eve Kosofsky Sedgwick develop a reading of performance predicated on Austin, and so on the strangely antitheatrical (or perhaps just theatrically uninflected, uninformed) emphasis that emerges in his work when stage performance is used as a trope. Perhaps because theatrical utterance is peculiarly "hollow," theatre itself – and, of course, the extensive theoretical literature on stage performance – is briskly sidestepped as a site of important "performative" work in their essay. Imagining theatre's "classical ontology" to be "the black box model" (2), a model in their view only recently displaced by wider conceptions of performance, Parker and Sedgwick recapitulate Austin's mistaken substitution of ontological for historical formations.

19 Dawson remarks, "For such critics, playgoing is a kind of rereading. When Barbara Hodgdon or Philip McGuire, for example, analyze in detail how particular moments of plays were realized theatrically in particular productions, their reading of those productions is itself conditioned by an array of literary understandings (parallels between scenes, or possible relations between verbal and visual images, for example), and even the method of analyzing the performance (teasing an interpretation out of it through selection, focus, and emphasis) is itself an instance of critical reading in which performance is construed as yet another text" ("Impasse over the Stage" 318).

20 Dawson rightly challenges my remarks in an earlier version of this chapter, suggesting that "by collapsing 'performance' on the stage into various other kinds of 'performance,' such as reading, or

writing criticism," I have tended "to flatten the debate instead of energizing it: if all signifying activity is to be seen as 'performance,' then we are left with no way of distinguishing acting from reading, courtly self-display, critical reproduction, political manipulation" ("Impasse over the Stage" 318 n.18). This is an important corrective, and has sharpened my thinking about my claims here.

21 I am thinking of Burke's remark that "Rhetoric is concerned with the state of Babel after the Fall. Its contribution to the 'sociology of knowledge' must often carry us far into the lugubrious regions of malice and the lie."

Works cited

Althusser, Louis. "Ideology and Ideological State Apparatuses (Notes towards an Investigation)." *Lenin and Philosophy and Other Essays.* Trans. Ben Brewster. New York: Monthly Review Press, 1971. 127–86.

Armstrong, Isobel. "Thatcher's Shakespeare." *Textual Practice* 3 (1989): 1–14.

Artaud, Antonin. "On the Balinese Theater." *The Theater and Its Double.* Trans. Mary Caroline Richards. New York: Grove, 1958. 53–67.

Austin, J. L. *How To Do Things with Words.* 2nd ed. Ed. Marina Sbisà and J. O. Urmson. Cambridge, MA: Harvard University Press, 1975.

Awashti, Suresh. "The Intercultural Experience and the Kathakali 'King Lear.'" *New Theatre Quarterly* 9.2 (1993): 172–78.

Barker, Francis. *The Tremulous Private Body: Essays on Subjection.* London: Methuen, 1984.

Barkworth, Peter. *More About Acting.* London: Secker and Warburg, 1984.

Barry, Jackson G. "Shakespeare with Words." *Shakespeare Quarterly* 25 (1974): 161–71.

Barthes, Roland. "The Death of the Author." *Image–Music–Text.* Ed. and Trans. Stephen Heath. New York: Farrar, Straus and Giroux, 1988. 142–48.

"From Work to Text." Barthes, *Image–Music–Text* 155–64.

Barton, John. *Playing Shakespeare.* London: Methuen, in association with Channel Four Television Company, Ltd., 1984.

"Set Speeches and Soliloquies." Dir. John Carlaw. 1982. Princeton: Films for the Humanities, 1988.

Bartow, Arthur. *The Director's Voice: Twenty-One Interviews.* New York: Theatre Communications Group, 1988.

Beckerman, Bernard. *Dynamics of Drama.* New York: Drama Book Specialists, 1979.

Benedetti, Robert L. *The Actor at Work*. 2nd ed. Englewood Cliffs: Prentice-Hall, 1976.

The Actor at Work. 5th ed. Englewood Cliffs: Prentice-Hall, 1990.

The Director at Work. Englewood Cliffs: Prentice-Hall, 1985.

Benjamin, Walter. "The Work of Art in the Age of Mechanical Reproduction." *Illuminations*. Ed. Hannah Arendt. Trans. Harry Zohn. New York: Schocken, 1969. 217–51.

Bennett, Susan. *Performing Nostalgia: Shifting Shakespeare and the Contemporary Past*. London: Routledge, 1996.

Berger, Harry, Jr. "Bodies and Texts." *Representations* 17 (Winter 1987): 144–66.

Imaginary Audition: Shakespeare on Stage and Page. Berkeley: University of California Press, 1989.

"Text Against Performance: The Example of *Macbeth*." *Genre* 15 (1982): 49–79.

Berry, Cicely. *The Actor and His Text*. New York: Charles Scribner's Sons, 1988.

Voice and the Actor. London: George G. Harrap, 1973.

Berry, Ralph. *On Directing Shakespeare: Interviews with Contemporary Directors*. London: Hamish Hamilton, 1989.

Shakespeare and the Awareness of the Audience. London: Macmillan, 1985.

Shakespeare's Plays in Performance: Castings and Metamorphoses. New York: St. Martin's Press, 1993.

Bevington, David. *Action is Eloquence: Shakespeare's Language of Gesture*. Cambridge, MA: Harvard University Press, 1984.

"Determining the Indeterminate: The Oxford Shakespeare." *Shakespeare Quarterly* 38 (1987): 501–19.

Black, George. *Contemporary Stage Directing*. Fort Worth: Holt, Rinehart and Winston, 1991.

Boal, Augusto. *Theatre of the Oppressed*. Trans. Charles A. McBride and Maria-Odilia Leal McBride. New York: Theatre Communications Group, 1985.

Bogdanov, Michael, and Michael Pennington. *The English Shakespeare Company: The Story of "The Wars of the Roses" 1986–1989*. London: Nick Hern, 1990.

Boleslavsky, Richard. *Acting: The First Six Lessons*. New York: Theatre Arts, 1933.

Bornstein, George, ed. *Representing Modernist Texts: Editing as Interpretation*. Ann Arbor: University of Michigan Press, 1991.

Bornstein, George, and Ralph G. Williams, eds. *Palimpsest: Editorial Theory in the Humanities*. Ann Arbor: University of Michigan Press, 1993.

Bowers, Fredson. *Bibliography and Textual Criticism*. Oxford: Clarendon Press, 1964.

Bradby, David, and David Williams. *Directors' Theatre*. New York: St. Martin's Press, 1988.

Braunmuller, A. R. "Editing the Staging/Staging the Editing." Thompson and Thompson, *Shakespeare and the Sense of Performance* 139–49.

Brecht, Bertolt. *Brecht on Theatre: The Development of an Aesthetic*. Ed. and Trans. John Willett. New York: Hill and Wang, 1964; London: Methuen, 1978.

Brett, Philip. "Text, Context, and the Early Music Editor." *Authenticity and Early Music*. Ed. Nicholas Kenyon. Oxford: Oxford University Press, 1988. 83–114.

Bristol, Michael. "How Good Does Evidence Have to Be?" Pechter, *Textual and Theatrical Shakespeare* 22–43.

Rev. of *Shakespeare's Characters: Rhetoric, Ethics, and Identity*, by Christy Desmet, and *Hamlet and the Concept of Character*, by Bert O. States. *Shakespeare Quarterly* 45 (1994): 226–31.

Shakespeare's America, America's Shakespeare. London: Routledge, 1990.

Brockbank, Philip. Foreword. Brockbank, *Players of Shakespeare* ix. Introduction. Brockbank, *Players of Shakespeare* 1–10.

Brockbank, Philip, ed. *Players of Shakespeare: Essays in Shakespearean Performance by Twelve Players with the Royal Shakespeare Company*. Cambridge: Cambridge University Press, 1985.

Brook, Peter. *The Empty Space*. 1968. New York: Atheneum, 1978. Foreword. Cicely Berry, *Voice and the Actor* 3.

The Shifting Point: Theatre, Film, Opera, 1947–1987. New York: Theatre Communications Group, 1987.

Brooks, Cleanth, and Robert Heilman. *Understanding Drama*. New York: Henry Holt, 1945.

Brown, John Russell. "Creating a Role: Shylock." *Shakespeare's Plays in Performance*. Rev. ed. New York: Applause Books, 1993. 63–85.

Discovering Shakespeare: A New Guide to the Plays. New York: Columbia University Press, 1981.

"The Nature of Speech in Shakespeare's Plays." Thompson and Thompson, *Shakespeare and the Sense of Performance* 48–60.

"Theatre Research and the Criticism of Shakespeare and His Contemporaries." *Shakespeare's Plays in Performance*. London: Edward Arnold, 1966. 223–37.

Bruder, Melissa, Lee Michael Cohn, Madeline Olnek, Nathaniel Pollack, Robert Previto, and Scott Zigler. *A Practical Handbook for the Actor*. Introd. David Mamet. New York: Vintage, 1986.

Bulman, James C. *Shakespeare in Performance: The Merchant of Venice*. Manchester: Manchester University Press, 1991.

Bulman, James C., ed. *Shakespeare, Theory, and Performance*. London: Routledge, 1996.

Bulman, James C., and H. R. Coursen, eds. *Shakespeare on Television: An Anthology of Essays and Reviews*. Hanover: University Press of New England, 1988.

Burke, Kenneth. *A Rhetoric of Motives*. Berkeley: University of California Press, 1969.

Butler, Judith. *Bodies that Matter: On the Discursive Limits of "Sex"*. New York: Routledge, 1993.

"Performative Acts and Gender Constitution: An Essay in Phenomenology and Feminist Theory." *Performing Feminisms: Feminist Critical Theory and Theatre*. Ed. Sue-Ellen Case. Baltimore: Johns Hopkins University Press, 1990. 270–82.

Buzacott, Martin. *The Death of the Actor*. London: Routledge, 1991.

Callow, Simon. *Being an Actor*. New York: Grove, 1988.

Calloway, Earl. "Peter Sellars' 'Merchant of Venice' is grossly baffling, boring." *Chicago Defender* 12 October 1994.

Carnovsky, Morris, with Peter Sander. *The Actor's Eye*. Introd. John Houseman. New York: Performing Arts Journal Publications, 1984.

Cartelli, Thomas. "Ideology and Subversion in the Shakespearean Set Speech." *ELH* 53 (1986): 1–25.

Case, Sue-Ellen, Philip Brett, and Susan Leigh Foster, eds. *Cruising the Performative: Interventions in the Representation of Ethnicity, Nationality, and Sexuality*. Bloomington: Indiana University Press, 1995.

Chaikin, Joseph. *The Presence of the Actor: Notes on the Open Theater, Disguises, Acting, and Repression*. New York: Atheneum, 1972.

Chaudhuri, Una. "The Future of the Hyphen: Interculturalism, Textuality, and the Difference Within." *Interculturalism and Performance*. Ed. Bonnie Marranca and Gautam Dasgupta. New York: PAJ Publications, 1991. 192–207.

Christiansen, Richard. "Provocative 'Merchant.'" *Chicago Tribune* 11 October 1994: 24.

Cima, Gay Gibson. "Strategies for Subverting the Canon." *Upstaging Big Daddy: Directing Theater as if Gender and Race Matter*. Ed. Ellen Donkin and Susan Clement. Ann Arbor: University of Michigan Press, 1993. 91–106.

Clurman, Harold. "The Principles of Interpretation." Gassner, *Producing the Play* 272–93.

Cohen, Philip, ed. *Devils and Angels: Textual Editing and Literary Theory*. Charlottesville: University Press of Virginia, 1991.

Cohen, Philip, and David H. Jackson. "Notes on Emerging Paradigms in Editorial Theory." Philip Cohen, *Devils and Angels* 103–23.

Cohen, Robert. *Acting Power*. Mountain View, CA: Mayfield, 1978.

Cohen, Walter. "Political Criticism of Shakespeare." Howard and O'Connor, *Shakespeare Reproduced* 18–46.

Cole, Susan Letzler. *Directors in Rehearsal: A Hidden World.* New York: Routledge, 1992.

Collier, Susanne. "Post-Falklands, Post-Colonial: Contextualizing Branagh as Henry V on Stage and Film." *Essays in Theatre/Études Théâtrales* 10 (1992): 143–54.

Cook, Judith. *Directors' Theatre.* London: Harrap, 1974.

Coursen, H. R. *Reading Shakespeare on Stage.* Newark: University of Delaware Press; London: Associated University Press, 1995.

Crowl, Sam. *Shakespeare Observed: Studies in Performance on Stage and Screen.* Athens, OH: Ohio University Press, 1992.

Csikszentmihalyi, Mihaly. *Flow: The Psychology of Optimal Experience.* New York: Harper and Row, 1990.

David, Richard. *Shakespeare in the Theatre.* Cambridge: Cambridge University Press, 1978.

Dawson, Anthony. "The Bard Goes to Univers(al)ity." Unpublished paper. Shakespeare Association Annual Convention, Kansas City, MO, April 1992.

"The Impasse over the Stage." *English Literary Renaissance* 21 (1991): 309–27.

"Performance and Participation: Desdemona, Foucault, and the Actor's Body." Bulman, *Shakespeare, Theory, and Performance* 29–45.

Watching Shakespeare: A Playgoers' Guide. New York: St. Martin's Press, 1988.

Dean, Alexander, and Lawrence Carra. *Fundamentals of Play Directing.* 4th ed. New York: Holt, Rinehart and Winston, 1980.

de Grazia, Margreta. *Shakespeare Verbatim: The Reproduction of Authenticity and the 1790 Apparatus.* Oxford: Clarendon Press, 1991.

de Grazia, Margreta, and Peter Stallybrass. "The Materiality of the Shakespearean Text." *Shakespeare Quarterly* 44 (1993): 255–83.

Derrida, Jacques. "The Theater of Cruelty and the Closure of Representation." *Writing and Difference.* Trans. Alan Bass. Chicago: University of Chicago Press, 1978. 232–50.

Dessen, Alan C. "Recovering Elizabethan Staging: A Reconsideration of the Evidence." Pechter, *Textual and Theatrical Shakespeare* 44–65.

Dobson, Michael. *The Making of the National Poet: Shakespeare, Adaptation and Authorship, 1660–1769.* Oxford: Clarendon Press, 1992.

Dollimore, Jonathan, and Alan Sinfield, eds. *Political Shakespeare: New Essays in Cultural Materialism.* Ithaca: Cornell University Press, 1985.

Donohue, Joseph. "Character, Genre, and Ethos in Nineteenth-Century British Drama." *Yearbook of English Studies* 9 (1979): 78–101.

Eagleton, Terry. *Criticism and Ideology: A Study in Marxist Literary Theory.* London: Verso, 1978.

Edmondson, Laura, and Jules Odendahl. "'A Ceaseless Revolution': An Interview with Sue-Ellen Case." *Theatre InSight* 6.2 (1995): 17–27.

Eliot, T. S. "Tradition and the Individual Talent." *The Sacred Wood: Essays on Poetry and Criticism.* 1920. London: Methuen, 1976. 47–59.

Ewbank, Inga-Stina. "From Narrative to Dramatic Language: *The Winter's Tale* and Its Source." Thompson and Thompson, *Shakespeare and the Sense of Performance* 29–47.

Felner, Mira. *Free to Act: An Integrated Approach to Acting.* Fort Worth: Holt, Rinehart and Winston, 1990.

Ferber, Michael. "The Ideology of *The Merchant of Venice.*" *English Literary Renaissance* 20 (1990): 431–64.

Filewod, Alan. "National Theatre/National Obsession." *Canadian Theatre Review* 62 (Spring 1990): 5–10.

Foster, Susan Leigh, ed. *Choreographing History.* Bloomington: Indiana University Press, 1995.

     Reading Dancing: Bodies and Subjects in Contemporary American Dance. Berkeley: University of California Press, 1986.

Foucault, Michel. "The Discourse on Language." *The Archaeology of Knowledge and The Discourse on Language.* Trans. A. M. Sheridan Smith. New York: Pantheon, 1972. 215–37.

     "What Is an Author?" *Textual Strategies: Perspectives in Post-Structuralist Criticism.* Ed. Josué V. Harari. Ithaca: Cornell University Press, 1979. 141–60.

Freedman, Gerald. "From Hitch-kick to Highgate." *American Theatre* 12.5 (May/June 1995): 30–33, 67.

Freeman, Neil. *Shakespeare's First Texts.* Vancouver: Folio Scripts, 1994.

Frey, Charles. "Teaching Shakespeare in America." *Experiencing Shakespeare: Essays on Text, Classroom, and Performance.* Columbia: University of Missouri Press, 1988. 122–43.

Gaines, Barbara. "Using Shakespeare's First Folio as an Acting Manual." Unpublished public lecture, Northwestern University, 3 March 1995.

Gaskell, Philip. *From Writer to Reader: Studies in Editorial Method.* Oxford: Oxford University Press, 1978.

Gaskill, William. *A Sense of Direction.* London: Faber and Faber, 1988.

Gassner, John. *Producing the Play.* With *The New Scene Technician's Handbook.* By Philip Barber. Rev. ed. New York: Holt, Rinehart and Winston, 1953.

Geertz, Clifford. "Blurred Genres: The Refiguration of Social Thought." *Local Knowledge: Further Essays in Interpretive Anthropology.* New York: Basic Books, 1983. 19–35.

     The Interpretation of Cultures. New York: Basic Books, 1973.

Gilbert, Helen, and Joanne Tompkins. *Post-Colonial Drama: Theory, Practice, Politics.* London: Routledge, 1996.

Goldman, Michael. *Acting and Action in Shakespearean Tragedy.* Princeton: Princeton University Press, 1985.
Shakespeare and the Energies of Drama. Princeton: Princeton. University Press, 1972.
Grady, Hugh. "Disintegration and its Reverberations." Marsden, *The Appropriation of Shakespeare* 111–27.
The Modernist Shakespeare: Critical Texts in a Material World. Oxford: Clarendon Press, 1991.
Granville-Barker, Harley. *Prefaces to Shakespeare.* 2 vols. Princeton: Princeton University Press, 1978.
Green, Amy S. *The Revisionist Stage: American Directors Reinvent the Classics.* Cambridge: Cambridge University Press, 1994.
Greenblatt, Stephen. "Invisible Bullets." *Shakespearean Negotiations* 21–65.
"Invisible Bullets: Renaissance Authority and its Subversion." Dollimore and Sinfield, *Political Shakespeare* 18–47.
Shakespearean Negotiations: The Circulation of Social Energy in Renaissance England. Berkeley: University of California Press, 1988.
Greetham, D. C. "[Textual] Criticism and Deconstruction." *Studies in Bibliography* 44 (1991): 1–30.
"Textual Forensics." *PMLA* 111 (1996): 32–51.
Grigely, Joseph. "The Textual Event." Philip Cohen, *Devils and Angels* 167–94.
Groden, Michael. "Contemporary Textual and Literary Theory." Bornstein, *Representing Modernist Texts* 259–86.
Gronbeck-Tedesco, John L. *Acting Through Exercises: A Synthesis of Classical and Contemporary Approaches.* Mountain View, CA: Mayfield, 1992.
Grotowski, Jerzy. *Towards a Poor Theatre.* New York: Simon and Schuster, 1968.
Guy, Joyce. Rev. of *Twilight: Los Angeles, 1992,* by Anna Deavere Smith. Mark Taper Forum, Los Angeles. June–July 1993. *Theatre Journal* 46 (1994): 115–16.
Hagen, Uta, with Haskel Frankel. *Respect for Acting.* New York: Macmillan; London: Collier Macmillan, 1973.
Halio, J. L. "'This Wide and Universal Stage': Shakespeare's Plays as Plays." *Teaching Shakespeare.* Ed. Walter Edens, et al. Princeton: Princeton University Press, 1977. 273–89.
Understanding Shakespeare's Plays in Performance. Manchester: Manchester University Press, 1988.
Hall, Peter. *Peter Hall's Diaries: The Story of a Dramatic Battle.* New York: Limelight, 1985.
Hamera, Judith. Rev. of *Twilight: Los Angeles, 1992,* by Anna Deavere Smith. Mark Taper Forum, Los Angeles. June–July 1993. *Theatre Journal* 46 (1994): 116–17.

Hapgood, Robert. *Shakespeare the Theatre-Poet.* Oxford: Clarendon, 1988.

Harbage, Alfred. "Elizabethan Acting." *PMLA* 54 (1939): 685–708.

Harrop, John. *Acting.* London: Routledge, 1992.

Hawkes, Terence. *Meaning by Shakespeare.* London: Routledge, 1992.
   That Shakespeherian Rag: Essays on a Critical Process. London: Methuen, 1986.

Hawkins, Sherman. "Teaching the Theatre of Imagination: The Example of *1 Henry IV*." *Shakespeare Quarterly* 35 (1984): 517–27.

Henning, Joel. "Shylock on the Beach." *Wall Street Journal* 21 October 1994.

Hernandez, Martin. Rev. of *Twilight: Los Angeles, 1992,* by Anna Deavere Smith. Mark Taper Forum, Los Angeles. June–July 1993. *Theatre Journal* 46 (1994): 113–14.

Hodgdon, Barbara. *The End Crowns All: Closure and Contradiction in Shakespeare's History.* Princeton: Princeton University Press, 1991.
   "He Do Cressida in Different Voices." *English Literary Renaissance* 20 (1990): 254–86.
   "Katherina Bound; or, Play(K)ating the Strictures of Everyday Life." *PMLA* 107 (1992): 538–53.
   "Looking for Mr. Shakespeare after 'The Revolution': Robert Lepage's Intercultural *Dream* Machine." Bulman, *Shakespeare, Theory, and Performance* 68–91.

Hodge, Francis. *Play Directing: Analysis, Communication, and Style.* Englewood Cliffs: Prentice-Hall, 1971.

Holderness, Graham. "Radical Potentiality and Institutional Closure: Shakespeare in Film and Television." Dollimore and Sinfield, *Political Shakespeare* 182–201.

Holderness, Graham, ed. *The Shakespeare Myth.* Manchester: Manchester University Press, 1988.

Homan, Sidney. *Shakespeare's Theater of Presence: Language, Spectacle, and the Audience.* Lewisburg: Bucknell University Press; London: Associated University Press, 1986.

Hornby, Richard. *The End of Acting: A Radical View.* New York: Applause, 1992.

Howard, Jean E. "The New Historicism in Literary Studies." *English Literary Renaissance* 16 (1986): 13–43.
   Shakespeare's Art of Orchestration. Urbana: University of Illinois Press, 1984.
   The Stage and Social Struggle in Early Modern England. London: Routledge, 1994.

Howard, Jean E., and Marion F. O'Connor. Introduction. Howard and O'Connor, *Shakespeare Reproduced* 1–17.

Howard, Jean E., and Marion F. O'Connor, eds. *Shakespeare Reproduced: The Text in History and Ideology.* New York: Methuen, 1987.

Howard, Michael. "A Method of One's Own." *American Theatre* 12.1 (January 1995): 24.

Huston, Hollis. *The Actor's Instrument: Body, Theory, Stage.* Ann Arbor: University of Michigan Press, 1992.

Iglarsh, Hugh. "If You Bore Us, Do We Not Walk?" *Context – Arts Journal of the Near Northwest Arts Council Graphic Resource Center* December 1994: 5.

Jackson, Russell, and Robert Smallwood, eds. *Players of Shakespeare 2: Further Essays in Shakespearean Performance by Players with the Royal Shakespeare Company.* Cambridge: Cambridge University Press, 1989.

　Players of Shakespeare 3: Further Essays in Shakespearian Performance by Players with the Royal Shakespeare Company. Cambridge: Cambridge University Press, 1993.

Jameson, Fredric. *Postmodernism, or, The Cultural Logic of Late Capitalism.* Durham: Duke University Press, 1991.

Jones, David Richard. *Great Directors at Work: Stanislavsky, Brecht, Kazan, Brook.* Berkeley: University of California Press, 1986.

Jones, Emrys. *Scenic Form in Shakespeare.* Oxford: Oxford University Press, 1971.

Joseph, B. L. *Elizabethan Acting.* Oxford: Oxford University Press, 1951.

Joseph, Bertram. *Acting Shakespeare.* 1960. New York: Theatre Arts, 1989.

Kaplan, Donald M. "Character and Theatre: Psychoanalytic Notes on Modern Realism." *Tulane Drama Review* 10.1 (1966): 93–108.

Kavanagh, James H. "Shakespeare in Ideology." *Alternative Shakespeares.* Ed. John Drakakis. London: Methuen, 1985. 144–65.

Kennedy, Dennis. Introduction. Kennedy, *Foreign Shakespeare* 1–18.

　Looking at Shakespeare: A Visual History of Twentieth-Century Performance. Cambridge: Cambridge University Press, 1993.

　"Shakespeare Without His Language." Bulman, *Shakespeare, Theory, and Performance* 133–48.

Kennedy, Dennis, ed. *Foreign Shakespeare: Contemporary Performance.* Cambridge: Cambridge University Press, 1993.

Knight, G. Wilson. *The Wheel of Fire.* 4th ed. London: Methuen, 1949.

Knowles, Richard Paul. "Focus, Faithfulness, and the *Shrew*: Directing as Translation as Resistance." Unpublished paper. Shakespeare Association of America/International Shakespeare Association World Congress, Los Angeles, April 1996.

　"Frankie Goes to Hollywood (North); or The Trials of the Oppositional Director." *Canadian Theatre Review* 76 (Fall 1993): 4–7.

　"Shakespeare at Stratford: The Legacy of the Festival Stage." *Canadian Theatre Review* 54 (Spring 1988): 39–45.

　"Shakespeare, 1993, and the Discourses of the Stratford Festival, Ontario." *Shakespeare Quarterly* 45 (1994): 211–25.

"Shakespeare, Voice, and Ideology: Interrogating the Natural Voice." Bulman, *Shakespeare, Theory, and Performance* 92–112.

Koltai, Judith. "Authentic Movement: The Embodied Experience of the Text." *Canadian Theatre Review* 78 (Spring 1994): 21–25.

Kott, Jan. *Shakespeare Our Contemporary*. New York: Norton, 1974.

Kotzin, Michael C. "Modern-day 'Merchant' leaves little to hold on to." *JUF News* November 1994: 77–79.

Lamb, Charles. "On the Tragedies of Shakespeare, Considered with Reference to Their Fitness for Stage Representation." *Prose of the Romantic Period*. Ed. Carl R. Woodring. Boston: Houghton Mifflin, 1961. 229–40.

Lanier, Douglas. "Drowning the Book: *Prospero's Books* and the Textual Shakespeare." Bulman, *Shakespeare, Theory, and Performance* 187–209.

Laqueur, Thomas. *Making Sex: Body and Gender from the Greeks to Freud*. Cambridge, MA: Harvard University Press, 1990.

Lee, Sae. Rev. of *Twilight: Los Angeles, 1992*, by Anna Deavere Smith. Mark Taper Forum, Los Angeles. June–July 1993. *Theatre Journal* 46 (1994): 118.

Levin, Richard. "The New Refutation of Shakespeare." *Modern Philology* 83 (1985–86): 123–41.

"Performance-Critics vs Close Readers in the Study of English Renaissance Drama." *Modern Language Review* 81 (1986): 545–59.

Levine, Lawrence W. "William Shakespeare in America." *Highbrow/Lowbrow: The Emergence of Cultural Hierarchy in America*. Cambridge, MA: Harvard University Press, 1988. 11–81.

Lieblein, Leanore. "Theatre Archives at the Intersection of Production and Reception: The Example of Québécois Shakespeare." Pechter, *Textual and Theatrical Shakespeare* 164–80.

Linklater, Kristin. *Freeing the Natural Voice*. New York: Drama Book Specialists, 1976.

Freeing Shakespeare's Voice: The Actor's Guide to Talking the Text. New York: Theatre Communications Group, 1992.

Living Theatre. *Paradise Now*. Written down by Julian Beck and Judith Malina. New York: Random House, 1971.

Loehlin, James Norris. Letter to the author. Undated [January 1995].

Rev. of *The Merchant of Venice*, by William Shakespeare, dir. Peter Sellars. Goodman Theatre, Chicago. 5 November 1994. *Theatre Journal* 48 (1996): 94–95.

Love, Lauren. "Resisting the 'Organic.'" Zarrilli, *Acting (Re)Considered* 275–88.

Lyons, Charles R., and James C. Lyons. "Anna Deavere Smith: Perspectives on her Performance within the Context of Critical Theory." *Journal of Dramatic Theory and Criticism* 9.1 (1994): 43–66.

Mann, Laurin M. "Teaching Acting: Four College Programs." *Canadian Theatre Review* 78 (Spring 1994): 32–37.

Marcus, Leah. *Puzzling Shakespeare: Local Reading and Its Discontents.* Berkeley: University of California Press, 1988.

"The Shakespearean Editor as Shrew-Tamer." *English Literary Renaissance* 22 (1992): 177–200.

Marowitz, Charles. "Lear Log." David Williams, *Peter Brook* 6–22.

The Marowitz Shakespeare. London: Marion Boyars, 1978.

Prospero's Staff: Acting and Directing in the Contemporary Theatre. Bloomington: Indiana University Press, 1986.

Recycling Shakespeare. New York: Applause, 1991.

Marsden, Jean I., ed. *The Appropriation of Shakespeare: Post-Renaissance Reconstructions of the Works and the Myth.* New York: Harvester Wheatsheaf, 1991.

Martin, Carol. "Anna Deavere Smith: The Word Becomes You – an Interview." *The Drama Review – The Journal of Performance Studies* 37. 4 (1993): 45–62.

Martin, Helen Saville. *On Some of Shakespeare's Female Characters.* London: William Blackwood, 1885.

Martin, Jacqueline. *Voice in the Modern Theatre.* London: Routledge, 1991.

Mazer, Cary M. *Shakespeare Refashioned: Elizabethan Plays on Edwardian Stages.* Ann Arbor: UMI Research Press, 1981.

McCullough, Christopher J. "The Cambridge Connection: Towards a Materialist Theatre Practice." Holderness, *The Shakespeare Myth* 112–21.

McGann, Jerome J. "The Case of *The Ambassadors* and the Textual Condition." Bornstein and Williams, *Palimpsest* 151–66.

A Critique of Modern Textual Criticism. Chicago: University of Chicago Press, 1983.

The Textual Condition. Princeton: Princeton University Press, 1991.

McGaw, Charles. *Acting Is Believing: A Basic Method.* 4th ed. New York: Holt, Rinehart and Winston, 1980.

McGuire, Philip. *Speechless Dialect: Shakespeare's Open Silences.* Berkeley: University of California Press, 1985.

McLuskie, Kathleen E. "The Shopping Complex: Materiality and the Renaissance Theatre." Pechter, *Textual and Theatrical Shakespeare* 86–101.

Meisner, Sanford, and Dennis Longwell. *Sanford Meisner on Acting.* New York: Vintage, 1987.

Mekler, Eva, ed. *The New Generation of Acting Teachers.* New York: Penguin, 1987.

Miles-Brown, John. *Directing Drama.* London: Peter Owen, 1980.

Miller, Jonathan. *Subsequent Performances.* New York: Elizabeth Sifton and Viking-Penguin, 1986.

Mitter, Shomit. *Systems of Rehearsal: Stanislavsky, Brecht, Grotowski, and Brook.* London: Routledge, 1992.

Montrose, Louis. "Professing the Renaissance: The Poetics and Politics of Culture." Veeser, *The New Historicism* 15–36.

Moore, Sonia. *Training an Actor: The Stanislavski System in Class.* Rev. ed. New York: Penguin, 1979.

Morrison, Hugh. *Directing in the Theatre.* 2nd ed. London: A&C Black; New York: Routledge, 1984.

Mueller, Martin. "Redrawing the Boundaries? Skeptical Thoughts About Literary Studies." *Centennial Review* 38 (1994): 603–22.

Orgel, Stephen. "The Authentic Shakespeare." *Representations* 21 (Winter 1988): 1–25.

Osborne, Laurie E. "Rethinking the Performance Editions: Theatrical and Textual Productions of Shakespeare." Bulman, *Shakespeare, Theory, and Performance* 168–86.

Parker, Andrew, and Eve Kosofsky Sedgwick. Introduction. *Performativity and Performance.* New York: Routledge, 1995. 1–18.

Pavis, Patrice. *Theatre at the Crossroads of Culture.* Trans. Loren Kruger. London: Routledge, 1992.

"Wilson, Brook, Zadek: An Intercultural Encounter?" Kennedy, *Foreign Shakespeare* 270–89.

Pechter, Edward. "Textual and Theatrical Shakespeare: Questions of Evidence." Pechter, *Textual and Theatrical Shakespeare* 1–21.

Pechter, Edward, ed. *Textual and Theatrical Shakespeare: Questions of Evidence.* Iowa City: University of Iowa Press, 1996.

"The Peter Sellars Interview." *Onstage: Newsletter of the Goodman Theatre Series* 9.1 (1994): 11–14.

Poel, William. *Shakespeare in the Theatre.* London: Sidgwick and Jackson, 1913.

Rabkin, Gerald. "Is There a Text On This Stage? Theatre/Authorship/ Interpretation." *Performing Arts Journal* 9.2–3 (1985): 142–59.

"The Play of Misreading: Text/Theatre/Deconstruction." *Performing Arts Journal* 7.1 (1983): 44–60.

Rayner, Alice. "Improper Conjunctions: Metaphor, Performance, and Text." *Essays in Theatre/Études Théâtrales* 14.1 (1995): 3–14.

Reinelt, Janelle. "Tracking *Twilight*: The Politics of Location." *TheatreForum* 6 (Winter/Spring 1995): 52–57.

Reinelt, Janelle G., and Joseph R. Roach, eds. *Critical Theory and Performance.* Ann Arbor: University of Michigan Press, 1992.

Reis, Kurt. "Defending NTS." *Canadian Theatre Review* 74 (Spring 1993): 81–84.

Richards, David. "Sellars Moves the Merchant to Venice Beach." *New York Times* 18 October 1994: B1–2.

Richards, Sandra L. "Caught in the Act of Social Definition: *On the Road* with Anna Deavere Smith." *Acting Out: Feminist Performances.* Ed. Lynda Hart and Peggy Phelan. Ann Arbor: University of Michigan Press, 1993. 35–53.

Roach, Joseph R. *The Player's Passion: Studies in the Science of Acting.* Newark: University of Delaware Press; London: Associated University Press, 1985.

Rodenburg, Patsy. *The Need for Words: Voice and the Text.* New York: Routledge, 1993.

Romain, Michael. *A Profile of Jonathan Miller.* Cambridge: Cambridge University Press, 1992.

Rosenberg, Marvin. *The Masks of Hamlet.* Newark: University of Delaware Press; London: Associated University Press, 1992.

The Masks of King Lear. Berkeley: University of California Press, 1972.

The Masks of Macbeth. Berkeley: University of California Press, 1978.

The Masks of Othello: The Search for the Identity of Othello, Iago, and Desdemona by Three Centuries of Actors and Critics. Berkeley: University of California Press, 1961.

"Subtext in Shakespeare." Thompson and Thompson, *Shakespeare and the Sense of Performance* 79–90.

Rouse, John. "Textuality and Authority in Theater and Drama: Some Contemporary Possibilities." Reinelt and Roach, *Critical Theory and Performance* 146–57.

Rutter, Carol, with Sinead Cusack, Paola Dionisotti, Fiona Shaw, Juliet Stevenson, Harriet Walter. *Clamorous Voices: Shakespeare's Women Today.* New York: Routledge/Theatre Arts, 1989.

Salter, Denis. "Acting Shakespeare in Postcolonial Space." Bulman, *Shakespeare, Theory, and Performance* 113–32.

"Body Politics: English-Canadian Acting at the National Theatre School." *Canadian Theatre Review* 71 (Summer 1992): 4–14.

"Declarations of (In)Dependence: Adjudicating the Dominion Drama Festival." *Canadian Theatre Review* 62 (Spring 1990): 11–18.

Samuelson, David. Preface. *Shakespeare: The Theatrical Dimension.* Ed. Philip McGuire and David A. Samuelson. New York: AMS, 1979. vii–xv.

Schechner, Richard. "Anna Deavere Smith: Acting as Incorporation." *The Drama Review – The Journal of Performance Studies* 37.4 (1993): 63–64.

"The Canon." *The Drama Review – The Journal of Performance Studies* 35.4 (1991): 7–13.

Environmental Theater. New York: Hawthorn, 1973.

"A New Paradigm for Theatre in the Academy." *The Drama Review – The Journal of Performance Studies* 36.4 (1992): 7–10.

"Once More, With Feeling." *The Drama Review* 30.1 (1986): 4–7.

"Performance Studies: The Broad Spectrum Approach." *The Drama Review – The Journal of Performance Studies* 32.3 (1988): 4–6.

"Toward the 21st Century." *The Drama Review – The Journal of Performance Studies* 37.4 (1993): 7–8.

Selbourne, David. *The Making of A Midsummer Night's Dream: An Eye-Witness Account of Peter Brook's Production from First Rehearsal to First Night*. Introd. Simon Trussler. London: Methuen, 1982.

Sellars, Peter. Untitled Commentary on *The Merchant of Venice*. *Onstage: Newsletter of the Goodman Theatre Series* 9.1 (1994): 4.

Shakespeare, William. *The Riverside Shakespeare*. Ed. G. Blakemore Evans. Boston: Houghton Mifflin, 1974.

The Shakespeare Laboratory: Peter Sellars' The Merchant of Venice. The Bard on the Box. BBC Version 1. 22 October 1994.

Sher, Antony. *Year of the King: An Actor's Sketchbook and Diary*. London: Chatto and Windus/Hogarth Press, 1985.

Shillingsburg, Peter L. *Scholarly Editing in the Computer Age*. Athens, GA: University of Georgia Press, 1986.

"Text as Matter, Concept, and Action." *Studies in Bibliography* 44 (1991): 31–82.

Sinfield, Alan. *Faultlines: Cultural Materialism and the Politics of Dissident Reading*. Berkeley: University of California Press, 1992.

"Give an Account of Shakespeare and Education, Showing Why You Think They Are Effective and What You Have Appreciated About Them. Support Your Comments with Precise References." Dollimore and Sinfield, *Political Shakespeare* 134–57.

"Royal Shakespeare: Theatre and the Making of Ideology." Dollimore and Sinfield, *Political Shakespeare* 158–81.

Skura, Meredith Anne. *Shakespeare the Actor and the Purposes of Playing*. Chicago: University of Chicago Press, 1993.

Slater, Ann Pasternak. *Shakespeare the Director*. Sussex: Harvester, 1982.

Smallwood, Robert. Introduction. Jackson and Smallwood, *Players of Shakespeare 3*: 1–20.

Smith, Anna Deavere. *Twilight: Los Angeles, 1992. On the Road: A Search for American Character*. New York: Doubleday, 1994.

Soloff, Emily D. "Merchant of Venom." *Chicago Jewish News* 21–27 October 1994: 20–24.

Spolin, Viola. *Improvisation for the Theater: A Handbook of Teaching and Directing Techniques*. Evanston: Northwestern University Press, 1963.

Spurgeon, Caroline. *Shakespeare's Imagery and What It Tells Us*. Cambridge: Cambridge University Press, 1939.

Stallybrass, Peter. "Transvestism and the 'Body Beneath': Speculating on the Boy Actor." *Erotic Politics: Desire on the Renaissance Stage*. Ed. Susan Zimmerman. New York: Routledge, 1992. 64–83.

Stanislavski, Constantin. "From the Production Plan of *Othello*." *Acting: A Handbook of the Stanislavski Method.* Comp. Toby Cole. New York: Crown, 1975. 130–38.

States, Bert O. *The Pleasure of the Play.* Ithaca: Cornell University Press, 1994.

Steen, Shannon. "'Surely This is Auteurist Direction Run Riot!' Authority and Authorship in the Work of Peter Sellars, Tadashi Suzuki, and Charles Mee, Jr." MA Thesis. Northwestern University, 1996.

Stephens, John Russell. *The Profession of the Playwright: British Theatre 1800–1900.* Cambridge: Cambridge University Press, 1992.

Strange Days. Screenplay by James Cameron and Jay Cocks. Dir. Kathryn Bigelow. Perf. Angela Bassett, Ralph Fiennes. Lightstorm, 1995.

Strasberg, Lee. *A Dream of Passion: The Development of the Method.* Ed. Evangeline Morphos. Boston: Little, Brown, 1987.

Styan, J. L. Rev. of *Shakespeare the Director*, by Ann Pasternak Slater. *Modern Philology* 83 (1985–86): 71–73.

The Shakespeare Revolution: Criticism and Performance in the Twentieth Century. Cambridge: Cambridge University Press, 1977.

Shakespeare's Stagecraft. Cambridge: Cambridge University Press, 1967.

"Stage Space and the Shakespeare Experience." Thompson and Thompson, *Shakespeare and the Sense of Performance* 195–209.

Suntree, Susan. Rev. of *Twilight: Los Angeles, 1992*, by Anna Deavere Smith. Mark Taper Forum, Los Angeles. June–July 1993. *Theatre Journal* 46 (1994): 114.

Suzuki, Tadashi. "Culture is the Body." Zarrilli, *Acting (Re)Considered* 155–60.

Swander, Homer. "In Our Time: Such Audiences We Wish Him." *Shakespeare Quarterly* 35 (1984): 528–40.

Swed, Mark. "'Merchant of Venice' Beach? Peter Sellars Strikes Again." *Los Angeles Times* 12 October 1994: F1, F5.

Tanselle, G. Thomas. "Editing Without a Copy-Text." *Studies in Bibliography* 47 (1994): 1–22.

"The Editorial Problem of Final Authorial Intention." *Studies in Bibliography* 29 (1976): 167–211.

Textual Criticism and Scholarly Editing. Charlottesville: University Press of Virginia, 1990.

Taylor, Gary. *Moment by Moment by Shakespeare.* London: Macmillan, 1985.

Reinventing Shakespeare: A Cultural History from the Restoration to the Present. New York: Oxford University Press, 1991.

"The Renaissance and the End of Editing." Bornstein and Williams, *Palimpsest* 121–49.

Taylor, Gary, and Michael Warren, eds. *The Division of the Kingdoms: Shakespeare's Two Versions of King Lear.* Oxford: Clarendon Press, 1983.

"Teaching Shakespeare." *Shakespeare Quarterly* 35 (1984): 515–656.

"Teaching Shakespeare." *Shakespeare Quarterly* 41 (1990): 139–267.

Therborn, Göran. *The Ideology of Power and the Power of Ideology.* London: Verso, 1982.

Thompson, Ann, Thomas L. Berger, A. R. Braunmuller, Philip Edwards, and Lois Potter. *Which Shakespeare? A User's Guide to Editions.* Milton Keynes: Open University Press, 1992.

Thompson, Marvin, and Ruth Thompson. "Performance Criticism From Granville-Barker to Bernard Beckerman and Beyond." Thompson and Thompson, *Shakespeare and the Sense of Performance* 13–23.

"Suggested Readings in Performance Criticism." Thompson and Thompson, *Shakespeare and the Sense of Performance* 252–56.

Thompson, Marvin, and Ruth Thompson, eds. *Shakespeare and the Sense of Performance: Essays in the Tradition of Performance Criticism in Honor of Bernard Beckerman.* Newark: University of Delaware Press; London: Associated University Press, 1989.

Tillyard, E. M. W. *The Elizabethan World Picture.* London: 16 Chatto and Windus, 1943.

Tropea, Silvana. "Ron Daniels Finds the Space Inside Shakespeare." *American Theatre* 11. 4 (April 1994): 40–41.

Twilight: Los Angeles 1992 – On The Road: A Search for American Character. Dir. Sharon Ott. Program. Berkeley Repertory Theatre. 16 March 1996.

Urkowitz, Steven. *Shakespeare's Revision of "King Lear".* Princeton: Princeton University Press, 1980.

Vanden Heuvel, Michael. "Textual Harassment: Teaching Drama to Interrogate Reading." *Theatre Topics* 3 (1993): 159–66.

Veeser, H. Aram. Introduction. Veeser, *The New Historicism* ix–xvi.

Veeser, H. Aram, ed. *The New Historicism.* New York: Routledge, 1989.

Villareal, Edit. Rev. of *Twilight: Los Angeles, 1992,* by Anna Deavere Smith. Mark Taper Forum, Los Angeles. June–July 1993. *Theatre Journal* 46 (1994): 111–13.

Warren, Roger. *Staging Shakespeare's Late Plays.* Oxford: Clarendon Press, 1990.

Watson, Ian. "Eastern and Western Influences on Performer Training at Eugenio Barba's Odin Teatret." Zarrilli, *Acting (Re)Considered* 129–36.

Wegener, Amy. "Playing Between The 'Other' and the Self: Actors, Performers, and (De)constructed Identities." Unpublished paper. Northwestern University, 1995.

Weimann, Robert. "Bifold Authority in Shakespeare's Theater." *Shakespeare Quarterly* 39 (1988): 401–17.

"Mimesis in *Hamlet.*" *Shakespeare and the Question of Theory.* Ed. Patricia Parker and Geoffrey Hartman. New York: Methuen, 1985. 275–91.

"Performance-Game and Representation in *Richard III.*" Pechter, *Textual and Theatrical Shakespeare* 66–85.

Shakespeare and the Popular Tradition in the Theater: Studies in the Social Dimension of Dramatic Form and Function. Ed. Robert Schwartz. Baltimore: Johns Hopkins University Press, 1987.

"Towards a Literary Theory of Ideology: Mimesis, Representation, Authority." Howard and O'Connor, *Shakespeare Reproduced* 263–72.

Weinraub, Bernard. "Condensing a Riot's Cacophony Into the Voice of One Woman." *New York Times* 16 June 1995: C15–C16.

Welker, David. *Theatrical Direction: The Basic Techniques.* Boston: Allyn and Bacon, 1971.

Wells, Stanley. General Introduction. Wells and Taylor, *William Shakespeare: The Complete Works* xiii–xxxviii.

Re-Editing Shakespeare for the Modern Reader. Oxford: Clarendon Press, 1984.

Wells, Stanley, and Gary Taylor, general eds. *William Shakespeare: The Complete Works. Original-Spelling Edition.* Oxford: Clarendon Press, 1986.

Whigham, Frank. "Ideology and Class Conduct in *The Merchant of Venice.*" *Renaissance Drama* n.s. 10 (1979): 93–115.

White, Hayden. "New Historicism: A Comment." Veeser, *The New Historicism* 293–302.

Whitmore, Jon. *Directing Postmodern Theatre: Shaping Signification in Performance.* Ann Arbor: University of Michigan Press, 1994.

Williams, Albert. Rev. of *The Merchant of Venice,* dir. by Peter Sellars. Goodman Theatre, Chicago. *Chicago Reader* 21 October 1994: I: 33–34.

Williams, David, comp. *Peter Brook: A Theatrical Casebook.* Rev. ed. London: Methuen, 1992.

Williams, Ralph G. "I Shall Be Spoken: Textual Boundaries, Authors, and Intent." Bornstein and Williams, *Palimpsest* 45–66.

Williams, Raymond. *Marxism and Literature.* Oxford: Oxford University Press, 1977.

Wills, J. Robert. *Directing in the Theatre: A Casebook.* 2nd ed. Metuchen: Scarecrow, 1994.

Wilson, Ann. "Staging Shakespeare." *Canadian Theatre Review* 75 (Summer 1993): 19–24.

Worthen, W. B. *The Idea of the Actor: Drama and the Ethics of Performance.* Princeton: Princeton University Press, 1984.

Modern Drama and the Rhetoric of Theater. Berkeley: University of California Press, 1992.

Rev. of *Imaginary Audition: Shakespeare on Stage and Page*, by Harry Berger, Jr. *Shakespeare Quarterly* 42 (1991): 96–99.

Rev. of *Shakespeare and the Sense of Performance: Essays in the Tradition of Performance Criticism in Honor of Bernard Beckerman*, ed. Marvin Thompson and Ruth Thompson. *Shakespeare Studies* 21 (1993): 300–12.

Zarrilli, Phillip B. "For Whom is the King a King? Issues of Intercultural Production, Perception, and Reception in a *Kathakali King Lear*." Reinelt and Roach, *Critical Theory and Performance* 16–40.

Introduction to Part I. Zarrilli, *Acting (Re)Considered* 7–21.

"'On the edge of a breath, looking': Disciplining the Actor's Bodymind through the Martial Arts in the Asian/Experimental Theatre Program." Zarrilli, *Acting (Re)Considered* 177–96.

Zarrilli, Phillip B., ed. *Acting (Re)Considered: Theories and Practices*. London: Routledge, 1995.

Zeller, Hans. "A New Approach to the Critical Constitution of Literary Texts." *Studies in Bibliography* 28 (1975): 231–64.

Zoglin, Richard. "Shylock on the Beach." *Time* 31 October 1994: 78.

Index

Printed in the United States
122564LV00001B/237/A